The Structuring of Pedagogic Discourse

The Structuring of Pedagogic Discourse

Volume IV
Class, codes and control

Basil Bernstein

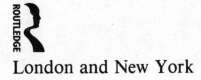

London and New York

First published 1990
by Routledge
11 New Fetter Lane, London EC4P 4EE

Simultaneously published in the USA and Canada
by Routledge
a division of Routledge, Chapman and Hall, Inc.
29 West 35th Street, New York, NY 10001

Typeset by Pat and Anne Murphy, Highcliffe-on-Sea, Dorset
Printed in Great Britain by Billings and Sons Ltd, Worcester

British Library Cataloguing in Publication Data

Bernstein, Basil
   The structuring of pedagogic discourse. — Class, codes
   and control; v.4
   1. Language, social aspects
   I. Title   II. Series
   401′.9

   ISBN 0-415-04568-1

Library of Congress Cataloging in Publication Data

Bernstein, Basil B.
   The structuring of pedagogic discourse / Basil Bernstein.
      p.   cm. – (Primary socialization, language and education: 4)
   (Class, codes and control: v. 4)
      ISBN 0-415-04568-1
      1. Sociolinguistics.   2. Educational sociology.   I. Title.
   II. Series.   III. Series: Class, codes and control: v. 4.
   P40.B39   1990   89-27304
   306.4′4 – dc20   CIP

To Marion

Contents

Acknowledgements   ix

Introduction   1

Part I   On codes

1   Code, modalities, and the process of cultural reproduction: a model   13

2   Social class and pedagogic practice   63

3   Elaborated and restricted codes: overview and criticisms   94

Part II   On pedagogic discourse

4   Education, symbolic control, and social practices   133

5   The social construction of pedagogic discourse   165

References   219

Index   228

Acknowledgements

I am very grateful to the many research students who, over the years, have been a crucial source of challenge, criticism, and enthusiasm, and most especially to Christian Cox, Mario Diaz, Ana Maria Domingos, Isabel Faria, Janet Holland, and to William Tyler for showing how much more there is to see, to Roger Hewitt for his steadfast dedication to finding out about language and culture, to Ruqaiya Hasan, whose courage, integrity, and generous scholarship I would like here to acknowledge. I am very grateful to Heidi Berry, who managed the transformation of written pages into manscript with immense tolerance and high competence.

The contents of this volume first appeared as or are based upon:

Chapter 1: 'Code, modalities and the process of cultural reproduction: a model', *Language and Society 10* (1981) 327–63.

Chapter 2: 'Education and democracy', Robert Finkelstein Annual Lecture, Adelphi University, New York, 1988.

Chapter 3: 'Class, codes and communication', in *Sociolinguistics: an International Handbook of the Science of Language and Society*, Vol. I, ed. U. Ammon, N. Dittmar, K. Mattheier, W. de Gruyter, Berlin, 1987.

Chapter 4: 'Education, symbolic control and social practice', public lecture under the aegis of CIDE, Santiago, Chile, 1988.

Chapter 5: 'On pedagogic discourse', in *Handbook of Theory and Research for the Sociology of Education*, ed. J.G. Richardson, Greenwood Press, New York, 1986.

The order of the papers, and sometimes their contents, in this volume, unlike the companion volumes, are not in the same order in which they were written, and this has created problems of presentation. With the exception of one, all the papers have their origins in the 1981 paper 'Code, modalities and the process of reproduction: a model', and therefore it was necessary to give that paper in its entirety. However, this has led unfortunately to some marked repetition (on pages 99–107 and 113–14). Further, the section on symbolic control which was originally part of the paper 'On pedagogic discourse' has been placed in Chapter 4 (pages 134–43) because a discussion of the field of symbolic control is essential to the argument in that chapter. There have been some additions to all of the original papers.

Introduction

Contents   Part I of this volume deals essentially with the concept of code and the modalities of pedagogic transmission and acquisition. The first chapter is entirely concerned with the integration, synthesis, and development of past attempts to formalize the concept of code. Chapter 2 is a revision and extension of chapter 6 in *Class, Codes and Control*, vol. 3 (1975). The original model of a visible pedagogy set out in that chapter is now shown to have, among its modalities, a relatively self-regulating autonomous mode (at least, until recently in the UK) and a market-oriented mode. The internal ordering rules of modalities are given, together with those of an opposing modality, an invisible pedagogy. The latter is shown to have both liberal and radical forms. All pedagogic modalities are generated by the same set of internal rules, whose realizations vary according to their classification and framing values. It is not appropriate to see these modalities as simple dichotomies. They are held to be opposing modalities, translations of power relations, ideologies, and interests of different class fractions.

The third chapter is essentially an overview of the theory of elaborated and restricted codes and of its research which concentrates on the more sociolinguistic features of the theory, discusses criticisms made by sociolinguists, and treats Labov's criticisms in some detail. I was not sure where to place this chapter, as thematically it belongs to Part I but it does make reference to some concepts which appear only in Part II.

Chapter 1 is placed first because subsequent chapters are based in part upon ideas outlined in the initial chapter. However, this chapter is a highly formal account of the thesis: some readers may well find it an advantage to reverse the order of chapters in Part I and commence with the general overview and criticisms of the thesis presented in chapter 3.

Whereas Part I is concerned with elaborated codes and pedagogic modalities and is concerned to make explicit their underlying generating rules, Part II is concerned essentially with an analysis of the social construction of pedagogic discourse and its relation to symbolic control. Chapter 4 is an explorative essay which, on the basis of an hypothesis of the changing relations both within and between the economic field and the field of symbolic control, attempts to trace the changing orientation, organization, and relation of education to both these fields from the medieval period to the twentieth century. It is argued that there is now a dehumanizing of pedagogic discourse, brought about by inserting a market principle between knowledge and the knower, between the inner relation to, and the outer form of, knowledge. This insertion has enabled the construction of two quite separate markets: one for knowledge and the other for creators and users. This essay takes for granted the social construction of pedagogic discourse. The final essay is an attempt to analyse the device which is thought to be the condition for any pedagogic discourse and models the processes underlying the various modalities of pedagogic discourse which the device makes possible. The starting point of this analysis is appendix 6 to the code modality paper (chapter 1) which discusses the production, recontextualizing, and reproduction of official pedagogic discourse. Appendix 6 has been repeated in chapter 5 simply for ease of reading. There have been a number of versions of the paper constituting chapter 5, involving minor changes of organization and content (Bernstein, 1986, 1987). The conclusions in this volume have been changed to incorporate a discussion of the fundamental pedagogic outputs of the device and to clarify the use of the concept of relative autonomy.

The form of analysis of pedagogic discourse is similar to the analysis of pedagogic practices in chapter 2, where a distinction is drawn between the rules of construction of pedagogic practices and the various realizations these rules make possible: a distinction between a relay and what is relayed by that relay. In the same way, the analysis of the social construction of pedagogic discourse begins with a distinction between the rules which constitute the pedagogic device, the stable form of the relay, and the rules regulating the vicissitudes of its realizations, the variable forms of what is relayed. This paper's fundamental concern (and probably the fundamental concern of the whole research endeavour) is to describe the device which constructs, regulates, and distributes official elaborated codes and their modalities.

Code and class The integrating concept of the papers in this volume (as in others) is the concept of code, which is formally defined in the first chapter and is discussed later in this introduction.

It should be clear from the early chapters that the concept of code is not simply a regulator of cognitive orientation but regulates dispositions, identities, and practices, as these are formed in official and local pedagogizing agencies (school and family). The past thirty years have been taken up almost wholly with the specification, development, and regulation of this concept, especially that of elaborated code and its several modalities, which form the focus of this volume. The concept of code bears some relation to Bourdieu's concept of habitus. The concept of habitus, however, is a more general concept, more extensive and exhaustive in its regulation. It is essentially a cultural grammar specialized by class position and fields of practice. It is by no means clear what are the rules of these class-specialized grammars and fields of practice, nor is it clear how the specialized grammars are constructed and relayed in the process of their transmission and acquisition. But these are not the special objects of Bourdieu's project. From the point of view here, code may be regarded as an attempt to write what may perhaps be called pedagogic grammars of specialized habituses and the forms of their transmission which attempt to regulate their acquisition. The concept of code is different in one important respect from the concept of habitus. In the process of acquisition of specific codes, principles of order are taken over but also at the same time tacit principles of the disordering of that order.

Although an account of the development of code is given in chapter 3 it might be relevant to fill in aspects of the development not covered in that chapter. Previous definitions of codes (1962–71) were given in terms of context-dependent/independent orientation to meanings whose realizations were regulated by positional/personal forms of control in familial socializing contexts (instructional, regulative, inter-personal, imaginative). Variations in the use of codes, both within and between social classes, were expected to be a function of positional/personal forms of control. The following remained obscure in such a formulation:

1 How transmission became a principle of acquisition. It was not clear how codes were acquired. There was a gap between the process of transmission and the process of acquisition.
2 How 'context', the basic unit of the analysis, could be formally described independent of its semantic focus, e.g. instructional/regulative.
3 How social class regulations regulated orientations to meanings. Social class relations were said to give rise to different forms of social solidarity (organic or mechanical) arising out of the

context of work, which produced different orientations to meanings. However, this could not be derived directly from code definitions. The link between forms of familial control, class fractions, and the economic field and the field of symbolic control were only vaguely adumbrated.

4 How to translate, in the same language, from macro levels (themselves considerably understated) to micro levels of acquisition.

The major drive to develop theory comes from problems of empirical investigation, from issues raised by doctoral students in the preparation, design, and interpretation of their research, and, of course, from relevant criticism. The decade following 1971 was taken up with dealing with early obscurities of the thesis.

The concepts of ground rule in Bernstein (1973) and performance rule in Bernstein (1977c)[1] opened the way to formulating how codes were acquired. The classification and framing paper (Bernstein, 1971b: ch. 11) spoke of how these concepts relayed the distribution of power and principles of control, but these relationships were only presented visually in diagrammatic form in note B to the paper 'Aspects of the relation between education and production' (Bernstein, 1977a: 197). The separation of and antagonism between dominant agents of production and symbolic control were also adumbrated in that paper. At the micro level, a more explicit formulation of context was given in terms of meanings, realization, and generating contexts (Bernstein, 1977c). Finally, and of considerable importance, the results of an empirical enquiry designed by Diana Adlam and myself, analysed and written up by Janet Holland (1981), pointed the way to defining coding orientations to meanings in terms of their relation to a material base. This made possible a more explicit relation between coding orientation, occupational location, and social relations as the major, but not the only, generator of coding orientation.

Thus the basic elements of the reformulation in the paper 'Codes, modalities and the process of cultural reproduction: a model' (Bernstein, 1981)[2] were available, albeit scattered across different papers. I attempted a fundamental formal statement of the theory in that paper which would incorporate all the earlier developments outlined above. I have always been attracted to Althusser's theory of ideology (despite the criticisms) and this was made the basis of the relation between classification, voice, and the construction of the subject. The relation between classification and recognition rules and framing and realization rules showed how differences in the strength of classification and framing controlled selection of the contents of these rules, so regulating the process of acquisition and giving rise to different code modalities.

In appendix 5 to the code modality paper the results of earlier empirical work which showed differences in the speech, forms of control, and meanings of middle-class and lower working-class children in formal contexts of elicitation were reinterpreted, using the new code formulation. Appendix 3 applied the concepts of classification and framing as code indicators of different contexts of industrial manual practice. Appendix 4 dealt with the production, recontextualizing, and reproduction of pedagogic discourse, which opened the way to the later analysis of the social construction of pedagogic discourse. The code modality paper (however difficult it was to read) was a release from the narrow theoretical and empirical constraints of earlier work and opened up more fundamental questions whilst providing more precise descriptions for the testing of hypotheses. Criticisms of this paper are discussed in chapter 3.

A number of researchers have used the formulations, in particular Daniels (1988), who tested the relation between different classification and framing values, recognition and realization rules, and different specializations of meanings. Daniels, who used the code formulation in the 1981 paper, showed that in schools with different classification and framing values (produced by different theories of instruction) children used different recognition and realization rules in discriminating between science and art texts. Daniels's study shows the delicacy of description the concepts of classification and framing make possible and their powers of creating indicators of difference between schools at the levels of organization, external relations, and pedagogic practice. Ruquaiya Hasan's (1988) research into social class differences in parents' and children's speech, obtained from natural dialogue within the family and teachers' classroom talk, provided an excellent test of the thesis, as it is one of the few studies which employs a relevant linguistic theory for the description of the speech.[3]

Whereas the code modality paper attempted to remedy earlier deficiencies with respect to the transmission/acquisition process, the defining of context, and macro—micro translations by the development of what was thought to be a more powerful language of description, it did little to deal with the criticisms of the theory with respect to the formulations of social class. Impetus to such reformulations arose initially from the analysis of 'progressive' and 'conservative' forms of pedagogic practice (visible and invisible pedagogies) which appeared in *Class, Codes and Control* vol. 3 (ch. 6) and is developed further in this volume in chapter 2. A form of analysis was created which distinguished between class fractions who controlled highly specialized principles of communication which were applied directly to the means, contexts, and possibilities of physical resources, and class fractions who controlled highly specialized principles of communication which were applied directly to the means, contexts, and possibilities of discursive resources. This distinction gave rise to a concept of the social division of labour of symbolic control, of its specialized agencies and agents. Dominant agents of symbolic control, as dominant agents of production, could function in the field of symbolic control, the cultural field, or the economic field. It was hypothesized that ideological orientation, interests, and modes of cultural reproduction would be related to *functions* of the agents (symbolic control or production), *field location*, and *hierarchical position*. This analysis of class fractions, field locations, ideological interests, and modes of cultural reproduction has been subject to empirical research. Holland (1986) studied adolescents' conceptions of the domestic and industrial division of labour as a function of the class and field location of parents. Jenkins[4] (1989) studied the social basis of progressive education. Cox (1984) examined political ideology and education in Chile as a function of class and field location. Aggleton (1987) in a detailed ethnographic study of middle-class youth, examined forms of their cultural reproduction.

Perspective The perspective adopted appears to give no place for individual agency. There appear to be no individuals, only the process whereby 'subjects' are selectively created and constrained in and by the process of their creation. The 'subject' never appears as an individual in his/her attempts to create meanings and purposes, to struggle for or against beliefs, to negotiate, or perhaps change, the initial order she/he finds. It appears that people are more acted upon than acting upon. A diagram with arrows confirms this impression, especially when it is explained by a language of transmitters, acquirers, agents, agencies, fields, codes, grammars, and rules. But the transmission/acquisition systems the thesis projects do not create copper etching plates in whose lines we are trapped. Nor are the systems, grids, networks, and pathways embedded in either concrete or quicksand. The transmission/acquisition systems reveal and legitimate the enabling and disabling functions of power relations which they relay and upon which they rest. Attempts to model the internal principles of such transmissions do not make them eternal. Such analysis may show the poles of choice for any set of principles and the assemblies possible within those poles. It calls attention to the selective effects of transmissions, their social costs, and the basis for change. It is the case that the individual is not conceptualized as the basic unit of the analysis. The basic unit of analysis is the social relation of transmission and acquisition, and the focus is upon its controls.

The perspective focuses upon the construction of rules which generate what may be called official pedagogic discourse/practices, whether these be in the school or the family. The perspective does not include the study of the full choreography of interaction in the context of the classroom or family. Nor does the perspective offer the possibility of a delicate description of the full repertoire of arabesques of interaction within any classroom, staff room, or family. Clearly, children do more than learn what is formally expected of them and teachers do more than teach what is formally expected of them. Some children do not learn what is formally expected of them and some teachers do not teach or are unable to teach what is formally expected of them. However, the principles of description, whilst not capable of describing the full repertoire of classroom interactions (for which they were not designed), are well capable of describing features relevant to the theory of classroom interactions, its organizational contexts, and their relation to external agencies (e.g. family and work).

Pedro (1981) carried out a study of classroom instructional and regulative discourse in three primary schools, drawing on children of different social class background. She observed and recorded lessons in Portuguese language and arithmetic which were analysed according to the theory's principles of description. The results showed how the social background of the pupils acted selectively on the form and content of the pedagogic transmissions. Many critics of the classification and framing concepts seem unaware of their power to create delicate descriptions of micro classroom interactions and to relate these micro levels of interaction to macro levels (Daniels, 1988). This may be because of the critics' obsessional regard for the original paper in which these concepts were presented and their ignorance of their development and empirical application. Critics, especially those who do not understand empirical research, seem to be unaware that a paper is often not terminal but a beginning, an opening to an enlarged problematic and an initial development of the language of its articulation and research.

Every exposition or criticism, if it is to be coherent and useful, issues from a position held by the critic. The issue is the nature of the critic's position and the extent to which it obscures or recontextualizes the original text. When this occurs it is often difficult to recover the original text or reconstitute it unadulterated by the criticism. It seems that criticism can become fact in its own right, to be endlessly recycled, reproduced with an authority whose basis is rarely challenged, an economical substitute for the original text. Of course, criticism is necessary; without it there would be less development and even, for some, little incentive to develop. Yet, whilst there are clear criteria which the results of research must satisfy, there are few criteria which recontextualizers have to meet. As a consequence, their position in the recontextualizing field (market) can itself become a major regulator of their relation to the appropriated text. In their acts of 'critical exposition' recontextualizers sometimes perform priestly functions of exorcism, celebration, charismatic divination, and ritual succession; sometimes warrior functions as guardians of the old and frontiersmen of the new; sometimes they function as thought police, the Fahrenheit corps, and sometimes they perform more humble functions, such as weeding, keeping borders neat, transplanting and exotic potting, the gardeners and garnerers of the field.

It may well be that some work, as in this volume, and its predecessors, which develops and enlarges a central theme ('inconsistent and contradictory') presents difficulties and may require special treatment.

Selective referencing is a process whereby, for example, a very early paper (say 1959), which inevitably sets out a very primitive statement of the theory, is soundly and perhaps justifiably criticized (after faint praise) in a Continental book published in 1970 and subject to much translation and reprinting. Between 1959 and the book's appearance in 1970 the original primitive statement has probably been replaced by more effective published formulations which rendered the original critique void.

A more altruistic process can be called secondary servicing. This is a process whereby one exposition/criticism becomes the primary source for a number of others. Schizzing is another process. Here the unity of the original corpus is split at least in two (creative schizzing can accomplish much more); one half is treated as the whole and the rest is then subject to what may be called discursive repression. Schizzing often gives rise to its complementary. This complementary process shows conclusively that the original theory ignored, failed to see the relevance of, or, more usually, was ideologically blind to, the significance of what has already been subject to discursive repression. This is clearly a case of the return of the repressed.

There is a more extensive process, over-determining. This is a process whereby exposition is kept to a minimum (or maybe even absent in the most skilled hands) and the text is composed entirely of the criticisms of others, so producing the ultimate recontextualized text.

In contrast to over-determining there is the process of pointillism. It is used by compilers of scholarly dictionaries and encyclopedias for the construction of individual entries. This is a higher art form than over-determining. The pointilliste, in a few lines, with well chosen words, creates an impression which gains greater validity the further one is from the original text. I personally must say that I have found pointillistes, after some initial pressure, more amenable to change. This is because pointillism is very much an art where the content is secondary to the form.

Finally, there is creative replacing, a process which produces the wholly imaginary text. Whereas schizzing is based upon a partial repression of the original text, creative replacing is a process based upon a thoroughgoing denial of the original text. The original text is transformed into a Rorschach blot, eliciting the projection of a wholly new text. Creative replacing replaces the author of the original text by the critic as author and authority. Paradoxically, both author and critic now disappear. Creative replacing thus produces the wholly imaginary text.

This discussion of functions and processes should not be regarded as exhaustive or determinist, nor as a denial of human agency and creativity.

Relevance   This volume of papers may appear today to be somewhat unusual, as the papers deal with highly abstract formulations, they rarely refer to the empirical studies they presuppose and have informed, and examples are few. The papers are not concerned with grand narratives, commentaries, critiques, or recommendations. There are no immediate policy implications, no indicators of effective economic performance, no diagnostics, and certainly no pedagogic utopias. Neither do the papers lead to close ethnographic classroom narratives, important as these clearly are. The papers represent an on-going attempt to understand the outer limits and inner constraints of forms of pedagogic communication, their practices of transmission and acquisition, and the conditions of their change, in such a way that the distribution of power and principles of control such communication presupposes may be modelled, described, and researched.

Notes

1   Code definitions in terms of meanings, realizations, and contexts were given in in this foreword, pp. vii−xv.

Introduction

2 A revision of this paper appeared in *C.O.R.E.* 12, 1 (1988). A further revision has been made to the paper in this volume. Both revisions are for purposes of greater clarity.
3 Hasan's speech sample is unusual in that it is based upon approximately 100 hours of mother–child dialogue. The findings, both of family and of school talk, are supportive of the code theory.
4 The thesis includes an excellent comparison of various itemizations of the membership of the new middle class.

Part I
On codes

Chapter 1

Codes, modalities, and the process of cultural reproduction: a model

'Class relations' will be taken to refer to inequalities in the distribution of power, and in the principles of control between social groups, which are realized in the creation, distribution, reproduction, and legitimation of physical and symbolic values that have their source in the social division of labour. This definition draws attention deliberately to the distributive function of class relations, as this function has been the enduring focus of the research, and the definition makes this explicit.[1] In terms of the particular problems of the relationship between class and the process of its cultural reproduction, as developed in this thesis, what has to be shown is how class regulation of the distribution of power and of principles of control generates, distributes, reproduces, and legitimates dominant and dominated principles regulating the relationships within and between social groups and so forms of consciousness.

What we are asking here is how the distribution of power and the principles of control are transformed, at the level of the subject, into different, invidiously related, organizing principles, in such a way as both to position subjects and to create the possibility of change in such positioning. The broad answer given by this thesis is that class relations generate, distribute, reproduce, and legitimate distinctive forms of communication, which transmit dominant and dominated codes, and that subjects are differentially positioned by these codes in the process of acquiring them. 'Positioning' is used here to refer to the establishing of a specific relation to other subjects and to the creating of specific relationships within subjects. In general, from this point of view, codes are culturally determined positioning devices. More specifically, class-regulated codes position subjects with respect to dominant and dominated forms of communication and to the relationships between them. Ideology is constituted through and in such positioning. From this perspective, ideology inheres in and regulates *modes of relation*.

Ideology is not so much a content as a mode of relation for the realizing of contents. The skeleton of the thesis can now be exposed diagrammatically (Figure 1.1).

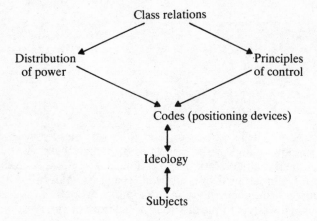

Figure 1.1

Codes: general

The first step towards filling out the entailed relationships in Figure 1.1 is to define codes, and the second step will be to derive from that definition propositions that will facilitate the defining of specific codes. In the Postscript to *Class, Codes and Control* vol. 1 (revised edition, 1974) there is a series of definitions of code that represent the evolution of the concept. Basically, there has been a movement from the giving of definitions in terms of linguistic indices to definitions in terms of their underlying semantic. In both cases the underlying semantic was considered to be the regulator of specific linguistic realizations. Specific linguistic usages were taken in the earlier definitions as indices of a specific semantic organization. The process of giving explicit primacy to the semantic systems is continued here. We shall now give the general definition of code.

A code is a regulative principle, tacitly acquired, which selects and integrates:

(*a*) relevant meanings	meanings
(*b*) forms of their realization	realizations
(*c*) evoking contexts	contexts

It follows from the definition that, if code selects and integrates relevant meanings, then code presupposes a concept of irrelevant or illegitimate meanings; that, if code selects forms of realization, then code presupposes a concept of inappropriate or illegitimate forms of realization; that, if code regulates evoking contexts, then again this implies a concept of inappropriate, illegitimate contexts. The concept of code is inseparable from the concepts of legitimate and illegitimate communication, and thus it presupposes a hierarchy in forms of communication and their demarcation and criteria (see appendix 1.1).

It also follows from this definition that the unit for the analysis of codes is not an abstracted utterance, or a single context, but relationships *between* contexts. Code is a regulator of the relationships between contexts, and, through those relationships, a regulator of the relationships *within* contexts. What counts as a context depends not on relationships within, but on relationships between, contexts. The latter relationships, *between*, create boundary markers whereby specific contexts are distinguished by their specialized meanings and realizations. Thus if code is the regulator of the relationships between contexts and, through that, the regulator of the relationships within contexts, then code must generate principles for distinguishing between contexts and principles for the creation and production of the specialized relationships within a context. We have previously called these principles, respectively, ground rules and performance rules.[2] However, in order to avoid confusion and irrelevant associations, the names of these two sets of rules will here be changed to *recognition* rules and *realization* rules. Recognition rules create the means of distinguishing between and so *recognizing* the speciality that constitutes a context, and realization rules regulate the creation and production of specialized relationships internal to that context. At the level of the subject, differences in code entail differences in recognition and realization rules. Later in this essay we shall be concerned to explicate *how* code generates recognition and realization rules.

Specific codes

The first step towards writing specific codes will require a rewriting of the original definitions so that it is possible to derive specific empirical relationships. The rewriting will also make explicit the causal chain of relevant meanings – realizations – context. Evoking contexts (*c*) will be rewritten as *specialized interactional practices*. Relevant meanings (*a*) will be rewritten as *orientations to meanings*. Forms of realization (*b*) will be rewritten as *textual productions*.

It may be useful first to put a gloss on 'orientations to meanings'. The latter refer to *privileged* and *privileging* referential relations.

'Privileged' refers to the priority of meanings *within* a context. 'Privileging' refers to the power conferred upon the speaker as a consequence of the selected meanings. Now the source of power and its legitimation, from our perspective, does not arise out of the social relationships *within* the context but out of a social base external to that context. That is, 'privileging' refers to relationships *between* contexts, whereas 'privileged' refers to relationships *within* a context. Looking ahead, relationships *between* contexts arise out of classificatory principles regulating communication within the context. For example, if we consider any pedagogic relation between doctor and patients, social worker and clients, teacher and pupils, parents and children, the power over the communication is extra-contextual of any one intra-contextual communication. *How* that power manifests itself within any one context, its local regulation of communication, depends upon the form of control of communication within a context (framing principles). Thus we can show these relationships diagrammatically (Figure 1.2). What counts as the textual production is a matter of the level of analysis.

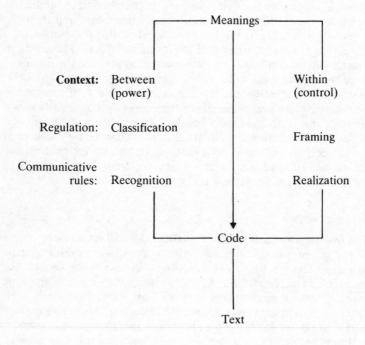

Figure 1.2

Thus we now obtain the following causal chain. The features that create the speciality of the interactional practice (i.e. the *form* of the social relationship) regulate orientations to meanings, and the latter generate, through *selection*, specific textual productions.[3] From this perspective the specific text is but a transformation of the specialized interactional practice; the text is the form of the social relationship made visible, palpable, material. It should be possible to recover the original specialized interactional practice from an analysis of its text(s) in its context. Further, the selection, creation, production, and changing of texts are the means whereby the positioning of subjects is revealed, reproduced, and changed.

We can now fill in a little more the inner structure of the thesis, which is shown in Figure 1.3. What is required is to show the means whereby it is possible to perform the following transformations: (1) class relations and positioning (via power and control); (2) positioning and codes; (3) codes and communication. If such transformations can be accomplished, then the invisible can be recovered from the visible.

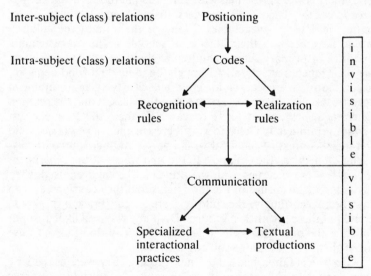

Figure 1.3

Elaborated and restricted codes

There are four aspects to consider: (1) orientations, (2) location, (3) distribution, (4) performance.

17

Orientations

We shall start by examining 'orientations to meanings', remembering that these look backward to specialized interactional practices and forward to textual productions. Our first approach is to recover specialized interactional practices from orientations to meaning. We shall then try to account for (2) and (3), the conditions for the *location* and *distribution* of such orientations.

We shall begin with a brief description of an enquiry into the social basis of classification carried out by the Sociological Research Unit (Holland, 1981). The Unit was concerned to create a means whereby it would be possible to discover children's orientation to principles of classification and the means of their change. The original sample consisted of thirty middle-class boys and girls and thirty lower working-class boys and girls aged 8 years and 11 years. The Unit wished to use, as the basis for classification, materials that would be equally familiar to all the children, although their *reading* of the materials in the experimental context was expected to be different, according to their class background. The children were presented with coloured pictures of food such as bread, cheese, bacon, hamburgers, fish fingers, sardines, soup, butter, and several vegetables. Many of these items the children would have eaten in their lunches at school, as the overwhelming majority of primary school children at the time of the experiment ate their lunches at school. Although the individual food items are a common experience for all children, clearly their grouping in specific dishes is likely to vary between the classes, and the relation between dishes is also likely to vary. Further, the frequency of certain groupings is likely to vary between the social classes, and the social context of the meal would be yet another source of class variation between the children. In the first stages of the experiment the SRU was concerned with the principle the children used when invited to make groups of the food items that they considered to go together. Accordingly, the children were asked, 'Do you think you could put these together in groups? Do it any way you like. Just put together the ones that seem to go together. You don't have to use all of them if you don't want to.'

After the children had made their groups, they were asked why they had made each group. It was possible for the children to give at least two broad principles for their groups. They could give a principle that had a direct relation to a specific local context of their lives and that took its significance from local activities and local meanings. In such a case the classification would relate to everyday life in the family (e.g. 'It's what we eat at home,' 'It's

what we have for breakfast,' 'It's what Mum makes'). In this case
it was proposed that the principle of classification has a relatively
direct relation to a specific local material base (a gloss on 'material
base' will be given below in the section headed 'Performance'.
However, the children could give a principle of classification that
related less to the specific, local context of their everyday
experience of food and its attendant social relations and practices
(e.g. 'These come from the ground,' 'These come from the sea,'
'These all have butter in them'). It is not that the latter examples do
not relate to a material base, for they do, but the relationship is
more indirect and less specific. It was found, as expected, that the
modal principle of classification of the middle-class children was
relatively independent of a specific context, whereas the modal
principle of classification of the lower working-class children was
relatively dependent upon a specific context.[4] In other words, the
crucial difference between the groups of children lay in the relation
of the classifactory principle to a material base; in one case the
relation was direct and specific; in the other the relation was more
indirect and less specific.

The children were then asked, 'Can you do it a second time? Can
you try to put them together in a different way this time?' This time
many middle-class children (a statistically significant number)
switched their principle of classification and produced principles
similar to those produced by the lower working-class children,
whereas the latter continued to use the principle they had used
before. (However, almost one-third of the lower working class had
changed their principle by the end of the experiment.) What is
interesting is that the middle-class children showed that they held
two principles and that these children held priority rules with
respect to the principles, such that those which had a relatively
direct relation to a specific material base were given second (i.e.
lower) priority. Indeed, I would argue that in the first four minutes
the middle-class children created orientations to meanings based
upon a *hierarchy* of principles, each of which had a different
relation to a material base, such that the principle which related to
a specific local material base in the experimental context was the
dominated (i.e. second) principle.

We have discussed the first section of the experiment in order to
prepare the ground for defining the *location* of elaborated and
restricted orientations to meaning. In previous papers we have
located these orientations in different modes of social solidarity,
mechanical and organic, which regulate different interactional
practices, and we argued that class relations regulated *how* these
orientations were made available in formal education and how

different class groups were differently placed with respect to their formal acquisition in the school. This formulation will now be modified so as to make more explicit the power relationships underpinning the location of these orientations and the distinctive feature of their materiality.

Location of elaborated and restricted orientations

We shall first give the general hypothesis. *The simpler the social division of labour, and the more specific and local the relation between an agent and its material base, the more direct the relation between meanings and a specific material base, and the greater the probability of a restricted coding orientation. The more complex the social division of labour, the less specific and local the relation between an agent and its material base, the more indirect the relation between meanings and a specific material base, and the greater the probability of an elaborated coding orientation.*

It is important to point out that in each case we are regarding the social division of labour *from the specific location of one of its agents*. Let us take the example of a peasant working on a sugar-cane plantation. From the point of view of that peasant, he or she would physically see himself or herself as part of a simple division of labour, and such an agent's interactional practices would have as their centre of gravity interactions within a simple division of labour regulating practices with respect to a local, specific material base. However, in the case of the patron, he (historically not she) would physically see himself as part of a complex division of labour, which would include the total *local* division of labour of the plantation, the local market, and circulation of capital, and which would also include national and international markets with their entailed capital circulations. The patron's centre of gravity would lie within a complex division of labour regulating practices with respect to a generalized material base.

Thus the most primitive condition for location of coding orientations is given by the location of agents in the social division of labour. Different locations generate different interactional practices, *which realize different relations to the material base* and so different coding orientations. At this point it is important to point out that we are here stating the *location* of different coding orientations, not their origins.[5]

Distribution

The conditions for the distribution of coding orientations in this model are clear. If agents become specialized categories of the social division of labour, and their location is fixed and so non-transposable, then coding orientations become specialities of position within the social division of labour. The condition for these conditions is the *principle of the social division of labour itself*. The group that dominates the principle of the social division of labour determines the extent to which positions in the social division of labour give access to specialized coding orientations. These coding orientations are in no sense inevitable consequences of any position. Coding orientations are not intrinsic to different positions. Whether they become so depends upon the distribution of power. Thus the distribution of coding orientations depends upon the distribution of power created by the principles regulating the social division of labour.

Performance: classification and framing

In this section we shall be concerned to show the regulation of the relation between orientations to meanings and the production and receiving of specific texts. Here we shall be examining the conditions for variations in and change of texts created by elaborated orientations to meanings. We shall see that in order to define specific codes it is necessary to state not only the regulation of *access* to positions in the social division of labour but also the regulation which constrains the *realization* of texts. Any definition of specific codes entails stating *orientation* and *realization* conditions.

Initial orientation conditions are located in the social division of labour and initial realization conditions are today almost co-terminous with formal educational agencies (schools, etc.). Thus access to orientations to meanings depends on the regulation of positions in the social division of labour of production, whereas the *form* of their realization is constituted by formal education. The availability, distribution, and realization of elaborated codes[6] depends fundamentally upon the relations between the modality of education and the mode of production. In as much as the relations *within* and *between* education and production are class-regulated, then code acquisition regulates cultural reproduction of class relations.

The division of labour and its social meanings

In the distinction between mode of production and modality of education there is clearly a distinction between different outputs; in the former physical objects are produced, exchanged, distributed, appropriated, whereas, in the latter,[7] discourses are produced/

reproduced, exchanged, distinguished, appropriated. The difference between those two products does not lie in the materiality of one and the non-materiality of the other. Discourse, as we shall see, has a material base, albeit it is less obvious and its relation to its materiality may be more opaque. *Agencies of symbolic control specialize in the production of specific discourses generated by elaborated codes.*

Despite differences in the dissimilarities of the outputs of production and education the social basis of these outputs is structurally similar. In both cases (objects/discourses) we have a social division of labour of production with its specialized categories of agents and their interrelations, together with the social relations *within* production. The former consists of the relation between the social categories of production (agents), and the latter consists of the specific realization of those categories (agents), that is, their specific practices/activities. Thus any production or reproduction has its social basis in *social categories* and *practices*. In the production of objects we have sets of differently specialized categories with their sets of differently specialized practices, and in the production and reproduction of discourses we have sets of specialized categories and sets of specialized practices (pedagogy). This analysis can be illustrated with reference to a family, which is a primary discourse reproducing/producing agency.

Here the social division of labour is constituted by the category set of kinship, whilst the social relations *within* production are the specific practices *between* the categories (e.g. between parents, between parents and children, between gender categories). We can apply the same analysis to school. Here the social division of labour is constituted by the set of categories of transmitters (teachers) and the set of categories which constitute acquirers, whilst the social relations refer to practices between transmitters and acquirers and practices between transmitters and practices between acquirers.

Any given social division of labour has two dimensions, horizontal and vertical. The horizontal dimension refers to specialized categories sharing membership of a common set, for example, school subjects in a given course, pupils, workers sharing a common status. The vertical dimension refers to the rank position of a category within a set and the ranking relation between sets. Power may be necessary to enter a set and is always necessary to change hierarchical positions within and between sets.

Classification and the social division of labour

Basic to the mode of production and modality of education are categories and practices that are regulated by the principles of a social division of labour and its internal social relations. Practices are the realization of categories. The form taken by these practices – that is, their degree of specificity, the extent to which practices are specialized to categories – depends entirely upon the relation between these categories. (Relation 'between' regulates relation 'within'.) Once categories are specialized it necessarily follows that their realization, their practices, are also specialized. The practice can be regarded as the 'message' of the category and is the *means of acquisition*. At this stage we shall simply state that specialized categories necessarily entail specialized 'voices', but we are as yet in no position to say anything about what is 'voiced'. We shall disconnect 'voice' from 'message'.

It does seem a little perverse to draw a distinction between voice and message, but the distinction is intrinsic to the logic of this approach. The voice of a social category (academic discourse, gender subject, occupational subject) is constructed by the degree of specialization of the discursive rules regulating and legitimizing the form of communication. In this sense voice is a little similar to register. However, accredited knowledge of these discursive rules is one thing and their realization in a local context quite another. Thus knowledge of the rules does not necessarily permit knowledge of their contextual use. The contextual use is, from this point of view, the *message*. Voice sets limits to message but, as we shall see, message becomes a means of change of voice. We can see that the distinctiveness of voice is a consequence of the relations between categories, whereas message is a consequence of the interactional practice *within* a context.

For purposes of exposition, we shall disconnect our analysis of the principles regulating the relations between categories from principles regulating their practices. We shall see later that there are also good analytic reasons for making such a separation.

If categories of either agents or discourse are specialized, then each category necessarily has its own specific identity and its own specific boundaries. The speciality of each category is created, maintained, and reproduced only if the relations between the categories of which a given category is a member are preserved. What is to be preserved? The *insulation between the categories*. It is the strength of the insulation that creates a space in which a category can become specific. If a category wishes to increase its specificity, it has to appropriate the means to produce the necessary insulation that is the prior condition to its appropriating specificity. The stronger the insulation between categories, the stronger the boundary between one category and another and the more defined the space that any category occupies and to which it is specialized.

It follows that, as the strength of the insulation between categories varies, so will the categories vary in their relation to each other, and so will their space, their identity, and 'voice'. Thus the *degree of insulation* is a crucial regulator of the relations between categories and the specificity of their 'voices'.[8] We can begin to see that the degree of insulation regulates criteria of demarcation between categories and so the *rules of their recognition*.

We are now in a position to state the fundamental principle regulating the relations between categories, that is, the fundamental principle regulating the social division of labour of production/reproduction. Different degrees of insulation between categories create different principles of the relations between categories and so different principles of the social division of labour.[9] If there is strong insulation between categories, then we shall say that there is a principle of strong classification, whereas if there is weak insulation between categories we shall say that this gives rise to a principle of weak classification. (Classification refers to the relations between categories, not to what is classified.) Any change in the principle of classification will require a change in the degree of insulation. Alternatively, the maintenance of a given principle depends upon preserving the strength of the insulation.

In order for insulation to be maintained there must be insulation maintainers (and a consequent division of labour, of reproducers, repairers, and surveyors) who work at constituting, sharpening, clarifying, repairing, defending boundaries. The principle of the classification is created, maintained, reproduced, and legitimated by insulation maintenance. Any attempt to change the classification necessarily involves a change in the degree of insulation between categories, which in itself will provoke the insulation maintainers (reproducers, repairers, surveyors) to restore the principle of the classification and themselves as the dominant agents. In order for this to be accomplished, the insulation maintainers must have power and the conditions to exert it. Thus insulation presupposes *relations of power* for its creation, reproduction, and legitimation.

We have shown, formally, that power relations regulate principles of classification by preserving or changing degrees of insulation between categories. In terms of our earlier analysis, power relationships establish the 'voice' of a category (subject/discourse) but not the 'message' (the practice). Power relations, in establishing the 'voice' of a category, necessarily establish demarcation markers and recognition procedures/rules. *Power relations position subjects through the principles of the classifications they establish.* If power relations are regulated by class relations, then class relations position subjects through the principles of classification they establish.

We can give examples of the relations between power, classification, and 'voice' by examining the division of labour according to gender. When this division of labour generates strong classification, then there is strong insulation between each category, and each category has its own specialized 'voice', and necessarily 'voice' will be specialized to gender. Further, any attempt to weaken the classification – that is, to reduce the insulation so as to change 'voice' (discourse) – will provoke the power relationship to re-establish the relations between gender categories by restoring the insulation.

We can see in this example another implication of insulation. Insulations are intervals, breaks, delocations, which establish categories of similarity and difference: the equal and the unequal; punctuations written by power relations that establish as the order of things distinct subjects through distinct voices. Indeed, insulation is the means whereby the cultural is transformed into the natural, the contingent into the necessary, the past into the present, the present into the future. In Bourdieu's terms, 'symbolic violence' is accomplished not by communication but by *delocations that regulate differences between voices*. Inasmuch as the insulation of strong classification of gender categories produces an arbitrary (contingent) specialization of gender 'voices', it has created imaginary subjects whose voices are experienced as real, as validating and constituting the specialized category (Althusser, 1971). Here the insulation attempts to suppress the arbitrariness of the principle of classification by suppressing the contradictions and dilemmas that inhere in the very principle of the classification. We can see that power relations can accomplish their reproduction by establishing a principle of classification that suppresses its own contradictions and dilemmas through the insulation it creates, maintains, and legitimates.

We can see that insulation has 'outer' and 'inner' consequences. On one level its maintenance is necessary for establishing and reproducing the principle of the classification and thus social order. In this process the contradictions and dilemmas which inhere in the principle of the classification are suppressed to the extent that the principle is taken for granted. At the level of the individual subject the contradictions and dilemmas which inhere in the principle of the classification are played out in some form, but any manifestation must be suppressed if it attempts to appear at the level of the social relation, or repressed if it appears at the level of fantasy or desire.

We are anticipating an important point. Insulation reproduces order both between and within individual subjects. But the contradictions and dilemmas which inhere in the principle of the classification are always in some sense active within and between individual subjects. In this sense the insulation creates not only order but also the potential of change in that order.

We can take another example from education. We can regard the social division of labour of a school to be composed of categories (transmitters and acquirers) and categories of discourse ('voices'). If the coding principle is one of strong classification, then there is strong insulation between educational discourse ('voice') and non-educational discourse ('voices'). Discourses are strongly insulated from one another, each with its own specialized 'voice' so that transmitters and acquirers become specialized categories with specialized 'voices'. Within the category of transmitter there are various 'sub-voices', and within the category of acquirer there are various 'sub-voices': age, gender, 'ability', ethnicity. In the process of acquiring the demarcation markers of categories (agents/discourse) the acquirer is constituted as a specialized category with variable subsets of voices depending upon age, gender, 'ability', ethnicity.

It may be as well to take up briefly the relation between 'voice' and its 'sub-voices'. In the case of school the dominant 'voice' is given by the category relation of teacher/pupil but the pupil may be subject to distributive rules which regulate the sub-voices (gender, race, ability, etc.). From another perspective pupils (and for that matter teachers) may be positioned within the category relations of social class and this may well become the dominant positioning voice, with pupil as the sub-voice. Whilst we may be criss-crossed by diverse voices (discourses), from our point of view these are arranged not horizontally but *hierarchically*.

In the same way that a strong classification of gender attempts to justify itself in terms of being a natural, non-arbitrary order, so the strong classification of educational agents/discourse attempts to justify itself in terms of a 'natural order' within discourse (logical), a 'natural order' of acquisition (biological), a 'natural order' of the relation between educational and non-educational discourse (specialized/lay).

It could be argued that, whereas the principle of the classification of gender categories and that of the categories of the mode of production have an arbitrary base, the principle of the classification of discourse ('voices') of education derives from features intrinsic to the specialized discourse and is therefore non-arbitrary. This may well be the case. We need, however, to distinguish between the distinctive features of a form of discourse that give its speciality and the social division of labour created for its transmission and reproduction; it is the latter that is the object of our concern.

From the point of view of the social division of labour of reproduction in education we can distinguish the following classificatory features, each constituted by its own arbitrary insulation features and power relations:

1 *Extra-discourse relations of education.* Educational discourse as a whole may be strongly or weakly insulated from non-educational discourse.
2 *Intra-discourse relations of education.* Organizational context:
   (a) *Insulation between agents and insulation between discourse.* In this situation agents and discourses are specialized to departments, which are strongly insulated from each other.
   (b) *Insulation between discourses but not agents.* Here agents and discourses are not specialized to departments but share a common organizational context.
3 *Transmission context.* Educational discourses within and/or between vocational and academic may be strongly or weakly insulated from each other.
4 *System context.* Education may be wholly subordinate to the agencies of the State, or it may be accorded a relatively autonomous space with respect to discursive areas and practices.

We can therefore distinguish classificatory principles between the category of educational discourse and the category of non-educational discourse, classificatory principles internal to educational discourse and classificatory principles regulating the context of the system. In all the above, 1–4, the question of the definition of discourse in terms of internal criteria is not at issue. What is at issue is the social basis of the insulation, the principle(s) of classification created by the insulation, and the power relations that maintain insulations (whatever their degree) and so the principle of the classification.

It may well be useful to make explicit the language used to discuss reproduction/production. We have earlier argued that production and reproduction have their social basis in categories and practices; that categories are constituted by the social division of labour and that practices are constituted by social relations within production/reproduction; that categories constitute 'voices' and that practices constitute their 'message'; message is dependent upon 'voice', and the subject is a dialectical relation between 'voice' and message. In this section we have dealt with the relation between the social division of labour, classification, and 'voice'.

Our view is this: the social division of labour is a relation between categories established by a principle of classification. The principle of classification establishes the degree of specificity of the 'voices' of the categories through the insulation it establishes. The insulation is the delocations produced by the distribution of power and through which power relations are given their voice. The subject is initially established by the silence through which power speaks.

Classification, voice, reproduction, and acquisition

We can present in diagrammatic form the structure of the arguments we have so far offered in our explication of the rules for defining specific codes (see Figure 1.4). The sets of relationships shown in Figure 1.4 are external to the subject and initially position the subject with respect to the social division of labour. The positioning of the subject creates the 'voice' of the subject but not the specific message. The 'voice' sets the limits on what can be a legitimate message. To create a message beyond those limits is to change 'voice'. Such a change entails changing the degree of insulation, which initially was the condition for the speciality of the original 'voice'. A change in the insulation produces a change in the principle of the classification, which in turn indexes a change in the social division of labour, which will then move its dominant categories (agents) to exert their power through the hierarchy(ies) they regulate to induce a return to the original 'voice'.

Distribution of power

|

Social division of labour

|

Hierarchical principles

|

Classification

Figure 1.4

We have also argued for a further set of relationships, which are the conditions for the *acquisition* of the 'voice' by the subject. We give these in diagrammatic form (Figure 1.5). The principle of the classification generates through its insulations the speciality of the categories and the markings of that speciality. The markings of the categories, from the point of view of the acquiring subject, provide a set of demarcation criteria for recognizing the categories in the variety of their presentations. The sets of demarcation criteria provide a basis for the subject to infer recognition rules. The *recognition rules* regulate what goes with what: what meanings may legitimately be put together, what referential relations are privileged/privileging. The recognition rules regulate the principles for generating legitimate meaning and in so doing create what we have called the *syntax of generation* of meaning.

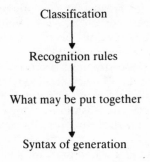

Figure 1.5

We shall give here an example of what we mean by the syntax of the generation of meaning. We shall take an example from the school, but we could as easily take the example from work. In a school operating with a strong classification of discourses (school subjects), or in one of its sections, there is a *level* of pupil acquisition which is positioned by the principle of the classification itself. Thus where there is a principle of strong classification this creates its set of specialized recognition rules for each of its categories (school subjects). This set of specialized recognition rules translates into the syntax for the generation of legitimate meaning. We shall see later that it is possible to have acquired the recognition rules of this syntax without acquiring the competence to produce what counts as effective messages in any one of the discourses (Daniels, 1988).

We can now trace a relation between the distribution of power external to the subject and the syntax of generation internal to the subject via the classificatory principle of the social division of labour. The subject creates, maintains, reproduces, and legitimizes the *distribution of power* through the development and establishing of the syntax of generation of meaning. This syntax is tacitly acquired in the sense that it develops through inferences the subject draws from the surface features of his or her on-going everyday interactions. We shall refer to this process as 'tacit practice'.

Here we shall distinguish two levels of tacit practice (in Figure 1.8 the unshaded and shaded levels). The first is that established by acquisition of the set of recognition rules translated into a syntax for the generation of legitimate meaning. This we can describe as the conscious level of tacit practice. We shall assert that at this level not only is the relation between dominant and dominated voices acquired but so also is a potential oppositional 'yet to be voiced'. As we have indicated earlier, there are potential contradictions and dilemmas in the order created by the principle of classification which serve as sources for a 'yet to be voiced', for alternative discourse, other subject-relations of power. These potential reordering features may be suppressed or rendered unthinkable by insulation. Even if these strategies are effective at the conscious level of tacit practice it will be asserted here that these reordering features have manifestations at a deeper level of the individual subject as metaphoric condensations of new category relations. And in turn these point to their controlling syntax for the generation of new meanings.

We do not want to give the impression that the stratum of tacit practice, the 'yet to be voiced' and its underlying condensed syntax, necessarily creates in each subject a potential theory of change. It should, however, provide a potential source of the arbitrary nature of the dominant classificatory principles and the power relations that speak through them. From this point of view it could provide the basis for anomie and so could speak either to a new imposition of order or change of power or to the tension of their relations. It may well be that for those dominating the power relations it would speak to anomie, whereas for those dominated it may well speak to change. The tension between order and change may be the distinguishing feature of the new agents of symbolic control (Bernstein, 1977d: ch. 8).

We can extend the diagrammatic illustration of our argument with reference to classification, 'voice' production, and acquisition (Figure 1.6).

It may be useful at this stage to summarize what has been so far proposed. In order to specify specific codes we are required to show how the distribution of power and principle of control are realized in the relationship within and between meanings, realization, and contexts. We rewrote the latter as interactional practices, orientations to meanings (privileged and privileging referential relations),

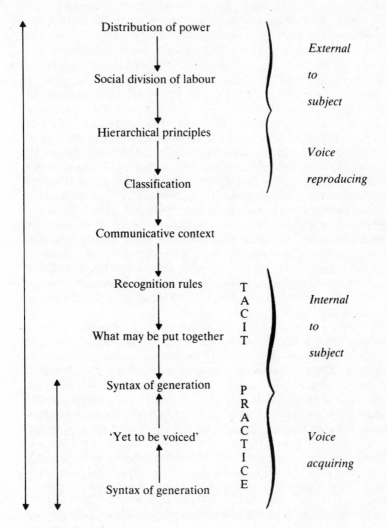

Figure 1.6

and textual productions. Orientations to meanings (privileged and privileging referential relations) are seen as generated by different locations (relations between dominant and dominated) within the social division of labour of the production of physical resources. Realizations of these meanings are specified in terms of specialized interactional practices. Realizations are a function of the social

31

relations within production. It was argued that the codes of education consist of elaborated orientations to meanings because of the indirect relation of these meanings to a specific material base. The realizations of the meanings in education are a function of the specific form taken by the interactional practices of education. Because the codes of education consist of elaborated orientations it does not follow that these are always transmitted and acquired by all groups of pupils.

The next step involved an analysis of interactional practices. Our analysis distinguished two crucial features: a category relation and its message. We considered that the category relation is created by the principle of the relation between categories, a classificatory principle which, in turn, is regulated by the social division of labour constituted by a given distribution of power. We then examined the relation between the classificatory principle and 'voice', and in this way we examined interactional practices in terms of 'voices'. We then made explicit the relations between the classificatory principle, 'voice', recognition rules, syntax of generation, and the distribution of power. In other words we specified a relation between *relations between categories* and *that which it is legitimate to mean*. We have as yet not specified the regulation on *the making public* of this meaning.

We have not as yet analysed *how* what it is legitimate to mean comes to have a specific realizational form. We shall see that it is through this realizational form, the message, that the code is acquired. The message is the means of socialization into the code. We have so far only theorized the constitution and acquisition of the 'what' of the code. Briefly, the code regulates the *what* and *how* of meanings: what meanings may legitimately be put together and how those meanings may legitimately be realized. We have so far concentrated on the 'what', and shown the relationship between the distribution of power and the regulation of the 'what' (see Figure 1.6).

We now turn to analysis of the regulation of the 'how', that is, to the relationships between principles of control and specific 'hows'. Here we shall be concerned with social relations and their regulation of 'message' and its contextualization. As we are going to discuss 'message' with reference to the acquisition of *discursive resources*, we shall be referring to the social relations within reproduction, that is, to *pedagogical relations*, essentially in education. However, we can extend the model to consider the social relations within production and the principles of their realization (i.e. the message). We have in fact carried out such an analysis in appendix 1.3, but we suggest that it be read after the completion of the discussion of framing.

Social relations, practice, and message

In the previous section we discussed the relations between the distribution of power, the social division of labour, the principle of its classification, the degree of specificity of categories, 'voice', recognition rules, and the syntax of generation of privileged and privileging relations. We shall now turn to an analysis of social relations, practices, and 'message'. There are difficulties in this discussion because 'message' is dependent on 'voice' and yet is the potential instrument of change of voice. 'Message' is dependent upon 'voice', for the voice limits the range of the legitimate potential of the message. Yet the cleavages, contradictions, and dilemmas, which are latent in the 'voice', are a potential of the realization of the message. Put in a less metaphoric way, the principle of the social division of labour necessarily limits the *realization* of its practices, yet the practices contain the possibility of change in the social division of labour and thus of their own change. The dynamic potential of the relation between 'voice' and 'message', between social categories and practices, between the social division of labour and its social relations, should be borne in mind throughout the subsequent analysis.

There is a further difficulty to this analysis. Empirically, it is not possible to separate 'voice' from 'message'. 'Voice' (implicitly or explicitly) is always announced, realized in 'message'. In an important sense the *classificatory principle* is continuously present in every pedagogical relation. All the 'voices' are invisibly present in any one 'voice'. Socialization into one 'voiced message' involves socialization into all (i.e. into the principle of the classification). If we consider, for example, a strongly classified array of school or university subjects, what is a school subject (its boundaries and their defining rules) is a function of the relationship with other subjects, e.g. what is sociology depends upon what is history, economics, geography, psychology. Entailed in the recognition of the voice and realization of any one subject is the invisible presence of the *classification* of all other subjects and of the power relations of their separateness and so distinctiveness.

Crucial to our perspective here is the analytic distinction between power and control, that is, between what is to be reproduced and the form of its acquisition. The latter directs out attention to the specific practices between transmitters and acquirers, which create the local context of reproduction. Social relations refer to the specific practices regulating the relationships between transmitters and acquirers, which constitute the context of acquisition. Essentially, social relations regulate the form of the pedagogic practice, and so the specific category-message. *The fundamental message of a pedagogic practice is the rule for legitimate communication*. Thus the social relations within reproduction control principles of communication, and in so doing regulate what we shall call the communicative context.

Context is a term frequently used but less frequently given the status of a derived term. Such a logical status is crucial when context is the basic unit of a theory or description. Among sociolinguists the definition of a context is often no more than the application of a botanical classification the principle of which is arbitrary, or which operates at a very low level of description.

The communicative context

If the degree of insulation is the crucial feature of the classificatory principle generated by the social division of labour, then the *form of the communicative context* is the crucial feature generated by their social relations, through the pedagogic practices the social relations regulate. These practices constitute, interrelate, and regulate the possibilities of two communication principles:

1 *Interactional.* This principle regulates the selection, organization sequencing, criteria, and pacing of communication (oral/written/visual) together with the position, posture, and dress of the communicants.
2 *Locational.* This principle regulates physical location and the form of its realization (i.e. the range of objects, their attributes, their relation to each other, and the space in which they are constituted).

Basically, these two principles represent the spatial and temporal features of the communicative context; the spatial feature is given by the locational principle, and the temporal feature is given by the interactional principle. We may well find that under certain conditions these two features are tied to each other in a one-to-one figure/ground relation (e.g. teacher/school, teacher/class), but this need not necessarily be the case. The interactional features may not be tied to a particular space. If we consider parents and children, the interactional feature is not necessarily tied to a particular space or sub-space. This points to a classificatory regulation of the communicative context. The stronger the tie between the temporal (interactional) and spatial (locational) features of the communicative context, the stronger will be its classification. The stronger its classification, the more likely that the array of objects, attributes, and their relation within the communicative context stand in a fixed relation to each other and so are specialized to that context.

We should note also that the possibilities of a communicative context include the marking of the relation between the locational and interactional features. It is possible for a specific practice to mark the locational feature more strongly than the interactional, or vice versa.

The *interactional principle* is the dominant feature of the communicative context, for it is this principle that establishes, interrelates, regulates, and *changes* the possibilities of the two principles.

We shall now show that recognition rules and realization rules establish the context. First, a classificatory principle, through its insulation, constitutes the degree of speciality of the communicative context and in so doing provides the limits of its communicative potential. The classification principle creates the specific recognition rules whereby a context is distinguished and given its position with respect to other contexts. Thus classification regulates spatial orderings and thus the *locational* principle. The interactional principle of the communicative context creates the specific message, that is, the specific rules for generating what counts as legitimate communication/discourse and so the range of possible texts. The interactional principle creates the specific realization rules for these texts and in so doing regulates temporal orderings. The communicative context is constituted by recognition and realization rules, and these rules when acquired by communicants create the competence. Classificatory principles establish recognition rules, and we shall see that framing principles establish realization rules.

Now although realization rules establish what counts as a legitimate text, these rules presuppose and are limited by recognition rules, and the classificatory principle these rules presuppose, which determines the limits of the legitimate potential of the communication. Thus, as we have seen, classification−recognition rules−voice−locational principle. And, as we shall see, framing−realization rules−message−*interactional* principle. There is a dynamic relation between voice and message. Whereas in the first instance the latter limits the former, the former is also the source of change of the latter and so of itself. In other words, social relations within the social division of labour have the potential of changing that social division of labour. Message is the means of changing voice.

Framing

We have so far discussed the interrelations within the social division of labour, the communicative context, and principles of communication. We now need to distinguish between various forms of these social relations and so various forms of the principles of communication. We shall use the concept of *framing* to describe these variations. Framing stands in the same relation to principles of communication as classification to the principles of the relation between categories. In the same way as relations between categories can be governed by strong or weak classification, so principles of communication can be governed by strong or weak framing. From this point of view, it does not make sense to talk about weak or strong principles of communication. Principles of communication are to varying degrees acquired, explored, resisted, challenged, and their vicissitudes are particular to a principle. Control is always present, whatever the principle. What varies is the *form* the control takes. The form of control is here described in terms of its framing.

Changes or variations in the classificatory principle produce changes or variations in the 'voices' of categories; changes or variations in framing produce variations or changes in pedagogic practices, which in turn produce changes or variations in principles of communication, and so changes or variations in the communicative context. Variations or changes in framing produce variations or changes in the rules regulating what counts as legitimate communication/discourse and its possible texts. In the same way that the distribution of power regulates the classificatory principle via the social division of labour, so principles of control regulate framing via its social relations.

Definition of framing. Framing refers to the principle regulating the communicative practices of the social relations within the reproduction of discursive resources, that is, between transmitters and acquirers. Where framing is strong, the transmitter explicitly regulates the distinguishing features of the interactional and locational principles, which constitute the communicative context. Where framing is weak, the acquirer has a greater degree of regulation over the distinguishing features of the interactional and locational principles that constitute the communicative context. This may be more apparent than real.

Variations in the degree and change of framing regulate variations and change in realization rules. In order to give a more precise definition of framing, we need to make explicit the phrase 'the distinguishing features of the communicative context'. These distinguishing features will vary according to whether the communicative context is generating physical or discursive resources (see appendix 1.3). If it is the latter, then the distinguishing features would be constituted by the selection, organization (sequencing), pacing, criteria of the communicants, together with the features of the physical location.

Strong framing: the transmitter controls the selection, organization, pacing, criteria of communication and the position, posture, and dress of the communicants, together with the arrangement of the physical location. *Weak framing:* the acquirer has more control over the selection, organization, and pacing, criteria of communication and over the position, posture, and dress, together with the arrangement of the physical location. It should be clear that the strengthening and weakening of framing may be confined to one or more of the features regulated by framing. Empirical studies of framing and of its internal features may be found in Cox (1986), Daniels (1988), Domingos (1987).

We can distinguish at a greater level of delicacy between the *internal* values of the strength of framing (F^i) and the *external* values of the strength of framing (F^e). If we consider a school where F^e is strong, then the transmitter regulates what features of non-school communication and practice can be realized within the school's pedagogic context, such as the classroom or equivalent F^e. Where F^e is weak, the acquirer has more regulation over what features of non-school communication and practice may be realized within the classroom or equivalent F^i. It is possible for F^e to be weak and F^i still to be relatively strong. Further, the relations between F^i and F^e may change over the time span of the transmission. When the acquirers are young, F^e may be relatively weak, whereas with advancing age F^e may increase in strength for one group of acquirers such as the successful, whereas F^e may be weakened or remain weak for the unsuccessful (social education, community projects, education for work, etc.).

In the same way we can consider C^e as the external value of classification and C^i as the internal value of classification within a context. In a classroom, for example, the locational position of pupils, teacher, desks, cupboard, wall ordering are a feature of the internal classification (C^i) together with the distribution of tasks among pupils (all doing the same or different tasks). In this way the principle of the internal and external classification of the pedagogic context is invisibly present in any communicative realization of the context. We can summarize our discussion in Figure 1.7.

In the previous section, devoted to classification, 'voice' reproduction, and acquisition, we indicated in Figure 1.6 a level of

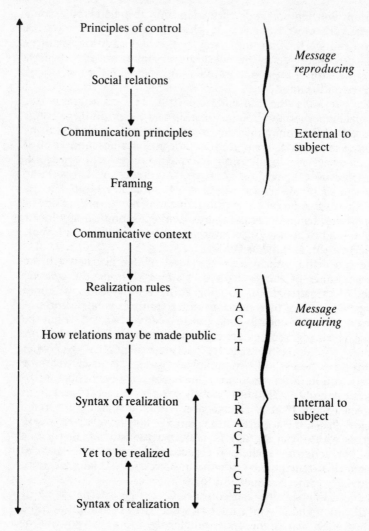

Figure 1.7

relation we called the 'yet to be voiced', which we argued was a potential of the contradictions, cleavages, and dilemmas generated by the classificatory principle itself. In Figure 1.7 we have distinguished a level of relation we have called the 'yet to be realized', which is a potential of the 'yet to be voiced'. It is a matter of some importance to distinguish between the *reactions to, or the challenge of, the realization rule* imposed by a given framing and the level we have called the 'yet to be realized'.

Any framing carries with it the procedures of its disturbance and challenge. Consider an elaborated code with values $+C+F^{ie}$ realized in the communicative context of a secondary school in which the pedagogical relations are between a teacher and a class of pupils who have been disabled by the code. The strategies for challenging the code are given by the code's principles. If the pupils are to challenge the code effectively, it cannot be done by one pupil. It requires changing the basic unit of acquisition, which is that of an isolated, privatized, competitive pupil, to communal, non-competitive classroom relations. There must be a change in pupils' principles of social integration. Given this change, the new group can substitute its own norm of production for the teacher's norms. The group can now impose its own realization rules. These may well include sabotaging the means of the pedagogic practice, subverting its rules, assuming aggressive postures. These disturbances and challenges are resistances called out by the specific code; they do not necessarily index a move even to declassify, let alone to reclassify. Challenge of, or resistance to, the framing of the pedagogic practice by transmitters or acquirers may be within the terms of the classificatory principles.

The level of tacit practice which we have called 'yet to be realized' operates at a deeper level. It is the 'message' of the 'yet to be voiced'. The 'yet to be voiced' is a potential challenge to the distribution of power and varies with its principles; the 'yet to be realized' is a potential answer to the principles of control and varies with those principles. Just as the classificatory principle may be realized by, and acquired through, different principles of communication ('message'), so the 'yet to be voiced' may be realized through different principles of communication ('message'). Its 'message' is a function of the dominant principle of control acting through a specific framing. What are the realizations of the 'yet to be realized'? The realizations, at this level, are not the product of a process of selection and orderings that can be consciously varied; they take the form of metaphors of new possibilitties. To say this is not to say that they are unregulated, for they are a potential of the code and of its change or variation.

We have distinguished two levels of tacit practices: (1) a level that is subject to conscious selection and ordering within the possibilities of a given syntax and realization; (2) a level that is not subject to conscious selection and ordering but interacts with the first level.

Specific codes and their modalities

We began this analysis with the statement that to define codes it is necessary to state both *orientation* and *realization* conditions. In class societies in general the primary distribution of elaborated and restricted orientation arises out of and is legitimated by the social division of labour of the mode of production and is transferred to the family. However, such transfer is not necessarily automatic, as it may be transposed by countervailing (oppositional) agencies arising out of the social matrix of the mode of production (trade unions, political parties) and discursive mediations of particular families. However, irrespective of the distribution of elaborated orientations to social groups in the mode of production, formal education is essentially predicated on the institutionalizing of elaborated orientations and the contingent forms of their realization irrespective of differences between social groups in their acquisition. Yet it may be the case that for certain groups of pupils (those who have been rendered disabled) a transmission may be suspended, because of the activities either of students or of their teachers. Further, restricted orientations may replace elaborated orientations for particular social groups of pupils where a limited, narrow concept of vocational skill training is substituted as the modal transmission.

Apart from these cases, education is predicated upon elaborated orientations, irrespective of the dominant principles of the social formation as these regulate the class structure and in particular the social division and social relations of production. But – and it is an important but – dominant principles select/limit the *mode of realization* of elaborated orientations in education and thus the code. Dominant principles of the social formation select/limit organizational, discursive, transmission, and relational practices, that is, the classification and framing values, and so the dominant codes. How effective is this selection/limitation is a matter of the space accorded to relative autonomies and a matter of the balance of power (see appendix 1.4).

Basically, specific elaborated codes, that is, codes with particular classification and framing values, are the means available for institutionalizing and relaying the dominant principles of a social formation in formal education. These codes have regulative consequences for the social distribution of their acquisition and for the formation of the consciousness of those who function in the specialized agencies of the field of symbolic control (see chapter 4). By extension, specific elaborated codes effect particular changes both in the forces and in the social relations of production. The form these codes take, their mode of regulation, varies according to the form of the dominant principle (capitalist, collectivist, dictatorship). Certainly in Western Europe and the USA, capitalism and its modes have been and are the dominant social principles and class relations their institutional form and arena. Whilst the analysis to follow is not limited to such formations, it will be here so applied.

Code modalities

In Figure 1.8 we have put together the two halves of the model that our exposition separated. The distribution of power and the principle of control of the dominant principle are realized in the social division of labour and its social relations, and they establish the classificatory and framing values, which define the mode of transmission/acquisition or practice in basic communicative contexts for the reproduction of discursive and the production of physical resources. The classificatory principles regulate recognition rules, what it is legitimate to put together, and so what we have called the syntax for generating legitimate meaning. Framing principles regulate realization rules, how relations may be made public, and so what we have called the syntax of realizations.

From this point of view the distribution of power and the principle of control translate into classificatory and framing principles, regulating the structure (organization), interactions, and communicative contexts of agencies for the production and reproduction of discursive and physical resources. The subject acquires classification and framing principles, which create for the subject, and legitimize, the speciality of his or her voice and message.

The unbroken lines of the model show the lines of imposition of what is to be reproduced and the process of its acquisition. Codes enable subjects not only to read and create texts that are legitimately available to be so constructed but also to read and create texts that are within the possibilities of the syntax of generation/realization as potential orthodox/heterodox texts. The diagonal lines show the process of resistance, challenge, or opposition. The diagonal shading shows the process shaping the response to the cleavages, contradictions, and dilemmas suppressed by the insulation of the classification. We do not want to give the impression that we are operating with a theory of variations, resistance, opposition which is based on isolated individual realization. Variation, resistance, challenge, opposition, struggle arise out of the structural relations between social groups.

We can now write specific codes regulating the reproduction/production of physical and discursive resources in terms of

41

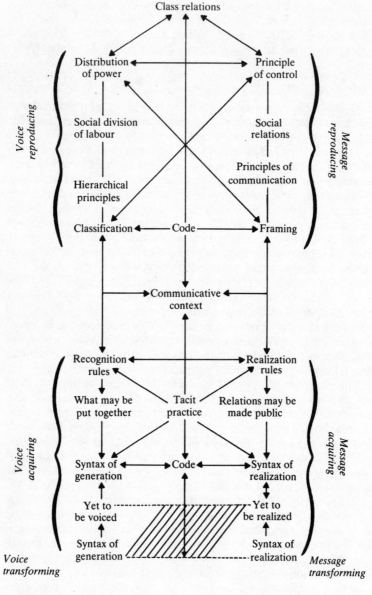

Figure 1.8

orientations to meanings and their realizations created by specialized interactional practices constituting communicative contexts. Codes can be specified by the following formula:

$$\frac{O}{\pm C^{i/e} \quad \pm F^{i/e}}$$

where O refers to orientations to meanings, elaborated or restricted (privileged/privileging referential relations); C refers to the principle of classification; F refers to the principle of framing; $\pm$ refers to the values of C and F with respect to strength (strong/weak); i refers to the internal values of C and F within a communicative context (e.g. family, school, or work); e refers to the external values of C and F, that is, the regulation of communicative relations between communicative contexts (e.g. family or community and school; school and work).

We can talk about the modality of a code and its change. The modality of a code or its change is given by the values of classification and framing. The values of classification and framing can vary independently of each other. Any one set of values for classification and framing constitutes the modality of the code.

Change of code

A change of code involves a change in the strength of a basic classification. We consider that there are two basic classifications which may or may not be interrelated, in the sense that changing the value of one does not necessarily lead to a change in the value of the other. We consider that the basic classificatory principle is created by the distribution of power constituting, reproducing, and legitimizing the social division of labour of physical resources. A change in this classificatory principle from strong to weak involves not a change in, but a change of, class relations. However, we must add immediately, while not diminishing the significance of such a change, that it would not, in itself, necessarily produce a change of institutionalized elaborated codes and therefore a change in the principle of cultural reproduction. In order (in the terms of this paper) for there to be a change in institutionalized elaborated codes and thus in the principles of cultural reproduction, the classificatory relation between the category 'education' and the category 'production' must be fundamentally weakened. This is the necessary condition for weakening the second basic classification, that between mental and manual work. In class societies the strengths of these two classifications are causally related. However, in societies dedicated to a change in the mode of production, few indeed have even attempted to institutionalize a weakening of the classificatory relation between education and production. On the contrary, such societies are as preoccupied with the systemic relations between education and production as are class societies (Bernstein, 1977d: ch. 8).

Code modalities defined

Code modalities are essentially variations in the means and focuses of symbolic control on the basis of a given distribution of power. Although modalities do not fundamentally change the principles of cultural reproduction or material production, as their effects are on the whole confined to changes in the process whereby the principle is transmitted and acquired, it would be inappropriate to dismiss variations in modalities as superficial phenomena. It is useful to classify such variations in modalities according to the *location* and *code value* of the modality:

1 *Location*
(a) The variation may regulate an agency or agencies *within* a field (e.g. symbolic control, production, or the various agencies of the State).
(b) The variation may regulate relations *between* agencies in different fields.
(c) The variation may be specific to either a dominant or a dominated modality or it may affect both.

2 *Code value*
The variation may affect only the principle of the classification, or only the framing, or it may affect both.

Classification

1 Within a given principle of classification there may be variations in different historical periods in the number, emphasis, and stability of categories (the set) regulated by the classification (the social division of labour).
2 There may be a substitution of categories within an existing set (e.g. applied, for pure; more, for less specialized).

Any variation within a code that affects the classification will create conflict, not over the general principle of the distribution of power, but over the distribution within the general principles.

Framing

Variation may affect only the internal values of the framing, or it may affect the external values, or both values.

We shall use the distinctions just made, based on locations and code values *within and between fields*, to give a more formal and concrete presentation of code modalities:

1 Within agencies/fields:
(*a*) *Variations within a dominant modality.* Examples of such variation would be historical variations in dominant academic curricula and practice in the various levels and department of the educational system, historical variations in the administration/management/practices of material production (Bourdieu and Boltanksi, 1978).
(*b*) *Variations within a dominated modality.* Examples of such variation would be historical variations in curricula and practice for non-elite pupils, or the shop-floor practices of material production.
(*c*) *Opposition within a dominant modality.* Examples of such opposition would be orthodox–heterodox, conservative–progressive practices, with respect to agencies within the field of symbolic control or the field of production – or State agencies.
(*d*) *Opposition between modalities.* A crucial and fundamental opposition here is the opposition between codes elaborated and restricted within education and within material production.

2 Between agencies/fields:
(*a*) Variations in the relation between different agencies, e.g. education and production. Framing relations within education may be relatively weakened in order to accommodate the requirements of different categories of labour, so as to strengthen the systemic or correspondence relation between the output of education and the requirements of work (Bernstein, 1977d: ch. 8).
(*b*) The degree of regulation (classification) by agencies of the State of agencies within the field of symbolic control or material production, or both, may vary. Variation in the strength of this classification regulates the degree of autonomy of the fields with respect to the State.

In the process of distinguishing locations of variations and change of elaborated codes we have utilized Bourdieu's concept of field and distinguished three related fields. We could say that code modalities establish and reproduce the practices specific to a field

45

and, again in Bourdieu's terms, create the specificity of a habitus. We have distinguished the field of symbolic control, whose ideologies and agencies regulate the means, contexts, and legitimate possibilities of cultural reproduction; the field of production, whose ideologies and agencies regulate the social basis of the means, contexts, and possibilities of physical resources; and the field of the State, whose various agencies and ideologies define, maintain, vary, and change what counts as legitimate order and the use of legitimate force.

The educational system today is a crucial producer and reproducer of discursive resources within the field of symbolic control. What is of interest is the process whereby productions of the educational system, theories, become decontextualized and recontextualized in other fields of practice, including different levels and functions of education. Theories in the natural sciences may alter the forces of production, but code modalities select, vary, or change their social relations. Theories in the social sciences establish an empirical basis for symbolic control, but code modalities regulate their selection, variation, and change. The issue is more complex. The positioning of theories within the intellectual field has itself to do with the relations between the principles of that field and the fields of specialized practice, especially that of the State. It is important to understand the social principles regulating the recontextualizing of theories in the fields of practice. This requires study of both recontextualizing agencies and agents (see appendix 1.6). In order to understand how it is that theories become dominant, we need to understand dominant code modalities.

Conclusion

We have been concerned in this paper:

1 To systematize developments that have been adumbrated in previous papers.
2 To create a model capable of generating class-regulated modalities of elaborated codes.
3 To show how the model may be used to write specific codes regulating agencies of cultural reproduction or agencies of production.
4 To show the specific principles regulating modes of transmission and acquisition.
5 To enable the possibilities of diachronic and synchronic comparison.

Our primary distinction is between *power* and *control*. At the most abstract level we have argued that power constitutes relations 'between', and control constitutes relations 'within'; that power constitutes the principle of the relations between categories, and control constitutes the principle of the realization of those relations. From this perspective, codes are transformations into specific semiotic principles or grammars of the relations and realizations of categories, where category relations represent the paradigmatic and realizations represent the syntagmatic. Class codes and their modalities are specific semiotic grammars that regulate the acquisition, reproduction, and legitimation of fundamental rules of exclusion, inclusion, and appropriation by which and through which subjects are selectively created, positioned, and oppositioned. These rules, while having their origin in the social division of labour and its social relations of material production, do not necessarily have the conditions of their cultural reproduction located in such a division and relations.

There are today, under conditions of advanced capitalism, many different sites of unequal relations between social groups – gender, ethnicity, religion, region – each having its own particular context of reproduction, generating (in the language of this paper) its specific 'voice message'. This paper has concentrated on the development of a model for understanding the process whereby what is regarded as a basic classification (class relations) is transmitted and acquired by codes that differentially, invidiously, and oppositionally position subjects with respect to both discursive and physical resources. Whether gender, ethnic, or religious categories (or any combination) are considered, it is held that these, today, speak through class-regulated modes, and it is the manner of the cultural reproduction of the latter that has been the concern of this paper. We would emphasize that despite the abstract language of the model we have proposed, it is not the intention to create a representation of a process ruled by some determination which inexorably fulfils some inner law. On the contrary, variation, opposition, and change inhere in the possibilities of code.

Appendix 1.1 Code, competence, and dialect

Although we have distinguished between the above concepts (Bernstein, 1974), it is unfortunately necessary to repeat the basis of the distinction.

Code and competence. Theories that operate with a concept of competence (linguistic or cognitive) are theories in which the conditions for the acquisition of the given competence require some innate facility, together with interaction with a culturally non-specific other who also possesses the competence. In other words, the crucial communication necessary for the acquisition of the competence is with a culturally non-specific other. Of course, no other who possesses a given competence can be culturally non-specific. There is no way of being a cultural subject without being culturally specific. Be that as it may, and it inevitably is, theories of competence necessarily abstract the non-culturally specific from the culturally specific. Code is transmitted and acquired in inter-actions that are culturally specific. Codes therefore presuppose specialized others. It is crucial to distinguish between theories that differ in the location of their problematic. The concept of code pre-supposes competences (linguistic/cognitive) that all acquire and share; hence it is not possible to discuss code with reference to cognitive deficiencies located at the level of competence. Code refers to a specific cultural regulation of the realization of commonly shared competences. Code refers to specific semiotic grammars regulated by specialized distributions of power and principles of control. Such grammars will have, among other realizations, specific linguistic realizations.

Code and dialect. The term 'dialect' refers to a variety of language that can be marked off from other varieties by phono-logical, syntactic, morphological, and lexical features. The term is descriptive. It should give the demarcation rules for a specialized usage of a language and the special rules of its internal orderings. In the same way that every language carries the same potential for generating codes as defined in this thesis, language varieties, dialects, have the same potential. There is no reason to believe that in our terms any language variety can generate only one code. It is therefore highly misleading and inaccurate to equate a standard variety with an elaborated code and a non-standard variety with a restricted code, even though there may well be a class distribution of language varieties. Codes and dialects belong to different theoretical discourses, to different theories, and address funda-mentally different problematics.

Appendix 1.2 Modality of culture and gender

Perhaps we can give an example of modality of culture and what we mean by general features of the cultural subject through a con-sideration of gender relations. Cultural subjects are generated by a distinct and highly specialized reproductive device. This device consists of reproducers (R) and reproduced (r). Reproducers may consist of a large set of categories (kinship) or a very small set. Three distinctive features of this device are culturally non-specific.

(1) The communicative principle, language, consists of an arbitary finite rule system capable of generating *n* number of other rule systems. (2) Communication principles between similars are different from communication principles between dissimilars as a consequence of the recognition of similarity and difference. (3) Sex markers are read off, usually and normally with the birth of r, by R.

If we now apply the above to the relations between R and r we obtain the model shown in Figure 1.9, where:

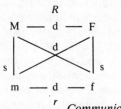

Categories	Communication
M refers to Reproducer Male	s refers to communication between similars
m refers to reproduced male	
F refers to Reproducer Female	d refers to communication between dissimilars
f refers to reproduced female	

Figure 1.9

Communication principles between RM and rm are different from communicative principles between Rm and rf, and similarly for RF and rm and RF and rf. Gender marking by communication is a feature intrinsic to the reproductive device. However – and it is a crucial however – the form the markings take, that is, their realizations, are always culturally specific. In our model we have given R as a male and a female and r as a male and female, but the same argument would hold if we limited the model to R Male and r male or R Female and r female. Nor is it necessary for R to be biologically responsible for r.

Appendix 1.3   Classification and framing of the codes of production

We can use the concepts of classification and framing to write the codes for the production of physical resources. We can consider the social relationships constituted by the mode of production in terms of classification and framing. We can ask what are the relationships between the various categories of production, that is, the relationships between the various agents – unskilled labourers, technologists, managers, administrators, and so forth. The relationships between these categories can be strongly or weakly classified. If the former, then the relationships are stable and sharply distinguished, the functions well insulated from each other, and the agents not interchangeable. If the latter, then the relationships between agents are less sharply distinguished, there is reduced insulation between functions, and agents are more interchangeable between categories. In the same way, we can consider the framing of the mode of production. This refers to the regulation of the realization of the categories, that is, to the form of communication constituted by the category system of the mode of production. If the primary unit of production is a repetitive, individually performed, strongly paced, explicitly sequenced, divisive act, we can say that this is strong framing. If the primary unit of production is relatively co-operative, group-based, and there are opportunities to vary the conditions and perhaps sequencing and pacing, where the outcome is less a fraction of the total object of production but bears a more direct relation to it, we can say that this represents a weak framing.

We shall consider the basic unit of production, the basic social relations of production, at the level of the shop floor. We have distinguished between the form of the productive act – what is made, what a worker produces – and the form of the relation between agents of production (workers). We distinguish between what is made and the relationships between those who are involved in making it. We call what is made, what is produced – that is, the social act of production – a realization of an agent. We examine the act in terms of the degree of fragmentation or divisiveness it entails. The degree of fragmentation or divisiveness refers to the relationship between the act and the final product. The more fragmented or divisive the act(s), the less like the final product is its (their) realization. The more integrated the act, the more like the final product is its realization, that is, its consequence. The act is a socially regulated realization of a category (agent). The act of production is a communicative consequence of an agent. We can therefore consider the regulation of the act in terms of framing. The more fragmented or divisive the act, the stronger the framing: the less fragmented or divisive, the weaker the framing.

The form of the social relationship between agents of the basic unit of production can be referred to the concept classification, because here we are considering the principle of the relationships between the categories (agents) of the social division of labour. The relationship between agents has two features, horizontal and vertical. The horizontal feature refers to the relationship between agents who share membership of a common category (e.g. un-skilled, skilled, supervisory, managerial). The vertical feature refers to the relationship between agents who are members of different categories. The vertical feature may, but not necessarily always, create a hierarchical ordering of the relationships between the categories. We can generate the following relationships between the primary agents of production in terms of the principle of their classification:

Very strong classification ($++C$). The primary act is the result of an isolated agent. The unit is an *isolated agent*.

Strong classification ($+C$). The primary act is the result of related agents within a category (e.g. a group of workers who are members of a common category). The unit is a *group*.

Less strong classification (C). The primary act is the result of related agents between adjacent categories. The unit is a team of workers: skilled, semi-skilled, variously skilled.

Weak classification ($-C$). The primary act is the result of integrated agents across categories. The unit entails an integration of workers of various skills and levels of supervision and management in the policy and practice of production.

Now if we put together the nature of the primary act in terms of its framing (divisive/integrated) and the form of the relation between agents in terms of the principle of their classification (isolated/integrated), we can obtain at least five forms of regulation of the basic unit of production. These codes of production are as follows:

1 Isolated agents; divisive act.	$++C++F$
2 Related agents within a category; divisive act.	$+C+F$
3 Related agents between adjacent categories; integrated act.	$C-F$
4 Integrated agents across categories; divisive act.	$-C+F$
5 Integrated agents across categories; integrated act.	$-C-F$

We can now identify four forms of ideological control over the mode of production in class societies.

We can identify an historical process in the development of these production codes, from entrepreneurial to corporate capitalism, from code 1 to code 3. We would argue that codes 4 and 5 would constitute a qualitative change in the production code were they to be fully implemented and generalized throughout the system of production. A necessary condition for this would be a change in the dominant cultural category – that is, a change in class structure.

We could link theories of control, which both legitimize and provide a scientific basis for exploitation of production, to the codes:

1   We might connect Taylorism with (1).
2   We might connect the human relations school with (2).
3   We might connect the socio-technical system theory with (3).
4–5 We might connect industrial democracy as a worker-based theory in opposition to the others.

As we move from 1 to 5 there is an important qualitative change occurring in the code value regulating the primary unit of production. Codes 1, 2, and 3 are variations of a restricted code, the capitalist relation of production, whereas codes 4 and 5 are variations of an elaborated code, realizing democratic relations of production.

Appendix 1.4   Class assumption of pedagogic codes

We shall give here a brief analysis of the class assumptions of a dominant modality of an elaborated code with strong classification and strong framing values ($+C+F$). Such a code is transmitted through what we have called a visible pedagogy, whereas where there is a major weakening of classification and framing ($-C-F$) the code is transmitted through what we have called an invisible pedagogy (see chapter 2).

We shall here be concerned with modes of transmission at the level of the primary and secondary schools. The secondary school in our terms may well contain a dominant code in which the values of C and F are strong and dominated codes where the values are weaker.

We distinguish between modes of transmission/acquisition in terms of rules regulating hierarchy, rules regulating sequence and pacing, and rules regulating criteria:

1 Hierarchical rules:
(*a*) *Explicit.* Where such rules are explicit, the power basis of the social relation is undisguised and visible.
(*b*) *Implicit.* Where such rules are implicit, the power basis of the social relation is masked, hidden, obscured by strategies of communication.
2 Sequential and pacing rules (pacing refers to the rate of expected acquisition of the sequencing rules):
(*a*) *Explicit.* Where such rules are explicit, the principles and signs of the progression of the transmission are explicit and made public. The educand has some awareness of his or her future state of expected legitimate consciousness and practice.
(*b*) *Implicit.* Where such rules are implicit, the principles and signs of the progression are known only to the transmitter. The

educand can have no knowledge (at least for some period of time) of the principles of his or her progression.

3. Criterial rules:

(a) *Explicit*. Where rules are explicit, the criteria to be transmitted are explicit and specific.

(b) *Implicit*. Where rules are implicit, the criteria to be transmitted are implicit, multiple, and diffuse.

Visible pedagogies can be defined as transmissions regulated by explicit hierarchy, explicit sequencing rules, strong pacing, and explicit criteria. There are a variety of such pedagogies. We can distinguish two main forms according to their autonomy of, or dependence upon, recruitment, selection, and training for relations of production.

We shall now give a brief analysis of the class assumptions and consequences of visible pedagogies at the school level (primary/secondary). Visible pedagogies are forms of transmission/acquisition of elaborated codes with at least values of $+C+F$:

Ideal form

1 Context of reproduction:

(a) A group homogeneous with respect to the following attributes: age, sex, ability.

(b) The act of acquisition will be solitary, privatized, and competitive.

2 Progression:

(a) It is crucial to read early in order to acquire the written code, for beyond the book is the textbook, which is the crucial pedagogical medium and social relation.

(b) Strong pacing regulates the acquisition of sequencing rules; failure to acquire sequencing rules is difficult to redeem. Usually, visible pedagogies have to create a vast, often inadequate repair system for those who cannot meet the requirements of the sequencing rules and pacing.

(c) The sequencing rules regulate the temporal ordering of the content such that the initial stages are concerned with the concrete and the learning of operations and relationships by rote, and later stages are concerned with the abstract and the learning of principles. Thus visible pedagogies separate 'concrete' and 'abstract' in time. This becomes the basis for the separation (strong classification) of manual and mental labour. Visible pedagogies create and distribute different forms of consciousness.

Criteria. The pedagogical intention is to show the child what is *missing* in his or her product; as a consequence, the criteria are explicit and specific. The latter create the possibility of 'objective' assessment and measurement and so facilitate the ideology of pedagogic neutrality.

Sites of reproduction
1 Visible pedagogies usually require two sites of acquisition: the school and the home. Two sites are possible because the medium of the textbook makes transfer possible. Not all homes can operate as a second site, and in as much as this does not occur, failure is highly likely.
2 The relation between the two sites is regulated by strong framing, that is, the school is selective of communications, practices, events, and objects, which may pass from the home into the pedagogical context.

Communication. Communication between transmitters and acquirers is specially constituted by the strong classification and strong framing (especially with respect to sequencing rules and pacing). Time is scarce, and discourses are strongly bounded. These affect the rules regulating spoken and written texts, question-and-answer format, their contexts, and social relations.

Economics. Although the cost of the building is higher for a visible than for an invisible pedagogy, the cost of transmission is relatively low. The space occupied by the learner is relatively small; the pacing is such that, often, as much time must be spent in the home as in the school. The hidden costs of visible pedagogies are the attributes of the home, physical, discursive, and interactional, which enable children to manage or fail to manage the class assumptions of the context and sites of reproduction, progression, and communication.

Modes of transmission ideologically create and position subjects.

Appendix 1.5   Code values and experimental contexts

The model we have developed may be used to generate relations between agencies and relationships within agencies, whether these be at so-called 'macro' or 'micro' levels. The latter (micro) would refer to what we have called the communicative context. This context is regulated by framing values on the basis of a given classificatory value. The classificatory principle is often invisibly present in the sense that it is presupposed. If we examine the communicative context established in the food experiment we discussed in the main text, from the perspective of our model we may be able to suggest an explanation of the differences between the middle-class and the lower working-class children. We shall begin by indicating the apparent opposition between the implicitly dominant code values constituting the communicative context and the spoken text with its apparently explicit code values.

The implicit dominant code values in our terms would be

$$\frac{E}{+C+F^{ie}}$$

which we will now elaborate:

Classification
Recognition rule:

1 This context is a sub-context of a specialized context; school $(+C)$.
2 This sub-context is specialized adult, instructional, evaluative. Thus: *elaborated orientation*.

Framing
Realization rule:

1 Select interactional practice and text in accordance with recognition rule $(+F)$.
2 Create specialized text; exhaustive principle, no narrative, no isolated situational exemplars or lists.

There are, of course, many other features of the communicative context regulated by framing values, but on the whole these resulted in practices shared by the children (sex, class).

However, when we look at the spoken text, their explicit code values are in apparent opposition. The instructions to elicit grouping and principles were of the order $-C-F$: 'Group the pictures any way you want' $(-C)$, with no indication of the spoken text required $(-F)$. The middle-class children, in the first request to group, ignored the $-C-F$ instruction and transposed it into its opposite, $+C+F$, whereas the lower working-class children read the instruction at its surface value and read it as the dominant code value. There can be little doubt that the lower working-class children were aware of the classifying principles used by the middle-class children, and indeed towards the end of the experiment some lower working-class children were using them as dominant principles. The difference between the children is therefore not a difference in cognitive facility but a difference in the recognition and realization rules the children used to read the context and to create their texts: a code difference (see also Bernstein, 1977c).

It is possible from this analysis to make explicit a variety of sources of differences in children's contextual practices: (1) inappropriate recognition rules, hence inappropriate realization rules; (2) appropriate recognition rules but inadequacy of realization rules either in creating the specific text or in the social relations of the performance, or both. We can give other examples of the selective effect of the formal setting upon the recognition and realization rules used by 7-year-old children from middle-class and lower working-class family backgrounds matched for 'intelligence' ('IQ') (see Adlam *et al.*, 1977: chs. 2–4).

Children were given a reproduction, about the size of a postcard, of a work by a Belgian naive painter, Trotin, and asked to talk about it. The probes were 'What is going on in the picture?' 'What are the people doing?' 'What is the picture all about?' (The last probe, after the children had finished talking about the card.) Such probes could be understood as a request for (*a*) narrative or (*b*) a description of persons, objects, events, relationships depicted on the card, i.e. a verbal demography.

We found that, in general, the focus of the child's speech was more a function of the child's class background than of the child's 'IQ'. The middle-class child, irrespective of gender, produced a text similar to or approximating (*b*), whereas the lower working-class child produced a text which was either oriented to (*a*) or which, although oriented to (*b*), was much more embedded in the context in the sense that it was less likely to be understood without the picture card. Other researchers or critics have interpreted this finding as indicating only that the lower working-class children were aware that both the researcher and the researched were looking at the picture card, and as a consequence there was no need to make verbally explicit a context which was shared. This 'explanation' is both *ad hoc* and selective, as it signally fails to explain (1) why the middle-class children produced little narrative (only six out of a total of sixty-four children did so), (2) why the lower working-class children produced narrative, (3) why it was the girls in the lower working-class who were mainly responsible for narrative texts, (4) why the lower working-class children's speech orientation was similar in other situations presented to the children in which the presumption of a shared perspective between researcher and researched could not be postulated (instructional and control situations).

Another situation offered to the children in the same interview required them to explain the rules of a game (hide-and-seek) to a child who did not know how to play, after first indicating to the researcher knowledge of the rules. We again found that social class of family background was more important than the child's 'IQ' in accounting for the orientation of the child's speech and referential relations. In general (but not uniformly) middle-class children created a relatively context-independent text, in the sense that the text was not embedded in a local context/practice. The text created by the lower working-class children was generally (but not uniformly) relatively context-dependent compared with the text of the middle-class children in that it was more embedded in a local context/practice and assumed knowledge of that context/practice. It does not necessarily follow that the middle-class child's text was a more effective instruction. Indeed, there may well be grounds for believing otherwise.

The children were given a third situation, based upon one created for their mothers two years earlier. The mothers were given six hypothetical situations in which their own child had done something wrong and they were asked what they would do or say. These same situations were presented to the children as if they were the mothers and were faced with *their* child having done something wrong. In general (independent of 'IQ'), there were marked differences in the forms of control the children used in terms of their family class background. While all the children tended to give imperative forms of control and forms which announced simple rules, the middle-class children used these forms less and gave forms which allowed for more options and contingencies.

Basically, the opening question to the children in all the above situations had the same general form as the opening question in the 'food' enquiry referred to earlier. It did not stipulate any particular relation between categories of referential relations, nor did the question explicitly direct the children to realize a particular text. We can account for the texts by the following recognition and realization rules.

Middle-class children: recognition rule

In all three situations (Trotin picture card, hide-and-seek, and mother–child control) the same rule would hold.

1 This context is a sub-context of a specialized context: school.
2 The sub-context is specialized adult, instructional, evaluative: elaborated orientation.

Thus the modal orientation of the middle-class children across the three contexts was elaborated, whereas the modal orientation of the lower working-class children was restricted. This does not mean that there was no variation. (Indeed, lower working-class girls produced more variations than lower working-class boys.)

Trotin picture card text

Middle-class children: realization rule

1 Use criteria true/false. Given this rule, there could be no narrative, and very few middle-class children gave any narrative. Further, given the true/false criteria, there would be a need to use modals ('might be', 'could be') and other forms indicating uncertainty. More middle-class children used such forms.
2 Make all referential relations explicit and specific. The rules (1) and (2) are sufficient to generate the structure and the modal middle-class text.

Lower working-class children: recognition rule

Relative to the middle-class children, the lower working-class children did not mark the context with the same speciality, therefore their modal orientation across the three contexts was restricted. In other words, for the middle-class child the context was relative to the lower working-class child, strongly classified ($+C$), whereas for the lower working-class child relative to the middle-class child it was weakly classified ($-C$).

Lower working-class children: realization rule

Given that the context was weakly classified, we could expect a range of texts, all selected from informal, everyday practices and modes.

1 Narrative.
2 Implicit referential relations.

Hide-and seek text

Middle-class children: realization rule

1 Make all sequencing rules, reference sets, and criteria explicit and specific.

Lower working-class children: realization rule

1 Similar to the Trotin realization rules.

In both the Trotin and the hide-and-seek situations the middle-class

children transformed an open question generated by apparent
$-C-F$ rules to $+C+F$. The lower working-class children carried
out this transformation significantly less frequently.

Mother–child control

Here we have a situation very different from the previous two
situations. The child is taking on the role of the mother, and what
we expect here are differences in recognition rules and realization
rules, which are less a function of the particular formal interview
setting than a function of the recognition and realization rules used
by the child's major controller in the family. Indeed, we know this
to be the case (see Cook-Gumperz, 1973).

Middle-class children's recognition and realization rules were of
the form $+C-F$ relative to the lower working-class children's
$+C+F$. The difference between the children at 7 years of age
showed in the strength of the framing, i.e. middle-class children
accorded more options of contingencies to the controlled than did
the lower working-class children.

We have extended our analysis to show how classification and
framing values act selectively on recognition and realization rules
which we *infer* are used by middle-class and lower working-class
children in the production of texts in a formal interview setting and
in the reproduction of familial texts (of control) in that setting.

Appendix 1.6   Primary, recontextualizing, and secondary contexts

We shall here make rather more explicit the importance of the
recontextualizing field, and of its agents, in the selective movement
of texts from the intellectual field created by the educational system
to that system's fields of reproduction.

Primary context: production of discourse. We shall distinguish
three crucial interdependent contexts of educational discourse,
practice, and organization. The first of these we shall call the
primary context. The process whereby a text is developed and
positioned in this context we shall call primary contexualization.
The latter refers to the process whereby new ideas are selectively
created, modified, and changed and where specialized discourses
are developed, modified, or changed. This context creates, appropriating Bourdieu, the 'intellectual field' of the educational system.
This field and its history are created by the positions, relations, and
practices arising out of the *production* rather than the reproduction
of educational discourse and its practices. Its texts, today, are
dependent partly, but by no means wholly, on the circulation of

private and State public funds to research groups and individuals.

Secondary context: reproduction of discourse. This context, its various levels, agencies, positions, and practices, refers to the selective reproduction of educational discourse. We shall distinguish four levels: tertiary, secondary, primary, and pre-school. Within each level there may be some degree of specialization of agencies. We shall call these levels and their interrelations, together with any specialization of agencies within a level, the secondary context of the reproduction of discourse. This context structures the field of reproduction. We can ask here questions referring to the classificatory and framing principles regulating the relations between and within levels and regulating the circulation and location of codes and their modalities.

Recontextualizing context: relocation of discourse. From these two fundamental contexts and the fields they structure we shall distinguish a third context which structures a field or sub-set of fields, whose positions, agents, and practices are concerned with the movements of texts/practices from the primary context of discursive production to the secondary context of discursive reproduction. The function of the position, agents, and practices within this field and its sub-sets is to regulate the circulation of texts between the primary and secondary contexts. Accordingly, we shall call the field and the sub-set structured by this context the *recontextualizing field*.

The recontextualizing context will entail a number of fields:

1 It will include specialized departments and sub-agencies (Schools Council) of the State and local educational authorities together with their research and system of inspectors.
2 It will include university and polytechnic departments of education, and colleges of education, together with their research.
3 It will include specialized media of education, weeklies, journals, etc., and publishing houses, together with their readers and advisers.
4 It may extend to fields *not* specialized in educational discourse and its practices but which are able to exert influence both on the State and on its various arrangements and/or upon special sites, agents, and practices within education.

When a text is appropriated by recontextualizing agents, operating in positions of this field, the text usually undergoes a transformation prior to its relocation. The form of this transformation is regulated by a *principle of decontextualizing*. This process refers to the change in the text as it is first *delocated* and then *relocated*. This process ensures that the text is no longer the same text:

1 The text has changed its position in relation to other texts, practices, and positions.
2 The text itself has been modified by selection, simplification, condensation, and elaboration.
3 The text has been repositioned and refocused.

The decontextualizing principle regulates the new ideological positioning of the text in its process of relocation in one or more of the levels of the field of reproduction. Once in that field, the text undergoes a further transformation or repositioning as it becomes active in the pedagogic process within an agency with a level. It is crucial to distinguish between, and analyse, the relations between the two transformations (at least) of a text. The first is the transformation of the text within the *recontextualizing field*, and the second is the transformation of the *transformed* text in the pedagogic process as it becomes active in the process of the reproduction of acquirers. *It is the recontextualizing field which generates the positions and oppositions of pedagogic theory, research, and practice.* It is a matter of some importance to analyse the role of departments of the State in the relations and movements within and between the various contexts and their structuring fields.

Notes

1 This paper follows closely the analyses developed in Part II of *Class, Codes and Control*, vol. 3 (revised edition, 1977) particularly chapter 8, 'Aspects of the relation between education and production'.
Indeed, this paper is a reordering, development, and refinement of a model presented in note C and a further elaboration of note A to that paper. I am very indebted to seminars held in a number of universities for constructive criticism, and especially to the University of Lund (Pedagogical Institute) and New York University (Department of Sociology). I am very grateful to students of the Department of the Sociology of Education, University of London Institute of Education, for lively discussion and debate.
2 'Ground rule' was first used in Bernstein (1973). Performance rules were distinguished from ground rules in Bernstein (1977c).
3 This formulation of the general definition of code was developed by Antonella Castelnuovo, Ph.D. student of the Department of the Sociology of Education, University of London Institute of Education.
4 This formulation closely follows earlier formulations (Bernstein, 1977c: introduction) in terms of context dependence and context independence. The latter is independent clearly not in any absolute but in a relative sense.

5 It is important to draw a distinction between the *location* of these
   orientations and their *origins*. While historically we can locate
   orientations in different positions of the mode of production, these
   orientations may not originate in that mode. In non-literate, small-
   scale societies with a simple division of labour (called 'primitive' by
   nineteenth-century anthropologists) elaborate orientations are found
   less in the social relations of material production than in the religious
   cosmologies (see chapter 5). This is not to say that these religious
   cosmologies have no relation to a material base; indeed, they often
   legitimated the categories and social relations of material production.
   Similarly, restricted orientations are likely to be found in relations of
   intimacy and close proximity. Elaborated orientations (where there is
   an indirect relation to a specific material base) are, however, always
   subject to strong regulation and surveillance, for these orientations
   have the potential of creating alternative realities, possibilities, and
   practices. Elaborated orientations are potentially dangerous, and those
   acquiring them have to be made safe.
6 Historically the institutionalizing of, access to, and distribution of
   elaborated codes were regulated by the Church's control of formal
   education (see Durkheim, 1938). We do not wish to transpose the
   technical term 'mode', as in the concept 'mode of production', to
   education. However, we do wish to distinguish between the various
   possibilities of a given elaborated code institutionalized as a dominant
   code in education. Modality refers to the specific values of a given
   elaborated code (its classification and framing values). See later
   discussion.
7 There is a problem in drawing a distinction between physical and
   discursive resources. For it implies that the latter are qualitatively
   different from the former. We do not take this view. On the contrary,
   we would hold that discursive resources/practices are a condition of
   and are constituted in physical resources. We are using these terms
   simply as low-level descriptions.
8 Silverman and Torode, in their impressive book *The Material Word*
   (1980), first drew my attention to the possibilities of 'voice'. I have,
   however, with apologies, put the concept to a rather different use.
9 From now on we shall use 'social division of labour' to refer to both
   production and agencies of cultural reproduction, in particular the
   agencies of education and the family.

Chapter 2

Social class and pedagogic practice

I shall start this paper[1] with an analysis of the basic social relation of any pedagogic practice. In this analysis I shall distinguish between pedagogic practice as a cultural relay and pedagogic practice in terms of what that practice relays – in other words, pedagogic practice as a social form and as a specific content. I shall argue that the inner logic of pedagogic practice as a cultural relay is provided by a set of three rules, and the nature of these rules acts selectively on the content of any pedagogic practice. If these rules constitute what can be called the 'how' of any practice, then any particular 'how' created by any one set of rules acts selectively on the 'what' of the practice, the form of its content. The form of the content in turn acts selectively on those who can successfully acquire. I shall examine in some detail the social class assumptions and consequences of forms of pedagogic practice.

On the basis of the fundamental rules of any pedagogic practice I shall generate:

1 What are regarded as opposing modalities of pedagogic practice, usually referred to as conservative or traditional and progressive or child-centred.
2 What are regarded as oppositions within what is considered the same basic form. Here the opposition is between a pedagogic practice dependent upon the market place for its orientation and legitimation, a practice emphasizing the assumed relevance of vocational skills, and a pedagogic practice independent of the market place, claiming for itself an orientation and legitimation derived from the assumed autonomy of knowledge. It will be argued that the pedagogic practices of the new vocationalism and those of the old autonomy of knowledge represent a conflict between different elitist ideologies, one based on the class hierarchy of the market and the other based on the hierarchy of knowledge and its class supports.

63

The structuring of pedagogic discourse

The basic argument will be that whether we are considering the opposition between conservative and progressive or the opposition between market and knowledge-oriented pedagogic practice, present class inequalities are likely to be reproduced.

I shall start first with some thoughts about the inner logic of any pedagogic practice. A pedagogic practice can be understood as a relay, a cultural relay: a uniquely human device for both the reproduction and the production of culture. As I have said earlier, I shall distinguish between what is relayed, the contents, and how the contents are relayed. That is, between the 'what' and the 'how' of any transmission. When I refer to the inner logic of a pedagogic practice I am referring to a set of rules which are prior to the content to be relayed (Figure 2.1).

The relationship basic to cultural reproduction or transformation is essentially the pedagogic relation, and the pedagogic relation consists of transmitters and acquirers. I shall examine the internal

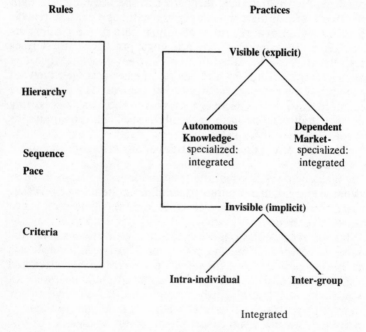

Figure 2.1 Pedagogic practices: generic forms and modalities. Whereas invisible pedagogies are always likely to relay integrated or embedded skills/subjects, visible pedagogies, especially of the autonomous type, are more likely to relay differentiated skills/subjects.

logic of this relationship. In fact, I consider the fundamental logic of any pedagogic relation.

I have drawn a distinction here between what I call the fundamental logic of the practice and the various practices to which this logic can give rise. This is rather similar to language, itself: a finite set of rules which can generate a great number of other rule systems. I will examine some of the realizations of these practices and I will analyse the social class assumptions of these practices.

If we look at the relationship between transmitters and acquirers I shall assert that this is essentially, and intrinsically, an asymmetrical relation. There may be various strategies for disguising, masking, hiding the asymmetry. For example, in certain modalities of practice the acquirer is perceived as a transmitter, and, perhaps, the transmitter appears to be the acquirer, but these are essentially arabesques. This may seem a very cynical view but we shall see whether it is of any value. Now it is the case that although this relation is intrinsically asymmetrical the realization of the asymmetry may be very complex.

The rules of pedagogic practice as cultural relay

I shall propose that the essential logic of any pedagogic relation consists of the relationship essentially between three rules. And of these three rules,[2] the first is the dominant one. I would now like to outline concretely the three rules.

Hierarchical rule

In any pedagogic relationship the transmitter has to learn to be a transmitter and the acquirer has to learn to be an acquirer. When you go to the doctor you have to learn how to be a patient. It is no good going to the doctor and saying, 'I feel really bad today, everything is really grey.' He says, 'Don't waste my time,' because he has many patients. 'Where is the pain? How long have you had it? What kind of pain is it? Is it acute? Is it chronic? Is it sharp? Is it persistent?' After a bit you learn how to talk to your doctor. He teaches you to be an acquirer. But how he teaches you is the function of a much more general set of forces which we shall go on to discover.

The acquirer, then, has to learn to be an acquirer and the transmitter has to learn to be a transmitter. The process of learning how to be a transmitter entails the acquiring of rules of social order, character, and manner which became the condition for appropriate conduct in the pedagogic relation. It is these rules which are a prerequisite of any enduring pedagogic relation. In any one such relation the rules of conduct may to different degrees permit a space for negotiation. These rules of conduct will here be called hierarchical rules which establish the conditions for order, character, and manner.

Sequencing rules

Now if there is a transmission it cannot always happen at once. Something must come before and something must come after. If something comes before and after, there is a progression. If there is a progression, there must be sequencing rules. Every pedagogic practice must have sequencing rules, and these sequencing rules will imply pacing rules. Pacing is the rate of expected acquisition of the sequencing rules, that is, how much you have to learn in a given amount of time. Essentially, pacing is the time allowed for achieving the sequencing rules.

Criterial rules

Finally there are criteria which the acquirer is expected to take over and to apply to his/her own practices and those of others. The criteria enable the acquirer to understand what counts as a legitimate or illegitimate communication, social relation, or position.

The internal logic of any pedagogic relation consists of hierarchical rules, sequential/pacing rules, criterial rules. We can distinguish, at another level, two more general rules. The hierarchical rules will be called the *regulative* rules and the other rules of sequence/pace criteria will be called instructional or *discursive* rules. The fundamental rule is the regulative one. Later on we shall see why this is the case.[3] Briefly, all education is intrinsically a moral activity which articulates the dominant ideology(ies) of dominant group(s). On the basis of these rules, I want to generate, to begin with, two different kinds of practices, and I shall do so on the basis of an examination of these rules.

In any teaching relation, the essence of the relation is to evaluate the competence of the acquirer. What you are evaluating is whether the criteria that have been made available to the acquirer have been achieved – whether they are regulative criteria about conduct, character, and manner, or instructional, discursive criteria: how to solve this problem or that problem, or produce an acceptable piece of writing or speech.

On the basis of the above rules of regulative and discursive order

I shall distinguish between two generic types or modalities of pedagogic practice. I must emphasize that these are types, and each can give rise to a range of practices, some of which will be discussed later in this paper.

Generating modalities of pedagogic practice

Hierarchical rules

If we take, first of all, the hierarchical rules, these rules can be explicit but they can also be implicit. If they are explicit, then the power relations in the relationship are very clear. The relationship is one of explicit subordination and superordination. This creates an explicit hierarchy. But a hierarchy need not necessarily be explicit. A hierarchy can be implicit. Let me give an example.

In 1968 the French took to the streets and the English studied a government report (Plowden, 1967) on primary education. The report was called *Children and their Primary Schools* – not 'Children and Primary Schools' or 'Primary Schools and Children'. In this book there were thirty-six pictures. If you look at those thirty-six photographs, there are children playing creatively by themselves: individual, productive play. There are pictures of children playing in groups, there are children in the school corridors and in the gardens surrounding the school, but it is difficult to find a teacher. This is the context created by an implicit hierarchy. The more implicit the hierarchy, the more difficult it is to distinguish the transmitter. We can define an implicit hierarchy as a relationship where power is masked or hidden by devices of communication. In the case of an implicit hierarchy the teacher acts directly on the context of acquisition but indirectly on the acquirer. Thus hierarchy can be either explicit or implicit.

Sequencing rules

These rules can be explicit. If they are explicit, then it means that children of 5 years of age are expected to develop particular competences, to behave in a particular way, and at 6 years of age they are expected to have different competences. Explicit rules regulate the development of the child, usually in terms of age. This means that the child is always aware of what her/his expected state of consciousness is supposed to be. He or she may not like it, but it is clear. Explicit sequencing rules construct the temporal project of the child. They construct temporal dislocations. These sequencing rules may be inscribed in syllabuses, in curricula, in behavioural rules, in rules of punishment and reward, and are often marked by transition rituals. However, sequencing rules can be implicit. Where sequencing rules are implicit the child initially can never be aware of his or her temporal project. Only the transmitter is aware of the temporal project of the child. We have a difference here. In the case of explicit sequencing rules, the child has some awareness of its temporal project; in the case of implicit sequencing rules only the teacher or the transmitter can be so aware.

We have to ask ourselves what is the basis of such a relationship, because if the child is not aware of his or her temporal project, then the child lives only in the present. When the sequencing rules are explicit, the child has some awareness of her/his temporal project although he or she lives in the past. The grammatical tenses of these pedagogic practices are opposed to each other. One child lives in the past although he or she can see his/her future, whereas the other child lives in the present of its own doings. Sequencing rules reveal what may be called the ideology of tense.

How does this come about? If sequencing rules are implicit, then they will be drawn from a range of theories. The theories that I am going to put forward here are not the only ones, but others will be structurally similar where they apply to children. The theories are set out in Figure 2.2. They construct a pedagogic *bricolage*.

If we look at these theories we can see that although they are very different they have certain things in common. First, almost all the

	Stage	Active	Learning	Abstracted	Implicit hierarchy
Piaget	1	2	3	4	5
Freud (neo-Freudian)	1	2	3	4	5
Chomsky	1	2	3	4	5
Ethological theories of critical learning	1	2	3	4	-
Gestalt	-	2	3	4	5

Figure 2.2

theories, with the exception of Gestalt, is a developmental theory. What is acquired has a meaning only in relation to a particular stage. (In the case of Freud there is the development from polymorphous perverse, the nirvana of babyhood, followed by oral, anal, phallic, and genital.) With one exception, all these theories are stage theories. Second, in every one of these theories the child is active in his or her own acquisition. Third, in all these theories the acquisition of the child cannot be readily modified by explicit public regulation, as learning is a tacit, invisible act. Fourth, in every one of these theories the child's institutional and cultural biography is excluded. The theories are asociological. At most the child has a family. Fifth, in every one of these theories, except the ethological, the relationship between the transmitter and the acquirer or the parent and the child is such that the socializer is potentially if not actually dangerous. These theories tend to be critical of the transmitter as an imposer of meaning. Every one of the theories, except the ethological, replaces domination by facilitation, imposition by accommodation.

The theories imply an implicit hierarchy. Now if you are going to apply this *bricolage* to the classroom as a teacher, or as a social worker, or as a counsellor, you have to have what is called a theory of reading. For in these theories the child is transformed into a text which only the transmitter can read. In other words, the teacher, the social worker, the psychotherapist is looking for certain signs, but the signs have meaning only to the teacher, and the child can never be aware of the meaning of its own signs, as their reading requires complex theories.

I was once in a classroom where a child was by himself. I happened to say that the child looked very unhappy, and the teacher said, 'Don't worry about that. He is just working through a problem.' The teacher, then, can read the child, and the teacher's behaviour to that child will depend on this reading, which in turn depends upon theories and upon how they have been transmitted, that is, recontextualized

Sequencing rules can be implicit or explicit. Where rules are implicit the acquirer initially can never know the meaning of her/his sign, as the meaning is derived from complex theories and their recontextualizing, and so available only to the transmitter.

Criterial rules

Criteria can be explicit and specific. For example, in a school the child may be making some facsimile of a person, drawing a person, and the teacher comes along, looks at the drawing and says (it does not have to be repressive; explicit criteria do not have to be repressively realized), 'That's a lovely man, but he's only got three fingers,' or 'That's a very good house, but where is the chimney?' In other words, the pedagogy works by making available to the child what is missing in the product. Now if it works in this way, by showing what is missing in the product, the criteria will always be explicit and specific, *and the child will be aware of the criteria.* He or she may not like them, but they will be articulated. However, criteria can be implicit, multiple, and diffuse. Imagine we go to another classroom. The children have very big pieces of paper. A whole series of media are available through which their unique consciousness can be graphically realized. And the facilitator happens to glance at the image and says to the child, 'Tell me about it.' 'Oh, that's very exciting.'

In the case of implicit criteria, by definition, the child is not aware except in a very general way of the criteria she/he has to meet. It is as if this pedagogic practice creates a space in which the acquirer can create his/her text under conditions of apparently minimum external constraint and in a context and social relationship which appears highly supportive of the 'spontaneous' text the acquirer offers (Daniels, 1989).

We can now say that we have distinguished between pedagogic practices in terms of those which have explicit hierarchical rules, explicit sequencing/pacing rules, and explicit criteria and those with implicit hierarchical sequencing/pacing and criterial rules.[4]

Types of pedagogic practice: visible and invisible

I shall now define two generic types of pedagogic practice, as follows. If the rules of regulative and discursive order are explicit (hierarchy/sequence/pace) criteria, I shall call such a type a *visible* pedagogic practice (VP) and if the rules of regulative and discursive order are implicit I shall call such a type an *invisible* pedagogic practice (IP).

Visible pedagogies

A visible pedagogy (and there are many modalities) will always place the emphasis on the *performance* of the child, upon the text the child is creating and the extent to which that text is meeting the criteria. Thus acquirers will be graded according to the extent that they meet the criteria. A visible pedagogy puts the emphasis on the external product of the child.

Visible pedagogies and their modalities will act to produce

differences between children: they are necessarily stratifying practices of transmission, a learning consequence for both transmitters and acquirers. It is here worth adding that because a visible pedagogy has explicit rules of regulative and discursive order it does not mean that there are no tacit rules or messages, only that their meaning must be understood in the context of a visible pedagogy.

Invisible pedagogies

In the case of an invisible pedagogy the discursive rules (the rules of order of instruction) are known only to the transmitter, and in this sense a pedagogic practice of this type is (at least initially) invisible to the acquirer, essentially because the acquirer appears to fill the pedagogic space rather than the transmitter. The concrete present of the acquirer is manifest rather than the abstract/abstracted past of the controlling discourse.

Invisible pedagogies are less concerned to produce explicit stratifying differences between acquirers because they are apparently less interested in matching the acquirer's text against an external common standard. Their focus is not upon a 'gradable' performance of the acquirer but upon procedures internal to the acquirer (cognitive, linguistic, affective, motivational) as a consequence of which a text is created and experienced. These *procedures of acquisition* are considered to be shared by all acquirers, although their realization in texts will create differences between acquirers.

But these differences do not signal differences in potential, as all acquirers are judged to share common procedures. Differences revealed by an invisible pedagogy are not to be used as a basis for comparison *between* acquirers, for differences reveal *uniqueness*. Thus whereas visible pedagogies focus upon an external gradable text, invisible pedagogies focus upon the procedures/competences which all acquirers bring to the pedagogic context. Invisible pedagogies are concerned to arrange that context to enable shared competences to develop realizations appropriate to the acquirer. Thus, in the case of invisible pedagogies, external non-comparable differences are produced by internal *commonalities* – that is, shared competences – whereas in the case of visible pedagogies external *comparable* differences are produced by internal differences in potential. In short, invisible pedagogies emphasize acquisition–competence and visible pedagogies transmission–performance.[5]

These differences in emphasis between visible and invisible pedagogies will clearly affect both the selection and the organization of what is to be acquired, that is, the recontextualizing principle adopted to create and systematize the contents to be acquired and the context in which it is acquired.

Different theories of instruction inhere in these two pedagogic types, which we illustrate in Figure 2.3 and, at the same time, show how modalities of the two types can be regarded as liberal, conservative, and radical practices.

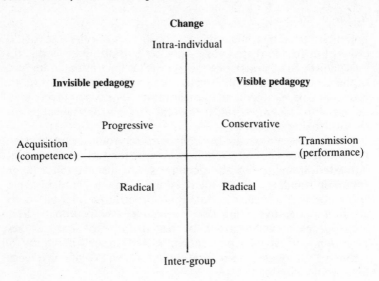

Figure 2.3

In Figure 2.3 the vertical dimension refers to the object of change of the pedagogic practice. Thus the primary object may be to produce changes in the individual or the primary object may be to produce changes not in the individual but between social groups. The horizontal dimension refers to the focus of the pedagogic practice, which can be either upon the acquirer or upon the transmitter. Clearly the latter indicates a visible and the former an invisible pedagogy. If we take the top left-hand quadrant, intra-individual−acquisition, then this would indicate what is often regarded as 'progressive' pedagogic practice whose theories of instruction are likely to be drawn from those listed earlier. However, if we take the bottom left-hand quadrant, acquisition−inter-group, the primary object of this pedagogic practice is to produce changes *between* social groups, that is, how the acquirer comes to understand the relation between social groups and through this new appreciation change his/her practice. This would be a radical rather than a liberal–progressive practice, e.g. Freire and, through Freire, the pedagogy of liberation theology. It would also include neo-Marxist formulations such as those of Giroux (1989).

The top right-hand quadrant, intra-individual–transmission, is likely to select behaviourist or neo-behaviourist theories of instruction which, relative to those selected in the top left-hand quadrant, are often regarded as conservative. It is a matter of interest that this top right-hand quadrant is regarded as conservative but has often produced very innovative and radical acquirers. The bottom right-hand quadrant shows a radical realization of an apparently conservative pedagogic practice

So far, then, we can see that these generic types can take either progressive, conservative, or radical modalities, and that theories of instruction will act selectively upon both the 'what' and 'how' of any pedagogic practice. Further, these different theories will act selectively upon what attributes of the acquirer become candidates for what labels. Finally, each theory will carry its own conditions of contestation, 'resistance', subversion.

I have proposed that it is important to distinguish between the fundamental grammar or ordering principles of a pedagogic practice and the forms of realization as pedagogic types. The ordering principles I have analysed as regulative (hierarchical) and instructional (selection, sequence/pace, and criteria). On the basis of this grammar I have generated two generic forms of pedagogic practice according to whether the ordering principles are explicit or implicit. These basic forms were shown to yield progressive, conservative, and radical modalities.

The next section will concentrate upon the social class assumptions of the generic types visible/invisible in their non-radical forms. We shall consider after this analysis two modalities of visible pedagogies, an autonomous modality and a market-oriented modality.

Social class assumptions of pedagogic practice

The fundamental proposition is that the same distribution of power may be reproduced by apparently opposing modalities of control. There is not a one-to-one relation between a given distribution of power and the modality of control through which it is relayed. In terms of this paper, pedagogic practices are cultural relays of the distribution of power. Although visible and invisible pedagogies are apparently opposing types, it will be shown that both carry social class assumptions. However, these social class assumptions vary with the pedagogic type. The class assumptions of visible pedagogies are different from the class assumptions of invisible pedagogies. These class assumptions carry consequences for those children who are able to exploit the possibilities of the pedagogic practices. The assumptions of a visible pedagogy are more likely to be met by that fraction of the middle class whose employment has a direct relation to the economic field (production, distribution, and the circulation of capital). Whereas the assumptions of an invisible pedagogy are more likely to be met by that fraction of the middle class who have a direct relation not to the economic field but to the field of symbolic control and who work in specialized agencies of symbolic control usually located in the public sector (see chapter 4). For both these fractions education is a crucial means of cultural and economic reproduction, although perhaps less so for that fraction directly related to the economic field.[6]

Social class assumptions of visible pedagogies

Sequencing rules

I shall start by looking at the sequencing rules of a visible pedagogy. In the case of a visible pedagogy the sequencing rules are explicit and mark the future of the child in very clear steps or stages. At 5 you should know and be this, at 6 you should know and be that, and at 7 you should know and be something else. Now it is quite clear that if a child comes to school at 5 and cannot meet the intitial requirements of the sequencing rules, it will have difficulty in meeting the requirements at 6. Gradually the child will fall further and further behind. Three strategies may be applied in this situation, or later in the life of the acquirer. Either a repair system will have to be introduced to cope with the children who have failed to meet sequencing requirements or the pacing rules will have to be relaxed so that the child is given more time to meet the requirements of the sequencing rules. Either strategy results in a stratification of acquirers. In the case of a repair system the stratification is explicit and public; in the case of relaxation of the pacing the stratification is implicit, and perhaps will not become explicit and public until later in the pedagogic life. A third strategy would be to maintain the pacing and sequencing rules but to reduce either the quantity or the quality of the contents to be acquired or both. All three strategies produce a more delicate system of stratification within an already stratifying pedagogic practice.

Early reading is crucial to a visible pedagogy and is an early requirement of the sequencing rules. Psychologists tell us that at a given age a child should be able to read. I am not certain I wholly accept this. The age by which a child should be able to read is a function of the sequencing rules of the pedagogic practice of the school. In the case of a visible pedagogy it is crucial that a child reads early, and this for many reasons.

Once a child can read, the book is there, and the book is the text-book or its equivalent. Once a child can read, independent solitary work is possible. He/she is also gradually introduced into a non-oral form of discourse, the rules of which are often at variance with oral forms. It is not only that reading involves the acquisition of a new symbolic relay but that *what* is relayed is itself different from the content of oral forms. Further, school reading is in many cases different from non-school reading. The difference is in what is relayed. In an important sense reading makes the child eventually less dependent upon the teacher and gives the acquirer access to alternative perspectives. Thus those children who are unable to meet sequencing rules as they apply to reading become more dependent upon the teacher and upon oral forms of discourse.

There is another aspect of sequencing rules which we should consider: the relation between the local, the here and now, the context-dependent, and the less local, the more distant, the more context-independent meanings. In pedagogic terms this refers to the acquisition of context-tied operations, on the one hand, and on the other to operations and understanding of principles and their application to new situations. In visible pedagogies there is usually a time interval between these different levels of discourse, in the sense that the local, context-dependent, context-tied operations come in the early stage of the pedagogic practice and the understanding and application of principles come at a later stage; the understanding of the principles of the principles even later. Visible pedagogies entail a distribution of expected age-related discourses.

However, if children cannot meet the requirements of the sequencing rules and are caught up in the strategies of the repair system, then these children, often the children of the lower working class (including other disadvantaged ethnic groups), are constrained by the local, context-dependent, context-tied skills; by a world of facticity. Children who can meet the requirements of the sequencing rules will eventually have access to the principles of their own discourse. These children are more likely to be middle class and are more likely to come to understand that the heart of discourse is not order but disorder, not coherence but incoherence, not clarity but ambiguity, and that the heart of discourse is the possibility of new realities.

We might ask ourselves, if this is the possibility of pedagogic discourse, why are the children of the dominant classes not demonstrating the possibilities of the discourses they have acquired? And the answer must be that socialization into a visible pedagogy tries, though not always successfully, to ensure that its discourse is safe rather than dangerous. In this way a visible pedagogy produces deformation of the children/students of both the dominant and the dominated social classes. In summary we can say that a visible pedagogy is likely to distribute different forms of consciousness according to the social class origin of acquirers. These different forms evolve from the sequencing rules.

Pacing rules: economy of pedagogic discourse

Pacing refers to the expected rate of acquisition, that is, the rate at which learning is expected to occur. Pacing is thus linked to sequencing rules and here refers to the rate at which the progression established by those rules is to be transmitted and acquired. Pacing rules, then, regulate the rhythm of the transmission, and this rhythm may vary in speed. Figure 2.4 illustrates pacing and sites of acquisition.

I shall propose that the schools' academic curriculum, if it is

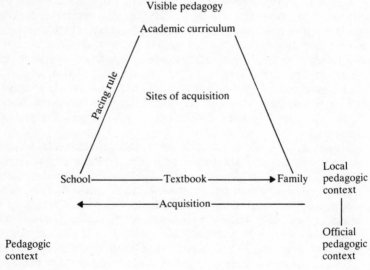

Figure 2.4

to be effectively acquired, always requires two sites of acquisition, the school and the home. Curricula cannot be acquired wholly by time spent at school. This is because the pacing of the acquisition is such that time at school must be supplemented by official pedagogic time at home, and the home must provide a pedagogic context and control of the pupil to remain in that context. There must be an official pedagogic discipline in the home. How does the school reproduce itself in the home? As the pupil gets older he/she is expected to do more and more school work in the home, and the family will be expected to ensure that the pupil has time at home for this work and will also have effective control over the peer-group practices of the child. The work the pupil is expected to do at home is, of course, homework. The basis of homework is usually a text-book. But the textbook requires a context, an official pedagogic context in the home. That is, a space – a silent space – and this is not usually available in the homes of the poor. Nor is pedagogic time available for poor children, as often time is used to work for money – the curriculum practice of the street. Under these conditions there cannot be an effective second site of acquisition with an effective official pedagogic context and support. Without a second site, acquisition will not be possible, still less so as the child grows older. Failure becomes the expectation and the reality.

Where the catchment area of a school draws upon a lower working-class community it is likely, as we have seen, that the school will adopt strategies, or have strategies forced upon it, which will affect both the content and the pacing of the transmission. The content is likely to stress operations, local skills rather than the exploration of principles and general skills, and the pacing is likely to be weakened (Domingos, 1987). In this way children's consciousness is differentially and invidiously regulated according to their social class origin and their families' official pedagogic practice. In the case of a socially mixed catchment area where pupils are drawn from a variety of class backgrounds some schools, through a variety of strategies of stratification (sometimes including repetition), will stream (or 'set') pupils according to the school's estimate of their ability, and these different streams or sets will follow curricula varying in their content and/or pacing.

However, there is a more fundamental effect of strong pacing rules which affects the deep sociolinguistic rules of classroom communicative competence. With strong pacing, time is at a premium, and this regulates examples, illustrations, narratives which facilitate acquisition; regulates what questions may be put, and how many; regulates what counts as an explanation, both its length and its form. Further, strong pacing will tend to reduce pupils' speech and privilege teachers' talk, and this the pupils come to prefer, as time is scarce for the official pedagogic message. In this way the deep structure of pedagogic communication is itself affected. Pacing creates the rhythm of the communication, and rhythms of communication have different modalities. The rhythm of narrative is different from the rhythm of analysis. A strong pacing rule for the latter constructs a principle of communication very different from the inner structure of the communicative principle children use in everyday life. The dominant modality of human communication is not that of analysis but that of narrative. We tell each other stories. However, some families not only construct an official pedagogic context but also socialize their children into official pedagogic communication and the inner structure generated by its pacing rules: an inner structure which points towards analysis rather than narrative, non-linear rather than linear communicative competences. In this way the pacing rule not only affects the social relations of communication but regulates the inner logic of communication.

The strong pacing rule of the academic curriculum of the school creates the necessity of two sites of acquisition. It creates a particular form/modality of communication which does not privilege everyday narrative. In this structure children of the disadvantaged classes are doubly disadvantaged. There is no second site of acquisition and their orientation to language, narrative, is not privileged by the pedagogic communication of the school, either in form or in content, for only some narratives are permissible in school. Thus the pacing rule of the transmission acts selectively on those who can acquire the school's dominant pedagogic code, and this is a social class principle of selection. To weaken the pacing rule would require a change in the allocation of cultural capital and economic capital to the school. A change in cultural capital, because a weakened pacing rule sets up different classroom practice and communications which will require a change in the training of teachers and an increase in economic capital, because the transmission of the same information will now cost more. It is likely, however, that the costs of yearly repetition in some societies will most certainly be reduced, together with the costs of alienated youth. Currently the visible pedagogy of the school is cheap to transmit because it is subsidized by the middle-class family and paid for by the alienation and failure of children of the disadvantaged classes and groups.

We can now see that the pacing rule carries invisible social class assumptions which act selectively on those who can acquire the dominant pedagogic code of the school through the distributive consequences of the visible pedagogy's strong pacing and its regulation of the deep structure of sociolinguistic competences. Indeed, where pacing is strong we may find a *lexical* pedagogic code where one-word answers, or short sentences, relaying individual facts/ skills/operations may be typical of the school class of marginal/ lower working-class pupils, whereas a *syntactic* pedagogic code relaying relationships, processes, connections may be more typical of the school class of middle-class children, although even here pupil participation may be reduced.[7]

We can regard pacing rules as regulating the economy of the transmission and so these rules become the meeting point of the material, discursive, and social base of the transmission.

It is important to point out that a visible pedagogy is not intrinsically a relay for the reproduction of differential school achievement among children from different social classes. It is certainly possible to create a visible pedagogy which would weaken the relation between social class and educational achievement. This may well require a supportive pre-school structure, a relaxing of the framing on pacing and sequencing rules, and a weakening of the framing regulating the flow of communication between the school classroom and the community(ies) the school draws upon. Such relaxation of the framing of a visible pedagogy raises the cost of the transmission and has crucial implications for teacher training and school management. An invisible pedagogy, as we shall see later, is likely to create a pedagogic code intrinsically more difficult, initially at least, for disadvantaged social groups (from the perspective of formal education) to read and to control.

I have discussed the social class assumptions of visible pedagogies only in respect to sequencing rule and pacing. The discussion of the social class assumptions of hierarchical rules will be deferred for purposes of exposition until the discussion of the social class assumptions of invisible pedagogies. I must point out that what has been analysed is the implicit ideological basis of the pedagogic relay itself, that is, the *bias in the relay* which acts selectively upon those who can acquire what is relayed. Clearly what is relayed, the instructional contents, the values these presuppose, and the standards of conduct, character, and manner which form the contents of the school's regulative discourse, carry cultural biases, including those of social class. These biases, the biases of what is relayed, are not the object of this analysis, as they are well documented in the literature.

Social class assumptions of an invisible pedagogy[8]

The class assumptions of an invisible pedagogy translate into cultural and economic prerequisites for the effective understanding and acquisition of this practice. I shall examine those assumptions with respect to the concept of space, the concept of time, and the concept of control. In the case of space and time I shall distinguish between economic and symbolic assumptions.

Space

Economic The material costs of the space of an invisible pedagogy relative to a visible pedagogy is high. For an invisible pedagogy presupposes movement on the part of the child – indeed, considerable freedom of movement. In a school class organized for a visible pedagogy the amount of space per child would be the size of the table or, later, a desk and chair. Under these conditions the school class can hold, and often does, a large number of acquirers. However, if the same space were to be organized for an invisible pedagogy most of the tables or desks would have to be removed to allow each child freedom of movement. But now it would not be possible to put the same number of children in the same space. The number would have to be reduced if the invisible pedagogy were to realize its potential. This reduction in the number of children necessarily increases the cost of the space. When the spatial requirement is translated into family space it is clear that the family cannot employ an invisible pedagogy where there are many members confined to a small space, as is the case with many working-class and lower working-class families, including, especially, disadvantaged families of minority ethnic groups. The spatial requirement is much more likely to be satisfied in the case of middle-class families.

Symbolic The rules whereby space is constructed, marked, and ordered contain implicit cognitive and social messages. In the case of a family operating with a visible pedagogy each room has its own function; within rooms objects may well have fixed positions, spaces may be reserved for special categories of person. There are strong explicit rules regulating the movement of objects, practices, communication from one space to another. Such space is strongly classified and pollution is necessarily visible. However, such strong classification can often provide privacy within its specialized boundaries. In general, this organization of space is predicated on a user rule: 'Leave the space as you find it'. Such a spatial grid carries cognitive and social messages.

However, in the case of a family operating an invisible pedagogy the spatial grid is very different. Relative to a visible pedagogy space it is more weakly marked. The rules regulating movements of objects, persons, practices, communications are less constraining. Meals may be provided on a cafeteria system. Living is more open-plan. Paradoxically, with greater freedom there is less privacy. If a visible pedagogy spatial grid is based on the fundamental rule that 'Things must be kept apart', with the rule of use 'Leave the space as you find it', then the spatial grid of an invisible pedagogy is based on the rule 'Things must be brought together', with the rule of use 'Make your own mark'. That is, the spatial grid of the invisible pedagogy facilitates, encourages individual representations in the sense of showing, revealing, individual representations. Cognitive and social messages are carried by such a space, and such is unlikely to be available and constructed by families disadvantaged by class or ethnicity.

Time

Economic If all children left school at 14 there would be no invisible pedagogies. An invisible pedagogy presupposes a long pedagogic life. Its relaxed rhythm, its less specialized acquisitions, its system of control (see later) entail a different temporal projection relative to a visible pedagogy for comparable acquisition. Indeed, this fact is explicitly taken into account by many middle-class families who favour this regime in the early years of their child's life before switching to a visible pedagogy at the secondary stage. Such favouring families often run a compensatory pedagogic programme dedicated to reading, writing, and counting whilst the child's creative potential may be facilitated by the invisible pedagogy of the infant school or pre-school.

Symbolic A child socialized by a familial visible pedagogy is involved in a particular symbolic projection in which time is punctuated by a series of dislocations in her/his treatment and expected behaviour. Time is symbolically marked as the child progresses through a series of statuses which define her/his relation not only to parents but also to the other siblings. The implicit theory of instruction held by parents which regulates their practice constructs age-specific communications/acquisitions. The child is developed in, and by, a particular construction of time.

However, in the case of an invisible pedagogy, the child is developed by, and is constructed in, a differently specialized construction of time. The child is constructed by implicitly held theories of instruction derived from the theories discussed earlier.

This construction of time appears to give priority to the child's time/space, rather than to the time/space of the parents; to the concrete present of the child, and age statuses give way to the unique signs of the child's own constructed development. In this sense the structuring of the child's time is through a different temporal grid. Visible and invisible pedagogies construct different concepts of the child's development in time which may or may not be consonant with the concept of development held by the school.

There are some implications of a visible pedagogy which I shall develop here. Where the child moves through a series of specialized statuses in time, his/her conduct, achievement, or aspiration is relative to a particular status and the child is subject to normative criteria. He/she is not measured against himself/herself but only against those sharing a similar temporal category. From this point of view the child competes only with those in a similar temporal category. In this way competition is reduced, for jealousies, envious feelings, operates towards his/her peers. This is not to say that the child does not direct negative feelings towards other than his/her peers, but that he/she is aware, or can be made aware of, a distributive rule which privileges older children; a rule which is not personal but public.

In the case of an invisible pedagogy, because statuses are relatively more weakly marked, because of the more individualized or, better, personalized realizations expected, the child, by apparently competing only with her/himself, competes with everybody. This may well be the charm of criteria referencing. Parents relate to the child in terms of the child's apparently unique showings and representations. Here the child, despite the apparent democracy of the pedagogic regime, is placed in a more competitive relation, as comparisons are less likely to be age-graded. Thus jealousies, envious feelings, aspirations are likely to be less specifically focused and so more difficult for both the parents and the child to deal with. From a cognitive and from a social point of view girls are less likely to be negatively constrained by invisible pedagogies than visible pedagogies. Conversely, for boys, under an invisible pedagogy practice, girls become successful competitors and a threat.

Control: hierarchical rules

Here I am concerned with how parents introduce and maintain principles of conduct, character, and manner – that is, concepts of social order, relation, and identity; in other words, with their regulative practice. In the case of a visible pedagogy the rules of social order are generally explicit and specific. The spatial and

temporal grids provide an explicit structure, a grammar of pro-
scriptions and prescriptions, and deviance is very visible. Once the
child has acquired the implicit grammar of the spatial and temporal
grids the problems of control are relatively reduced. Clearly, they
do not evaporate. If the child disobeys, then privileges are with-
drawn and explicit rules are articulated. In the extreme, strategies
of exclusion and physical punishment may be used. I would like it
to be clear that visible pedagogies are not necessarily 'authori-
tarian' but they are certainly positional. Control functions to
clarify, maintain, repair boundaries. However, in the case of
invisible pedagogies we can ask, where does the control lie in a
context of weakened spatial and temporal grids, of encouraged
personalized representations, especially in a context where we could
reasonably expect a greater potential for issues of control to arise?

I want to propose that in this apparently relaxed familial context
control lies almost entirely in inter-personal communication: a
form of communication which works round the areas of motivation and intentionality as read by the parents. The communication
is multi-layered. In order to facilitate this multi-layering of communication a progressive weakening takes place of the classification between the inside of the child and the outside. The parents
encourage the child to make more of his/her inside public and
facilitate the process. More of the child's feelings, fantasies, fears,
and aspirations are expected to be made public. The surveillance of
the child is total. In this sense it is difficult for the child to hide and
also difficult for the parents to. The communication process works
to make the invisible visible, through language, and this may carry
its own pathology.

In the case of a visible pedagogy we said that one of the strategies
of control is exclusion but that this strategy carries difficulties in
the case of an invisible pedagogy. For if the child is excluded (or as
a strategy of self-defence excludes him/herself by withdrawing),
then the communication process is weakened and so is the means of
control. This gives the child a powerful strategy for controlling the
parents by withdrawing, by excluding him/herself, by not being
there, symbolically or physically. The parents must then develop
strategies of retrieval in order to return the child symbolically or
physically to the communication system. In this way the child
acquires a particular elaborated variant of communication which
gives rise to an elaborate repertoire of manipulative skills.

Invisible pedagogies give rise to procedures of control based
upon multi-layered class patterns of communication necessary to
support and promote their concept and practice of social order.
And the construction of these communicative competences is likely

to be class-based. Where these competences are not made available in the family the child is less likely to be self-regulating in school, according to the requirements of its invisible pedagogy practice, and is likely to misread both the practice and its pedagogic context.

I have argued that the assumptions of invisible pedagogies as they inform spatial, temporal, and control grids are less likely to be met in class or ethnically disadvantaged groups, and as a consequence the child here is likely to misread the cultural and cognitive significance of such a classroom practice, and the teacher is likely to misread the cultural and cognitive significance of the child.

We have focused upon different pedagogic sites in our analysis of the social class assumptions of visible pedagogies and invisible pedagogies in their generic form. In the case of visible pedagogies we focused upon the school and in the case of invisible pedagogies we focused upon the family. This is because the *surface* features of a visible pedagogy can be understood by all, as it is a standard pedagogic form, whether or not its underlying principles and practices are reproduced in the family. Thus it was necessary to analyse the underlying ordering principles of the official – that is, the school's – pedagogic practice in order to show that the ordering principles may militate against the acquisition of this practice by class or ethnically disadvantaged groups. In the case of invisible pedagogies we focused on the family to show the supporting domestic pedagogic practice required if the classroom context and practice were to be understood for their pedagogic significance.

What we find, as I have pointed out before, is rarely a pure form of an invisible pedagogy but rather an embedded pedagogic practice where the invisible pedagogy is embedded in a visible pedagogy:

$$\frac{IP}{VP}$$

Here —— indicates embedded. The specific specialized skills and attributes of a visible pedagogy are beneath the surface of an invisible pedagogy, or surface at special occasions. And this holds in the family. What is of interest is when the strong classification of a visible pedagogy emerges as a pedagogic form in itself or surfaces to interrupt an invisible pedagogy. It is clear that, even for ardent sponsors of invisible pedagogies, this practice is generally confined to the child's early years; certainly by the secondary level the demand is for a visible pedagogy, as it is this practice which leads to professional occupational placement. Given this situation, the socialization of a fraction of the middle class is perhaps unique as a modal type. We mean by modal that the form of socialization is not confined to individual families but is a publicly recognized form: a form in which the primary pedagogic socialization principles and practices are at variance with those of the secondary stage. Or where weak classification is embedded in a latent strong classification; and this, we suspect, has many complex consequences.

Whilst it is certainly not true to say that a visible pedagogy is a capitalist practice, it is the standard European pedagogic practice, in one form or another, of every elite secondary curriculum, whether in the East or the West. The strong classification of the visible pedagogy probably has its roots in the medieval university, in the major classification between the Trivium and the Quadrivium and in their sub-classifications, and in the subordination of both to religion. The strong classification between mental and manual practice probably dates from the same period, when manual practice had its own specialized relays, either within the family or in specialized guilds, so creating the concept of the autonomous or abstract visible pedagogy. Such a visible pedagogy, autonomous with respect to control over its own practices, won its independence from the Church, but remained abstract in the sense that its discourse referred only to itself rather than to work. After gaining independence of the Church it became progressively regulated by the State. Whilst, in origin, the visible pedagogy as a relay is not itself a class product, *even though what it relayed was*, its institutionalization in either the private or the public sector led to a selective class-based acquisition.

In the case of the invisible pedagogy, certainly in the UK and probably elsewhere, the sponsors of this as a public form, its dissemination and construction as a practice, were members of that fraction of the middle class discussed earlier. Celia Jenkins (1989) has clearly shown that the members of the New Education Fellowship who were highly influential throughout the 1920s and 1930s in promoting and constructing the 'new education' were drawn almost entirely from professional agents of symbolic control functioning in specialized agencies of symbolic control. Those who opposed invisible pedagogies (other than pedagogues) were likely to be those members of the middle class whose work had a direct relation to the production, distribution, and circulation of capital.

The opposition between these fractions of the middle class is an opposition not over the distribution of power but over principles of social control. At economic and political levels the opposition is an opposition over the role of the State. On the whole the middle-class sponsors of invisible pedagogy support State intervention and the expansion of agents and agencies of symbolic control, and thus growth in public expenditure. For this is the ground and opportunity of their own reproduction and advancement, whereas the middle-class sponsors of visible pedagogy drawn from the economic sector and the entrepreneurial professions are opposed to growth in public expenditure. Thus there are opposing material and symbolic (discursive) interests.

We have so far discussed the class assumptions which act selectively on those who can achieve in visible and invisible pedagogies as generic types. We have earlier said that these generic types can generate a variety of modalities. We shall now consider two modalities of the visible pedagogy, modalities which are opposed to each other and which today are likely to be found in opposition in Europe and North and South America.

Autonomous and market-oriented visible pedagogies[9]

School systems and university systems are now more and more engaged in a struggle over what should be transmitted, over the autonomy of transmission, over the conditions of service of those who transmit, and over the procedures of evaluation of acquirers.

I shall conclude by looking, somewhat cursorily, at the present conflict between knowledge and market-oriented forms, that is, between 'autonomous' and 'dependent' forms of visible pedagogies. That is, between visible pedagogies justified by the intrinsic possibilities of knowlege itself and visible pedagogies justified by their market relevance. In a sense the autonomous visible pedagogy is both a sacred and a profane form, depending essentially upon one's position as either transmitter or acquirer. From an acquirer's point of view an autonomous visible pedagogy is instrumental to class placement through symbolic means. Yet it has the cover of the sacred. However, a market-oriented visible pedagogy is a truly secular form born out of the 'context of cost-efficient education', allegedly promoting relevant skills, attitudes, and technology in an era of large-scale chronic youth unemployment. The explicit rules of selection, sequence, pace, and criteria of a visible pedagogy readily translate into performance indicators of schools' staff and pupils, and a behaviourist theory of instruction readily realizes programmes, manuals, and packaged instruction. Specialization of curricula within a dominant market-oriented visible pedagogy allows for an almost perfect reproduction of the hierarchy of the economy within the school, or between schools (as in the case of 'magnet' schools), through the grading of curricula, e.g. managerial/administrative/business, through the various technological specializations, clerical, and imaginary trade apprenticeships for the lower working and marginal class groups. It is but a small step to encourage industry-based training and, as in Chile, State-sponsored privatized schools. Both autonomous and market-oriented visible pedagogies are relays of the stratification of knowledge, of social inequalities. However, the ideological base of the market-oriented visible pedagogy is more complex and, if I may be allowed, perhaps more sinister.

The autonomous visible pedagogy justifies itself by the intrinsic worthwhileness and value of the knowledge it relays and by the discipline its acquisition requires. Its arrogance lies in its claim to moral high ground and to the superiority of its culture, its indifference to its own stratification consequences, its conceit in its lack of relation to anything other than itself, its self-referential abstracted autonomy. The market-oriented visible pedagogy is ideologically a much more complex construction. It incorporates some of the criticism of the autonomous visible pedagogy, much of it originating from left-wing positions: criticism of the failure of the urban school, of the passivity and inferior status of parents, which combine to reduce their power over schools and teachers, of the boredom of working-class pupils and their consequent disruption of and resistance to irrelevant curricula, of assessment procedures which itemize relative failure rather than the positive strength of the acquirer. But it assimilates these criticisms into a new discourse: a new pedagogic Janus.

The explicit commitment to greater choice by parents and pupils is not a celebration of a participatory democracy but a thin cover for the old stratification of schools and curricula. New forms of assessment, profiling, criteria-referenced rather than norm-referenced assessment, allegedly to recognize and liberate individual qualities, allow of, and mark, greater control of assessment. At the same time periodic mass testing of pupils concentrates new distribution procedures for homogenizing acquisition and, at the same time, creates performance indicators of its effectiveness.[10] Vocationalism appears to offer the lower working class a legitimation of their own pedagogic interests in a manual-based curriculum, and in so doing appears to include them as significant pedagogic subjects, yet at the same time closes off their own personal and occupational possibilities.

The situation is indeed complex. At the same time as the economy is moving towards a greater concentration upon mergers and corporate growth, at a more micro level an entrepreneurial 'artisan' culture is being encouraged in the service sector. This is reflected in market-oriented visible pedagogies to develop imaginary apprenticeships into the skills for this function, e.g. decorating, plumbing, carpentry for the self-employed. Even the pedagogic regimes are mixed, drawing on features of invisible pedagogy, e.g. in the 'negotiation' of pupils' profiles, life skill programmes.[11] The new pedagogic discourse recontextualizes and thus repositions within its own ideology features of apparently oppositional discourses.[12]

The market-oriented visible pedagogy, at least in the UK, creates apparently greater local independence for, and competition between, schools and teachers, yet at the same time the schools and teachers are tied more directly to State regulation. And finally we can detect that the State is now operating on quite different principles with respect to the principles and practices of the economy and the principles and practices of specialized agencies/ agents of symbolic control, especially education. In the economy privatization rules but competition is reduced as mergers proceed apace. As the State reduces its control, corporations and multi-nationals take up the vacated space. In the sector of the specialized agencies of symbolic control, especially in education, we see that privatization, the local autonomies of agencies, are there to encourage greater competition between units. Indeed, we might say that the major site of competition is not the economy in total but increasingly within the sector of publicly regulated symbolic control. Yet despite the greater competition within this sector it is subject to greater and more complex forms of State regulation. Thus the essential shift which appears to be taking place is the shift of State regulation from the economy to symbolic control. Yet State management of symbolic control is accomplished more and more by the exclusion of its own agents and their replacement by managers, administrators, industrialists of the economy.

The ideological message of a market-oriented visible pedagogy is less the regulation and realization of the pedagogy of the new 'relevance' than the new regulation and realization of symbolic control in the transition to capitalism's latest transformation: communications.[13]

Addendum

This paper is a revision of an earlier paper, 'Class and pedagogies: visible and invisible' (in *Class, Codes and Control*, vol. 3, revised edition 1977). It develops and extends the discussion of rules and their class assumptions and provides a more general model for generating types and modalities of pedagogic practices. Further, it includes a discussion of market-oriented pedagogies and specula-tions on their origin, function, and linkage to macro changes in the form of symbolic control. It does not, however, replace the earlier paper but extends and builds upon it. The paper does show that the basic underlying logic of this and other papers can deal with the question of content, as well as linking macro and micro levels of analysis.

In terms of the general classification and framing analysis, much of the focus of the paper in the discussion of specific pedagogic practices is upon framing rather than upon classification. It should be borne in mind that principles of classification are always invisibly present in any pedagogic practice in the sense that any context of that practice presupposes a relationship with other contexts, other pedagogic practices/communications, either within the institution or external to it. Further, principles of classification are visibly present within any pedagogic practice and are realized in the arrangement of acquirers, the distribution of tasks, and in the organizational features of the context. Thus principles of classification, as principles of framing, always have internal as well as external values.

Notes

1 This paper has benefited from seminars held at CIDE, Santiago, Chile, in 1985, and at the University of Valle, Cali, Colombia, in 1986. The present form arose out of an invitation from Adelphi University, New York, to deliver the Robert Finkelstein Annual Lecture, 1987. I am grateful to Dr Alan Sadovnik of Adelphi University for comments and discussion, and also to Celia Jenkins, of the Department of the Sociology of Education, University of London Institute of Education, whose Ph.D. thesis investigated the social class basis of progressive education in Britain.

2 For the purposes of this paper this logic has been reduced to three rules, but there is a fourth, a recontextualizing rule which creates the content to be transmitted. This is a complex matter, fully presented in chapter 5.

3 See chapter 5 for detailed analysis.

4 It is, of course, possible to have explicit hierarchical rules but degrees of implicitness of sequential/pacing rules, which indicate a weakening in the framing of these rules.

5 It is a matter of some interest that in the 1960s in the major disciplines of the human sciences, psychology, linguistics, and anthropology, the concept of competence underlined the structuralist theories of Piaget (child development), Chomsky (linguistics), and Lévi-Strauss (anthropology). Competence in all three theories refers to an in-built grammar. Chomsky's theory of syntax, Piaget's theory of the development and transformation of cognitive operations,

Lévi-Strauss's theory of cultural assemblies and reassemblies are all competences triggered by interaction with non-culturally specific others. That is, competence arises out of two facilities, an in-built facility and an interactional facility. From this point of view competence-acquisition takes place, analytically speaking, at the level of the social, *not* the cultural, because acquisition is dependent not upon any cultural arrangement but upon *social* interaction.

Competence theories, then, integrate the biological with the social, but both are disconnected from the cultural. Competence theories point to competence-acquisition as entailing active participation on the part of the acquirer. Indeed, competence-acquisition arises out of the creative possibilities of the acquirer in inferring rules (Chomsky) in the process of accommodation (Piaget) in *bricolage* (Lévi-Strauss). In a sense competence theories announce a fundamental democracy: all are equal in their acquisition, all actively participate in their acquisition, creativity is intrinsic to becoming social. Differences between individuals are then a product of culture. From this point of view competence theories may be regarded as critiques showing the disparity between what we are and what we become, between what we are capable of and our performance. However, this idealism is bought at a price: the price of severing the relation between power, culture, and competence, between meanings and the structures through which meanings become possible. The democracy of competence theories is a democracy removed from society.

6 An analysis of symbolic control, its agents, agencies, and its relation to the economic field may be found in Bernstein (1986), and set out in chapter 4. For empirical study of differences in the socialization of adolescents whose parents function in the field of symbolic control and the economic field see Holland (1986), Aggleton and Whitty (1985), and Cohen (1981).

7 It is important to point out that what we have called 'lexical' and 'syntactic' pedagogic practices are within the general thesis that the privileging code of the school is elaborated. We may now be finding that this code is officially suspended and replaced by a 'lexical' pedagogic practice relaying less the exploration of principles than context-specific operations which develop low-level skills. In the past, the suspension of an elaborated code with respect to groups of pupils, usually lower working-class, including racially disadvantaged groups, was not official policy but came about because of the context that teachers and pupils alike found themselves in.

8 King (1978 and elsewhere) criticizes the analysis of invisible pedagogy on the grounds that his empirical study of primary schools found no evidence of its existence. As has been pointed out here and in the original paper it is more likely that what will be found is an embedded

pedagogic practice, the invisible embedded in the visible. The pure form is more likely to be found in the private sector. Invisible pedagogy was institutionalized under the name of *dialog-pedagogike* in Sweden in the 1970s. Empirical support for the practice of invisible pedagogy in middle-class families may be found in the references cited in note 5, and at the level of the classroom in Daniels (1988, 1989). An enquiry into different forms of special school organization, pedagogic practice, and pupil discrimination is to be found in *CORE* 12, 2. See also Jenkins (1989).

9 'Autonomous' in the sense of independent is clearly *relative* to 'market-oriented' in the sense of dependent upon economy. Certainly in the United Kingdom (and, for that matter, elsewhere) all levels of the educational systems have for the past thirty years become more and more subject to central control. University research funding is now severely constrained both by the reduction in governmental funding (especially in the social sciences) and by governmental criteria regulating approved research. Market-oriented visible pedagogies indicate a shift of focus of central government, both with respect to the knowledge which is transmitted and with respect to the change in the controlling agents, which now include industrialists. This shift of focus involves not only the development of specialized curricula but also the development of specialized schools.

10 I am indebted to Patricia Broadfoot (1986) for these points.

11 The discussion of invisible pedagogies has occurred in a context where such a practice is dominant within the institution (e.g. family, primary school, pre-school). It has been noted that an invisible pedagogy is less likely to appear in a pure form in the public sector but more likely to be embedded in a visible pedagogy. However, it is possible that features of invisible pedagogy will be found as specialized practices within a predominantly visible pedagogy modality. Here such a specialized practice is likely to be particular to a part of the curriculum (e.g. life skills), addressed to a particular social group (e.g. disadvantaged class or ethnic groups), or may even form part of an assessment procedure. In general invisible pedagogies and/or 'integrated' pedagogic practices are more likely to be formed at primary level or, if at secondary level, associated with disadvantaged social groups as means of their social control. In general, shifts towards invisible pedagogies or similar 'progressive' practices which imply a weakening of classification and framing are more likely to occur in times of 'economic buoyancy'. Such practices are more expensive, both with respect to the training of the transmitters and with respect to the cost of the transmission, than visible pedagogies. In times of economic boom/growth the demand

side is less powerful than the supply side, and as a consequence hierarchies may well take a more indirect, less explicit form as well as being less able to be as selective with respect to ideas, personnel, and interests. However, in times of slump and chronic unemployment demand is more powerful than supply, hierarchies may be expected to become more explicit and directive, more selective of ideas, personnel, and interests. As a consequence, in general, classification and framing relations are likely to strengthen in conjunction with stronger central control. However, as pointed out earlier, specialized invisible pedagogic practices are still likely to be inserted as devices of social control.

In summary we could hypothesize that shifts in modal state pedagogic practices away from, or towards, weak classification and weak framing ('progressive' practices) are likely to be mediated by shifts in the economy which change the social basis of the influencing dominant agents of the state, the degree of explicitness of hierarchies, and the terms of supply of and demand for pedagogic practitioners. In the case of development/expansion of the economy, there is likely to be an increase in public expenditure on education, medical, and social services, and influencing dominant agents are likely to be drawn from agents of symbolic control specializing in agencies of symbolic control, whereas in the case of a downturn in the economy there is likely to be a reduction in public expenditure on education, medical, and social services, and influencing dominant agents of the state are likely to be drawn not from symbolic control but from the economic field.

12 Whilst it can be hypothesized that the more abstract the principles of the forces of division of labour then the more simple its social division of labour, because many of the lower (and increasingly the higher) functions are in information chains and feedback loops of the computer, it is also likely that, as the social division of labour of the economic field becomes both simplified and reduced, that of the field of symbolic control is likely to increase in complexity and size. Further, there is likely to be an attempt to develop an entrepreneurial service structure of the artesan type. Much of the vocational training of sections of the working class is directed towards this end.

13 The transition is linked to high levels of unemployment, changes in occupational functions and conditions, an increase in mergers, recurrent dangers of severe recession, which together may produce instabilities in the social order. The overall movement to greater state control in the field of symbolic control often announces itself through an ideology of the family and nation. This new individualism regulating the field of symbolic control contrasts

sharply with the corporative potential of the communications revolution in the economic field.

Chapter 3

Elaborated and restricted codes: overview and criticisms

Elaborated and restricted codes: an overview, 1956–87

It might be useful to give an account of the development of the code theory and research. Although the research had its origins in specific questions raised by demographic studies in Britain, which showed the persistent patterns of differential achievement of middle-class and working-class pupils and the under-representation of the working class at the higher levels of the educational system, this issue was embedded in a more general theoretical question of classical sociology: how does the outside become the inside and how dow the inside reveal itself and shape the outside? Such a question involves a detailed specification of the principles constituting the outside: an explanation of how these principles are transformed into a process whereby the inside is given an initial form and how that initial form is transformed by the individual in her/his encounters with the world. Thus in the beginnings of the research in 1956 there were two questions, one very specific, the other general.

Between 1954 and 1960 I was teaching in a school in the East End of London and I was aware of the discrepancy between the forms of communicative practice required by the school and the form of communication which the pupils spontaneously moved towards. It was clear that these were oppositional forms. I saw the issue as requiring an explanation of the principles which generated these opposing forms of communication and their social basis. For at that time in the 1950s their basis was seen to lie in an inherited, unchanging attribute, 'IQ'. My first studies attempted to show that 'IQ' was not responsible for these forms of communication. Accordingly, I carried out a number of studies in which I compared the test results of so-called non-verbal and verbal 'IQ' tests given in a group situation to middle-class and lower working-class boys (Bernstein, 1958, 1960). The results showed quite clearly that within the lower working-class group of boys the higher the scores on the non-verbal test the greater the difference between the scores of the two tests. That is, the verbal scores tended to cluster around the mean of the test, whereas the non-verbal scores were distributed across the full range of the non-verbal test, with a pronounced clustering at the higher scores. These results could not be accounted for by the test situation, as it was similar for both tests. This distribution of scores was not found in the middle class; the mean scores on both tests were more similar.

I then argued that social relations acted selectively on principles and focuses of communication and these in turn created rules of interpretation, relation, and identity for their speakers. In other words, social relations regulate the meanings we create, and issue through roles constituted by these social relations, and that these meanings act selectively on lexical and syntactic choices, metaphor and symbolism. In essence the causal linkage flowed from social relations, roles, meanings, language, communications. This emphasis has not changed, although the concept of role now has no place in the conceptual language of the thesis. Between language and speech is social structure. However, in the beginning and throughout the research the problem was the description of the forms of communication and their regulative functions. It is very important to bear in mind the distinction between the generation of the speech forms – that is, social relations – and the *description of the indicators* of the speech forms. What has happened over the decades of the research is a continuous attempt to obtain a more general and more delicate formulation of the generating principles of these speech forms, the social relations, and a more systematic, more general, and more delicate description and specification of the speech forms.

Between 1958 and 1961 I used a list of unreliable features as an initial attempt at a description which included as one of the ten features 'short, simple, often unfinished sentences with poor syntactic structure'. I would add that this indicator was never used in the empirical research. It was made exceptionally clear that all the characteristics were generated not by a linguistic feature but by a semantic feature, an orientation to implicit meaning. I certainly would not wish to defend indicators of what was called then a 'public language use' but would argue emphatically that it was made abundantly clear and stated that such a framework of communication should not be confused with dialect, that in my terms all languages and their varieties carried the same potential for producing either of the associated speech forms. However, this did not prevent 'public language use' being identified with a non-standard form and 'formal language usage' with the standard form.

The description of the speech forms in terms of the ten indicators was inadequate and it was consequently modified in 1961–6. The terms 'public language use' and 'formal language use' were transformed into elaborated and restricted codes, which differentially regulated the range and combinatory possibilities of syntactic alternatives for the organization of meaning. Elaborated codes were considered to regulate a greater range of combinatory possibilities than restricted codes and their syntactic alternatives were considered less predictable. Again it is important to stress that the level of analysis I was using was at the level of performance, not at the level of competence. It referred to how sets of social relations in which people were embedded acted selectively on what was chosen from common linguistic resources. At the same time (Bernstein, 1962) as the definition of code indicators was changed, its semantic basis was referred to in terms of particularistic, local, context-dependent meanings in the case of restricted codes and in terms of universalistic, less local, more context-independent meanings in the case of elaborated codes. Clearly, in a fundamental sense, all meanings are context-dependent, but meanings can differ with respect to their relationships to a local context and in the nature of the social assumptions upon which they rest. The social relationships generating these different orders of meaning were also made more explicit.

Two family types were modelled on the basis of their role relations and procedures of social control. *Positional* families had segregated, specialized roles and well marked boundaries regulating spatial and temporal features of family socialization. Such a family type was expected to be found within all social classes. The second type was called *personal*; here roles were blurred and social control was achieved essentially through complex forms of interpersonal communication. Both family types were expected to be found in different degrees in both the middle and the working class, although it was expected that their distribution would be different in different social classes. The movement towards 'personal' family modes was originally considered to be a function of the movement of complex societies to service societies (Bernstein, 1970a). Later, these types in the middle class were seen to be typical of the old middle class (positional) and the new middle class (personal) and linked to different forms of organic solidarity created by changes in symbolic control of corporate capitalism (Bernstein, 1975, 1977a). These family types were considered both to generate and to produce modalities of codes in both classes. It was possible to distinguish between *orientations of codes with respect to orders of meaning* and *realizations of codes* in terms of positional and personal control.

Thus by the end of the 1960s differences within class groups as well as between class groups were possible and capable of being empirically tested (Cook-Gumperz, 1973; Robinson, 1973; Turner, 1973; Aggleton, 1984, 1987; Wells, 1985). Further, these family types were considered to be generated by different forms of social solidarity. Positional types within the working class were carriers of mechanical solidarity, whereas positional and personal family types were seen as two realizations of two forms of organic solidarity within the middle class ('positional' forms, the old middle class, and 'personal' forms, the new middle class). Class relations generated by the mode of production were held to distribute different forms of solidarity – mechanical solidarity in the lower working class and organic solidarities in the middle class – and these in turn regulated both the orientation to different orders of meaning and the form of their realization.

During 1961–5 extensive research took place which resulted in a number of problems and reformulations of the thesis (see Bernstein, 1970b). (1) The codes could not be described in terms of the relative predictability of their syntax (although I think now it might be possible) and so their description was given in semantic terms and their specific linguistic realizations were described in terms of Halliday's systemic grammar, or, as it was called in those days, scale and category grammar (Halliday, 1973, 1978). (2) The context-free definition of codes was replaced by a formulation which specified the relation between codes and their regulation of specific context, each context having its own specific semantic base and linguistic realization. I distinguished, reformulating Halliday, four crucial socializing contexts in the family: 'regulative', which positioned the child in the moral system, its backings, and practices; 'instructional', which gave access to specific competences for managing objects and persons; 'inter-personal'; and 'imaginative'. I proposed that a code was restricted or elaborated to the extent that the meanings in these four contexts were context-dependent or context-independent. Thus by the end of the 1960s distinctions were made between codes and speech variants. Contexts critical for the empirical testing of the theory were isolated. Procedures for the empirical investigation were created and executed. It was clear that a code could be inferred only from the underlying regulation of four contexts and minimally two, the regulative and the instructional (Bernstein, 1971a).

The method of analysing speech in different context was also developed during this period. The specific meaning potential (the expected referential relations derived from the modelling of the context according to the theory) is expressed in a network, the sub-systems of which open into a binary chain of contrasting choices. The choices at the left of the network represent the most likely choices within a sub-system, whereas proceeding towards the extreme right of the network reveals dependent, more idiosyncratic choices. In this way, in principle, the speech meaning can be transformed into data relevant to the exploration of the theory. Further, any semantic entry into the network can have a range of linguistic realizations. It is then possible to write the linguistic realizations of the semantic entry.

Thus the network becomes the instrument for translating the social relations and their specific practices into a set of contrasting semantic choices and into their linguistic realization. The instrument for the exploration of the theory condenses in itself the sociological, semantic, and linguistic levels. It is pertinent here to draw attention to the research of Hasan (1988), whose research included an intensive analysis of mother–child natural dialogues, each approximately 100 hours, drawn from different social class groups. Hasan also analysed the talk of the teachers of the children. She used Halliday's linguistic theory for the description of the speech and followed the contextual specifications of the code theory. Hasan's results are as predicted by the code theory. For other applications see Turner (1973), Pedro (1981), Holland (1983), Faria (1983), and Bliss *et al.* (1983). It is a matter of interest that this method for the exploration of the theory has rarely been adopted by others. This leads to an important point of method. *A theory should generate the criteria for its evaluation, the contexts necessary for its exploration, the principles for their description, and the rules for interpretation.*

Finally, in Bernstein (1973) ground rules and performance rules were formulated. The latter referred to the control of the selection of the orientation to meaning, that is, whether an elaborated or restricted orientation was required by a given context. This is briefly the development of what has been called the 'speech code' thesis; however, it is important to point out (because it is normally ignored) that a series of papers concerned with the assumptions, principles, and practices of educational agencies together with their external regulation began in 1964. Those papers analysed how class relations penetrate the assumptions, principles, and practices of the school so as to position pupils differentially and invidiously according to their class background: legitimizing the few, invalidating the many. A set of concepts was developed which permitted the translation of power relations into structural relations and the translation of procedures of control into principles of communication (Bernstein, 1971b, 1977a, 1981). The distribution of power is considered to maintain, reproduce, and legitimize the positions within any social division of labour, whether the social division is that of the mode of production, the modality of education, family, or gender. In the case of the school we would be concerned with the social division of labour of teachers, administrators, discourses, practices, contexts, acquirers, together with the social division of pedagogic practices between the school and the family, or the school and work. Any position in a social division of labour is a function of the relations between positions. The relations between positions is given by the degree of insulation. The degree of insulation defines and regulates the degree of specialization (difference) of a position. Thus, if there is strong insulation, then positions have unambiguous identities, sharp boundaries, specialized practices. Conversely, if the insulation is weak, then identities are more generalized, boundaries reduced, and practices more integrated. From this point of view the principle of a social division of labour is the relations between its positions, or, more generally, its categories, and this relation is a function of the degree of insulation.

We use the concept of classification to define the principle of a social division of labour. Thus strong classification ($+C$) refers to positions/categories of a social division of labour which are strongly insulated from each other, whereas weak classification ($-C$) refers to positions/categories where insulation is much reduced and as a consequence each position/category is less specialized. To change a classificatory principle the insulation between categories must be changed. If this occurs, then the power relations upon which the social division of labour is based will be challenged and exposed, and this is likely to lead to attempts to restore the insulation and thus the classificatory principle. *Thus the distribution of power maintains itself essentially through the maintenance of the appropriate degree of insulation between the categories of the social division of labour it legitimizes.* Insulation maintains social order at the level of agency, and, at the level of the agent, insulation (provided it is taken for granted as necessary rather than contingent) suppresses the contradictions, cleavages, and dilemmas which inhere in the principle of the classification. In a sense the classificatory value ($C\pm$) establishes the 'voice' of the category: that is, the limits of its legitimate communicative potential.

We consider that the social relations within a social division of labour are subject to principles of control which can vary independently (within limits) of the classificatory principles of the social division of labour. These principles of control regulate the legitimate rules of the social relations through the location of the source of control over the legitimate selection, organization, sequencing, pacing, and criteria of the communication, together with the posture, position, and dress of the communicants. In agencies of cultural reproduction (e.g. school, family, prison, hospital, etc.) the social relations with which we are concerned are pedagogic relations between transmitter and acquirers. We use the concept of framing to refer to the location of control over the rules of communication. Thus strong framing ($+F$) locates control with the transmitter, whereas weak framing locates control more with the acquirer. If classification regulates the 'voice' of a category, then framing regulates the form of its legitimate message. Framing is the means of socialization into the classificatory principle (for dynamics and change see Bernstein, 1981). Power and control are transformed into rules of legitimate communication and intepretation, through the acquisition of classification and framing values. Challenge and opposition are also acquired.

Variations in or changes of the distribution of power produce variations in changes of the degree of insulation between the categories of a classification, so varying or changing its principles (be these categories of teachers, pupils, contexts, discourses, or practices). Variations in changes of the procedures of control, framing, produce variations in/changes of the social relations of pedagogic practice (e.g. parents/children, doctor/patient, teacher/pupil, social worker/client, etc.), so as to create variations in/changes of the location of the control over the selection, sequencing, pacing, and criteria intrinsic to the communicative principles. Thus variations in/changes of power and procedures of control are translated into strengthening/weakening of the principle of the classification ($\pm$) and of the framing ($\pm$).

The classificatory principle can also be used to determine external relations between categories of agencies according to the degree of their insulation from each other (e.g. school/family community, school/work, school/State). Classification can thus have an internal value, i, which refers to category relations within an agency, between transmitters, between acquirers, between transmitters and acquirers, and an external value, e, which refers to the relations between categories of communication between agencies. The values of C and F can vary independently of each other. In this way it is possible to write the underlying regulative principles to be transmitted/acquired in an agency as $\pm C^{ie}F^{ie}$. Application of this approach at the level of agencies of cultural reproduction can be found in Tyler (1983), Moore (1984), Bernstein and Diaz (1984), Cox (1984); at the level of student classifications, in Holland (1985): at the level of students' contextual rules, in Bernstein (1981) and Dahlberg (1985).

Modalities of elaborated codes and restricted codes could now be defined according to the classification and framing rules of the transmitting agency. The classification and framing rules translate power and control relations into interactional practices and their communicative principles, together with modes of resistance and opposition. The concepts of classification (structural relations) and framing (interactional practices) were developed to translate external power/control relations into power/control relations within and between agencies of cultural reproduction and social production. The concepts create the linkage between macro structures and micro interactional communicative practices. From this point of view ideological positioning and oppositioning are realized in, transmitted, and legitimated by classification and framing rules.

Prior to the development of the above model the code thesis distinguished between coding orientations, elaborated/restricted in terms of implicit/explicit, context-dependent/independent meanings, and code modalities in terms of positional/personal structures of interaction. The development of the macro linkages of the theory and the empirical research at the micro contextual level led to a new definition of code from which could be derived specific modalities. Basically, there has been a movement from the giving of definitions in terms of general linguistic indices (which proved impossible to operationalize and robbed the thesis of any contextual specificity) to the giving of definitions in terms of a *generating contextually specific semantic*. However, in all definitions the underlying semantic was considered to be the regulator of linguistic realization.

The general definition of codes which has been used since Bernstein (1977c) and developed in Bernstein (1981) emphasizes the relation between meanings, realizations, and context. *Thus a code is a regulative principle, tacitly acquired, which selects and integrates relevant meanings, forms of realizations, and evoking contexts.* It follows from this definition that the unit for the analysis of codes is not an abstracted utterance or a single context but relationships between contexts. Code is a regulator of the relationships *between* contexts and, through that relationship, a regulator of relationships *within* contexts. What counts as a context depends not on relationships within but on relationships between contexts. The latter relationships, *between*, create boundary markers whereby specific contexts are distinguished by their specialized meanings and realizations.

Thus if code is the regulator of the relationships between context and, through that, the regulator of the relationships within contexts, then code must generate principles for distinguishing between contexts (classification) and principles, for the creation and production of the specialized relationships within a context (framing). We previously called the speech rules, respectively, ground rules and performance rules. However, in order to avoid confusion and irrelevant associations, the names of these two sets of rules have been changed to *recognition* rules and *realization* rules. Recognition rules, a function of classification, create the means of distinguishing between, and so recognizing, the *speciality* that constitutes a context, and realization rules, a function of framing, regulate the creation and production of specialized relationships internal to that context. At the level of the subject, differences in code entail differences in recognition and realization rules.

It follows from the above definition that, if code selects and integrates relevant meanings, then code presupposes a concept of whose relevance and whose legitimacy; that if code selects forms of realization, then code presupposes a concept of inappropriate or illegitimate forms of realization; that if code regulates evoking contexts, then, again, this implies a concept of inappropriate, illegitimate contexts. The concept of code is inseparable from a concept of legitimate and illegitimate communications, and thus it presupposes a hierarchy in forms of communications, and in their demarcation and criteria.

It can be shown that this general formulation of code operates not only at the level of interaction but also at the macro level of agency. Relevant meanings at the level of interaction translate at the level of agency into discursive practices; realizations translate at the level of agency into transmission practices; and contexts, at the level of agency, translate into organizational practices.

Relevant meanings, relevant to codes, are privileged and privileging referential relations. Privileged in the sense that such meanings within a context have priority, and privileging in the sense that such meanings confer differential power upon speakers. Privileged meanings are a function of control procedures within a context and are a product of its framing rules, but privileging means are a function of power relations between contexts and are a product of the classificatory rules. We shall illustrate the classification and framing of relevant meanings with reference to empirical studies.

A study designed by Bernstein and Adlam and analysed and published by Holland (1981) showed that when white middle-class and lower working-class children, aged 7, were invited to sort pictures of different kinds of food, at one time provided as part of the primary school lunch, the two groups of children gave different reasons for the grouping of pictures they made. The lower working-class children gave principles that had a direct relation to a specific local context of their lives and which took their significance from local activities and meanings, e.g. 'It's what we have for breakfast', 'It's what Mum makes', 'I don't like those'. These sorting principles have a direct relation to a specific material base. The middle-class children gave principles for their sorting which had an indirect relation to a specific material base: 'They're vegetables', 'They've got butter in them', 'They come from the sea'. The crucial difference between the two groups of children lay in the relation of the grouping principle selected to a material base; in one case the relation is direct and specific, and in the other the relation is more indirect and less specific.

After the children had made their first sort they were asked, 'Can you do it a second time? Can you try to put them together in a different way?' This time many middle-class children (a statistically significant number), when asked why they had grouped the pictures as they did, switched their principle and produced principles similar to those produced by the lower working-class, whereas the latter continued to use the principle they had initially selected. (However, by the end of the experiment almost one-third of the lower working-class children had changed their principle of classification. This switching was one of the aims of the experiment.) Here we can see that the middle-class children held two grouping principles and that these children held priority rules with respect to those principles such that the principle which had a relatively direct relation to a specific material base was given second (i.e. lower) priority. Indeed, we would argue that in the first four minutes of the experiment the middle-class children selected relevant meanings based upon a hierarchy of principles each of which had a different relation to a material base. In the experimental context the principle which related to a specific, local material base was the dominated (i.e. the second principle), whereas, from the perspective of the middle-class children, the dominant privileging principle was a principle indicating a relatively indirect and less specific relation to a material base.

We shall now show how these coding orientations on the part of the two groups of children were produced by different readings of the classification and framing values of the experimental context.

The surface value of the interaction in the experimental context is essentially $-C$ ('Group pictures in any way you like') $-F$ ('Talk about them as you wish'). However, we argue that the middle-class children ignored the surface rule and produced its opposite, $+C+F^{ie}$. These children selected a strongly classified recognition rule which marked the context specialized. That is, the experimental context is marked off ($+C$) from other external contexts (e.g. play-group, domestic). The recognition rules marked the context as (1) a sub-context of a specialized context – school – and (2) the sub-context as specialized: adult instructional, evaluative, therefore elaborated orientation.

The framing value selected is also strong ($+F^{ie}$) in that it excludes the realizations of meanings/practices in other contexts (e.g. play-group, domestic). The strong framing leads to the selection of the realization rules, (1) select interactional practice and text in accordance with recognition rules; and (2) create a specialized text, exhaustive taxonomic principle, no narrative. Thus a $-C-F$ coding rule is transformed in the case of the middle-class children into its opposite $+C^{ie}+F^{ie}$ as a consequence of the children's underlying code, elaborated. In the case of the lower working-class children the coding rule $-C-F$ is taken as *the* rule and the children, from their point of view, select a non-specialized recognition rule which in turn regulates their selection of a non-specializing recognition rule. By non-specialized we are referring to the selection of a rule of everyday practice.

The difference between the children is not a difference in cognitive facility/power but a difference in recognition and realization rules used by the children to read the context, select their interactional practice, and create their texts.

We shall now give other examples as further illustrations. Middle-class and lower working-class children were given a reproduction (see Adlam *et al.*, 1977) about the size of a postcard of a work by a Belgian naive painter, Trotin, and asked to talk about it. The probes were 'What is going on in the picture?' 'What are the people doing?' 'What is the picture all about?' (The last probe, after the children had finished talking about the card.) Such probes could be understood as a request for (*a*) narrative or (*b*) a description of persons, objects, events, relationships depicted on the card, i.e. a verbal demography. We found that in general the focus of the child's speech was more a function of the child's class background than of the child's 'IQ'. The middle-class child (irrespective of gender) produced a text similar to or approximating (*b*), whereas the lower working-class child produced a text which was either oriented to (*a*) or which, although oriented to (*b*), was much more embedded in the context in the sense that it was less likely to be understood without the picture card.

Other researchers or critics have interpreted this finding as indicating only that the lower working-class children were aware that both the researcher and the researched were looking at the picture card, and as a consequence there was no need to make verbally explicit a context which was shared. This 'explanation' is both *ad hoc* and selective, as it signally fails to explain (1) why the middle-class children produced little narrative (only six out of a total of sixty-four children did so), (2) why the lower working-class children produced narrative, (3) why it was the girls in the lower working-class who were mainly responsible for narrative texts, (4) why the lower working-class children's speech orientation was similar in other situations presented to the children in which the presumption of a shared perspective (researcher and researched) could not be postulated (instructional and regulative situations), (5) why embedded meanings were preferred by the lower working-class mothers of the children (Henderson, 1971) in a non-shared situation.

Basically, the opening probe(s) is/are the same as in the previous example. The probe(s) is/are 'open', yet we can account for all the texts the children produced as follows. The middle-class children's recognition rules are the same as those given earlier and lead to the selection of an elaborated orientation; their realization rules are as follows. (1) Select criteria, true/false. Given this rule, there can be no narrative, and very few middle-class children gave narrative. Further, given the selected criteria, true/false, there is a need to hedge bets and so use modals ('might be', 'could be', etc.), indicating uncertainty. More middle-class children used such forms (Turner and Pickvance, 1973; Turner, 1977). (2) Make all referential relations explicit and specific. Realization rules (1) and (2) are sufficient to generate the distinctive features of the texts produced by the middle-class children. In the case of the lower working-class children relative to the middle-class children the context was less distinctively marked; for the middle-class children the context was strongly classified ($+C$); in the case of the lower working-class children it was much more weakly classified ($-C$). The latter affects the realization rules of the lower working-class children, which as a consequence have the form $-F$. Thus the texts were selected from the children's everyday practice and so were more likely to be narrative or entail implicit referential relations.

Another situation offered to the children in the same interview required them to explain the rules of a game (after first indicating to the researcher knowledge of the rules) to a child who did not know how to play hide-and-seek. We again found that social class family background was more important than the child's 'IQ' in accounting for the orientation of the child's speech and referential relations. In general (but not uniformly), middle-class children created a relatively context-independent text, less directly related to a special material base in the sense that the text was not embedded in a local context/practice. The text created by the lower working-class children was generally (but not uniformly) relatively context-dependent compared with the text of the middle-class children in that it was more directly related to a specific material base and so embedded in a local context/practice and assumed knowledge of that local context/practice.

It does not necessarily follow that the middle-class child's text was a more effective instruction. Indeed, there may well be grounds for believing otherwise. In this situation the middle-class children's recognition rule was, as before, a function of their reading of the context as $+C$. The selected realization rule required the making of sequencing rules, referential sets, and criteria explicit and specific. The lower working-class children, again using a weak framing principle $(-F)$, selected a realization rule in accordance with their everyday practice of playing the game and their everyday interactions with their peers. We suggest that in all the above situations the middle-class children transformed an apparently 'open' question $(-C-F)$ into $+C^{ie}+F^{ie}$ and that the lower working-class children carried out this transformation much less frequently.

These examples show that code realizations vary with the situation and/or task but the underlying code – the transformation of $-C-F$ into $+C+F$ – does not vary, and this, we suggest, is a function of the underlying code (Adlam *et al.*, 1977). The middle-class children operate with the view that the instructional contexts of the school require specialized rules of communication and inter-actional practices; the lower working-class children operate less as a group with such specialized rules. These specialized rules privilege meanings, realizations, and instructional practices and confer privilege upon those who use them. But the distribution of the fundamental rules, the recognition and realization rules, is class-regulated. In this way the sociolinguistic rules acquired are a function of the distribution of power. Thus distribution of power $\rightarrow$ principles of classification $\rightarrow$ recognition rules $\rightarrow$ relevant meanings; principles of control $\rightarrow$ framing $\rightarrow$ realization rules. From the perspective of the school, where the external classification of the code is strong $(+C)$, the school regulates the recognition rules its code requires, and this acts selectively upon the meanings, realizations, and practices of the children that the school will legitimate.

In the examples we have given it is possible to see how the distribution of power and principles of control operate at the micro level and are transformed through classification and framing procedures into differentially valued communications. Although the examples we have given have all been drawn from formal interview contexts, the analysis can be extended to include 'naturally' occurring classroom talk (see Pedro, 1981).

We have used the term 'context' throughout without giving any indication of its external demarcation and internal features. In the code theory a context is defined by its classificatory and framing values $\pm C^{ie}$ F^{ie}. These regulate the *interactional* principle with respect to the selection, organization (sequencing), pacing, and criteria of oral, written, or visual communication, together with the position, posture, and dress of communicants, and the locational principle with respect to physical location and the form of its realization (the range of objects, their attributes, and relation to each other in space).

We would argue that many of the sociolinguistic studies of classrooms have ignored underlying coding rules as given by the classification and framing of the elaborated code of the school, which regulates its internal and external category relations and interactional practices between teachers, between discourses, between contexts, between acquirers, and between teachers and acquirers. For example, the sequencing and pacing rules of strong framing regulate the fundamental form of all written and oral communication. The sequencing and pacing (rate of expected acquisition of the sequencing rules) of strong framing require that an official pedagogic ideology, context, practice be embedded in the local pedagogic ideology, context, practice of the family if the child is to manage successfully the rules of communication and interactional practice (Domingos, 1984).

It has been argued by some that classroom talk in primary schools and sometimes in secondary schools is, if anything, code-restricted (Cooper, 1976). This is to misinterpret the concept. Because classroom talk at the surface level may consist of short question, answer, check, solicit, expand – teacher-controlled routines – this does not mean that it is restricted in the terms of the theory, only that there is strong framing. Nor does it mean that it is restricted because in some areas the teacher may use a series of short sentences! Instructional routines are essentially a function of the classification and framing values, and as these change so will the routines and the positioning of acquirers in social relations, talk, and language. The referential relations of the dominant curriculum are, however, still elaborated.

Further, any given framing positions the acquirer in an embedded pedagogic discourse. Rules of social order, relation, and identity are embedded in rules of discursive order (selection, sequence, pace, and criteria). The first we have called *regulative* and the second *instructional* discourse. It is possible that the regulative discourse of the school, as it is realized in speech, may be highly positional and imperative but this does not mean that the underlying code is restricted, only that it realizes strong framing of regulative discourse. The framing values of regulative and instructional discourse may not be the same. It may well be the case that in some circumstances the school's instructional discourse is suspended and the discourse then is wholly regulative. (For an analysis of pedagogic discourse see Bernstein and Diaz, 1984; Bernstein, 1986).

This analysis attempts to show the translation of the distribution of power into classificatory principles (within and between contexts) which regulate recognition rules, and the translation of principles of control into framing procedures, which regulate realization rules, and in this way create ideological positioning and oppositioning, and the communicative practices of pedagogic relationships of different code modalities. Daniels (1988) tested the relation between different classification and framing values, recognition and realization rules, and different specializations of meanings in his study of pupils' discriminations and realizations of science and art texts in schools differing in their organization, pedagogic practice, and external relations. He showed that pupils' discriminations and realizations of such texts were related to the classification and framing values of the school's organization, pedagogic practice, and external relations.

Codes can now be classified by the formula

$$\frac{O}{\pm C^{ie}\ F^{ie}}$$

where O refers to orientation to meanings elaborated/restricted (privileged/privileging referential relations); C refers to the principle of the classification; F refers to the principle of framing; $\pm$ refers to the values of C and F with respect to strength, strong or weak; i refers to internal relations, e to external relations. The line ———— indicates that meanings are embedded in power and control principles. The modality of a code is given by the values of classification and framing. The values of classification and framing can vary independently of each other. Any one set of values for classification and framing constitutes the modality of the code.

We regard variations of $C^{ie}F^{ie}$ as regulating variations of control within a given distribution of power. In general, and put simply, the values of $C^{ie}F^{ie}$ will tend to increase in strength in times of economic crisis (except possibly e values), whereas the values of all functions will tend to weaken in times of economic buoyancy. A $+C^{ie}+F^{ie}$ modality is a relatively cheap training, administrative, transmission, and evaluation system, whereas a $-C-F$ modality is a much more costly training, administrative, transmission, and evaluation system. Further, the latter is a relatively unstable reproductive procedure, as its reproduction depends less upon positions in an explicitly hierarchical structure and more upon dense interpersonal communication within an explicit shared ideology. In times of full employment, innovation (moves to change power relations) is likely to come from below, as labour is scarce, whereas in conditions of severe unemployment power lies in the demand for rather than the supply of labour. Here we are pointing to the material base of modalities of communication, but we do not wish to present nor do we subscribe to an economistic model (Bernstein, 1977b). Although the code modalities here refer to agencies of cultural reproduction and their pedagogic processes (family, school, prisons, etc.) the same model has been applied to agencies of production (Bernstein, 1977b; Moore, 1984).

We shall now turn to an explicit formulation of the relation between class relations and the distribution of codes. Earlier, when giving examples of recognition rules and the selection of relevant meanings, we distinguished between orders of meaning in terms of meanings which were directly related to a specific material base and those where the relation was more indirect and less specific. This formulation was preferred to earlier definitions (universalistic/particularistic, context-dependent/independent, implicit/explicit) because the social class regulation of distribution and location is more transparent.

We shall first give general conditions for the location and distribution of codes. First, *location*. The simpler the social division of labour and the more specific and local the relation between an agent and its material base, then the more direct the relation between meanings and a specific material base and the greater the probability of a restricted code. The more complex the social division of labour, and the less specific and local the relation between an agent and its material base, then the more indirect the relation between meanings and a specific material base and the greater the probability of an elaborated code.

It is important to point out that in each case *we are regarding the social division of labour from the specific location of one of its agents.* Let us take the example of a peasant working on a sugarcane plantation. From the point of view of the peasant, he or she would physically see himself or herself as part of a simple division of labour, and such an agent's interactional practices would have as their centre of gravity interactions within a simple division of labour regulating practices with respect to a local, specific material base. However, in the case of the patron, he (historically not she) would physically see himself as part of a complex division of labour which would include the total local division of labour of the plantation, the local market, and the local circulation of capital, and which would also include a complex division of labour of national and international markets, with their entailed capital circulations. The patron's centre of gravity would lie within a complex division of labour regulating practices with respect to a generalized material base. Thus the most primitive condition for the location of coding orientations is given by the location of agents in the social division of labour of production. Different locations generate interactional practices, which realize different relations to the material base and so different codes. At this point it is important to point out that we are here stating the conditions for the location of different coding orientations, *not* their origins.

Distribution. The conditions for the distribution of coding orientations in this model are clear. If agents become specialized categories of the social division of labour, and their location is fixed and so non-transposable, then coding orientations become specialities of position within the social division of labour. The condition for these conditions is the principle of the social division of labour itself. The group that dominates the principle of the social division of labour determines the extent to which positions in the social division of labour give access to specialized coding orientations. These coding orientations are in no sense inevitable consequences of any position. Coding orientations are not intrinsic to different positions. Whether they become so depends upon the distribution of power created by the principles regulating the social division of labour, i.e. the classificatory principles. If the principle regulating the social division of labour is that of class relations, then positions are likely to be fixed and non-transposable, one set of dominated positions generating mechanical solidarity in opposition to the set of dominant positions generating organic solidarity.

It is the case that the class principles of the social division of labour and its social relations locate and distribute production codes (elaborated and restricted) differentially within its hierarchy.

Access to those codes is differentially acquired via the credentialism of State education according to the social class background of students, whether as a consequence of the ideological positioning of the practices of transmission or of the refusal of students to be incorporated.

It is important to note that this model generates what can be called the official or class-regulated location and distribution of code orientations and interactional practices regulating a code modality. Education is the official State agency for the location and general distribution of elaborated codes and their modalities of reproduction, which selectively create, position, and evaluate official pedagogic subjects. It is equally important to point out that oppositional restricted and elaborated codes may be generated both in school and at work, and that oppositional elaborated codes arise out of agencies of defence, challenge, opposition (trade unions, political parties, and counter-hegemonic sites: Moore, 1984; Holland, 1985).

The origins of elaborated codes lie not in the mode of production but in the agencies of symbolic control, essentially in religious systems. In the case of 'simple' societies the thought worlds (cosmologies) of the religious systems are made possible because of elaborated orientations but the possibilities of such orientations are policed by the thought world itself and the practices to which it gives rise. The link between religion and education in medieval Europe (Durkheim, 1938) established the institutionalizing of elaborated codes. The possibilities of these official codes are still subject to policing practices, and such practices are likely to be intrinsic to their very transmission. Codes are sites of contradictions, challenge, and change (Bernstein, 1986).

The above gives a highly general formulation of conditions for the location and distribution of codes in the mode of production. In terms of empirical research there are considerable difficulties in the specification of the boundaries, relations, and internal differentiation of social classes. The conceptual analysis of class relations is one thing, their empirical descriptive specification another, and the relation between the conceptual and the empirical an even more bothersome thing. Measures of hierarchically arranged groups according to occupational/functional/educational level leads to an unwarranted homogeneity of groups and to the construction of scales whose use is possible only in European societies, and there is little agreement between those societies in the construction of such scales. The specification of modalities of elaborated code requires greater delicacy in the specification of the hypothesized social class location.

We distinguish (1) between types of occupation location, that is, whether an agent is located in economic agencies (public/private) or agencies specializing in symbolic control (public/private), (2) whether the agent is specialized as an economic agent in the economic field or specialized as an agent of symbolic control in that respective field, (3) whether an agent of symbolic control is located in an economic agency or in an agency of symbolic control, (4) the hierarchical position of an agent within an agency.

On the basis of these distinctions it is possible to make distinctions within the customary middle class or working class according to the field in which an agent is located, economic or symbolic control (public/private). Thus we might expect differences in ideological positioning, communicative practices, and interests despite a common occupational function according to field location. In the case of the customary middle class we can distinguish 'new' middle-class agents located in economic or symbolic control fields functioning as specialized economic agents or as specialized agents of symbolic control. The latter may function in economic agencies or agencies specializing in symbolic control. Thus we might expect differences in ideological positioning, communicative practices, and interests within the middle class according to field location, specialization, and agency. For empirical application see Holland (1985) and Faria (1984) for sociolinguistic studies in class differences in self-reference.

We consider that different fractions of the middle class (those who are directly related to the mode of production as distinct from those who are directly related to specialized agencies of symbolic control) may be sponsors of different modalities of elaborated codes and in this way influence the public shaping of communication rules, interactional practices, and their ideological positioning (Bernstein, 1975, 1986). These fractions may have opposing interests towards public expenditure by the State. The middle-class fraction located in the mode of production may well have an interest in limiting public expenditure. This is more likely to promote code modalities of $+C+F$, whereas that fraction located in specialized agencies of symbolic control may have opposing interests and support increases in public expenditure. This is more likely to promote code modalities whose classification and framing values are weakened. The restriction and expansion of public expenditure by the State have consequences for the social division of labour of the field of symbolic control, for its social relations, and thus for its code modalities.

Behind the research is an attempt to create a language which will permit the integration of macro and micro levels of analysis; the recovery of the macro from the micro in a context of potential change. The project could be said to be a continuous attempt to understand something about the rules, practices, and agencies regulating the legitimate creation, distribution, reproduction, and change of consciousness by principles of communication through which a given distribution of power and dominant cultural categories are legitimated and reproduced. In short, an attempt to understand the nature of symbolic control.

Criticisms of the theory

Code, competence, dialect, and deficit

Code and competence

Theories that operate with a concept of competence (linguistic or cognitive) are theories in which the conditions for the acquisition of the given competence require some innate facility, together with interaction with a culturally non-specific other who also possesses the competence. In other words, the crucial communication necessary for the acquisition of the competence is with a culturally non-specific other. Of course, no other who possesses a given competence can be culturally non-specific. There is no way of being a cultural subject without being culturally specific. Be that as it may, and it inevitably is, theories of competence necessarily abstract the non-culturally specific from the culturally specific. Code is transmitted and acquired in interactions that are culturally specific. Codes therefore presuppose specialized others. It is crucial to distinguish between theories that differ in the location of their problematic. The concept of code presupposes competences (linguistic/cognitive) that all acquire and share; hence it is not possible to discuss code with reference to cognitive/linguistic deficiencies located at the level of competence. Code refers to a specific cultural regulation of the realization of commonly shared competences. Code refers to specific semiotic grammars regulated by specialized distributions of power and principles of control. Such grammars will have, among other realizations, specific linguistic realizations.

Code and dialect

The term 'dialect' refers to a variety of language that can be marked off from other varieties by phonological, syntactic, morphological, and lexical features. The term is descriptive. It should give the demarcation rules for a specialized usage of a language and the special rules of its internal orderings. In the same way that every language carries the same potential for realizing codes as defined by this thesis, language varieties, dialects, have the same potential. There is no reason to believe that in our terms any language variety can realize only one code. It is therefore highly misleading and inaccurate to equate a standard variety with an elaborated code and a non-standard variety with a restricted code, even thogh there may well be a class distribution of language varieties. Codes and dialects belong to different theoretical discourses, to different theories, and address fundamentally different problematics.

> A verbal deficit theory is any hypothesis that (i) seeks to explain differential educational attainment to any significant degree in terms of the intrinsic nature of two fundamentally different varieties of language used by schoolchildren, both at the commencement of their school careers and subsequently; and (ii) seeks to explain the unequal social distribution of educational attainment in terms of which social groups are deemed to speak one of the two varieties rather than the other.

This quotation from a linguist (Gordon, 1981: 60) contains all the confusion which attempts to identify codes, varieties, deficit. What is at stake is not the issue of the intrinsic nature of different varieties of language but different modalities of privileged meanings, practices, and social relations which act selectively upon shared linguistic resources. A language variety cannot be defined with respect to meanings, practices, and social relations. Codes are not varieties. Educational failure (official pedagogic failure) is a complex function of the official transmission system of the school and the local acquisition process of the family/peer/group/ community.

Deficit and difference

This opposition received much of its power from Labov's paper 'The logic of non-standard English' (1969), in which he contrasts the arguments of two black speakers, one middle-class and the other working-class. He shows that the working-class youth's argument is succinct, pithy, and logical, whereas the middle-class black adult is verbose, redundant, hesitant. This is an unwarranted conclusion. Both arguments are logical, as judged by rules of inference, but the modalities of the argument are different. They follow different paradigmatic forms and in consequence they should not be judged by anthitheses such as verbose–succinct, redundant–pithy, economic–uneconomic, hesitant–fluent. Larry's argument is essentially by assertion and denial: some say if you are good you go to heaven and if you are bad you go to hell, but there is no god and so no heaven. The middle-class black is not redundant, verbose; he is producing an argument based upon a different paradigmatic form entailing rules of evidence, falsification, abstraction, generalization. The crucial difference lies not in the content but in the form of the argument offered by the two speakers.

It is a matter of interest that in the endlessly recycled account of Larry's discussion of black and white gods it is rarely noted that Larry is given five probes to assist in the structuring of his argument. 'What?' 'What happens to your spirit?' 'And where does your spirit go?' 'On what [does it depend]?' 'Why?' Further, in another exhange (p. 217), which appears later in the paper but may have preceded the interchange referred to above (p. 214), Larry is specifically asked what colour God is, white or black, and is given three probes to focus the answer. In contrast, the question to the black middle-class speaker is, 'Do you know of anything that someone can do to have someone who has passed on visit him in a dream?' (p. 218). Not the clearest question to answer. The respondent is given no probes to assist in the structuring of his reply. The first half of the reply is concerned with the relation between dreams and reality and the second half is concerned with whether it is possible to induce a dreamer to dream of something specific. In the light of the question, perhaps not a bad effort. However, this is not Labov's view, nor of those who recycle the quotations and interpretations unmediated by an analysis. The 'liberal' ideology of white sociolinguists paradoxically here transforms difference into deficit.

Nothing is shown by this comparison because no comparison using Labov's criteria should be applied. The issue which is raised refers to the social origins of the forms of argument and the rules of their selective, contextual realization and interactional practices. It may well be the case on this analysis that the middle-class black adult has access to two argumental forms whereas the black working-class youth may well have access to only one. This would require further investigation.

Later in the same paper Labov presents spoken texts of a black child who in a formal experimental context was virtually silent, but when placed in a context with a friendly black adult interviewer who sat on the floor and where the child was accompanied by his friend sharing a Coke spoke freely and managed the interaction effectively. The example is used to illustrate the effect of context upon speech and the management of interaction, and this it undoubtedly does, but it also raises more fundamental questions. How was it necessary for the context to be changed so drastically and what was the relation between the distinguishing features of the changed context and the management of interaction and communication? In terms of the theory offered here an analysis of the child's speech shows that it is a restricted variant, which is precisely what it should be, given the distinguishing features of the context. In both cases offered in the paper the sociological level of analysis is bypassed in order to demonstrate an underlying competence, and this is not unusual where a 'difference' position is to be favoured, but I would submit that the fundamental issue is not an illustration of a communicative competence but the question of the *controls on the distribution of sociolinguistic rules of contextualized performance.*

We shall consider in more detail Labov's second major example, taken from the speech of a black boy under different contextual constraints. It is worth spending time over these examples, as they have been received enthusiastically and repeated, usually without comment. In the first situation the boy is expected to make comments in response to the elicitation 'Tell me all you can about this.' The reference is a toy space ship. Even with six probes offered by the white interviewer the boy rarely replies in more than one nominal group. In another context the white interviewer is replaced by a black (Clarence Robins), who interviews Leon (aged 8). The latter again gives minimal responses to the following question accompanied by eleven probes: 'What if you saw somebody kickin' somebody else on the ground or was using a stick, what would you do if you saw that?' No other description of the contexts is given in Labov (1969). Labov's explanations are that here Leon is defending himself against possible accusations, and in the first example it is the asymmetry of the relationship, not the ineptness of the interviewer, which is responsible for the silence.

Further, Leon is interviewed by a skilled black interviewer raised in Harlem and offered, 'You watch – you like to watch television?' (Leon nods.) 'What's your favourite programme?' Despite eight probes Leon's replies are minimal. Labov comments that despite the skills, sensitivities, and experience of the black interviewer, Clarence Robins, Leon is not communicative and Robins is unable to break down what Labov calls the 'prevailing social constraints'. For Labov it is because the social relationship is asymmetrical, not because of the race of the interviewer. But is it? Is it, the asymmetry, a property of the form of the social relationship or is it the form of the discourse?

In all the contexts so far described the child is positioned in an interrogative, instructional discourse, whether official within the school or informal in the case of interrogation on a moral issue or a favourite television programme. This discourse is specialized, first, with respect to the child's social relation to the discourse and, second, as an interrogative of an open form. The child is positioned within a request for unique information, that is, information which only he can give. In this sense the social basis of the child's relation to the discourse is egocentric. He is differentiated from his social base and its competences, as a figure differentiated from its ground. As a consequence the child cannot draw upon communicative competence deriving from a sociocentric relation to the discourse. The fact that the interrogative is of an open form intensifies the egocentric social base.

Now in the contexts which follow the asymmetry is no less explicit, but on the argument offer here, the child's relation to the discourse is sociocentric and in consequence he can draw upon competences which make that position possible. Thus when Clarence Robins sits on the floor, introduces taboo words, topics, when Leon is with his best friend, then a lively interaction takes place. Yet in this interaction the lead is taken by Leon's friend Greg. Labov argues that Greg and Leon talk as much to each other as they do to Robins, the black interviewer. In fact this is not the case. Robins makes eleven interventions, all of them interrogative. In other words the asymmetry holds in the context despite its apparent informality. The interchange is lively between boys because they both draw upon common rules and shared knowledge.

In the next section, which consists of eighteen interchanges, Robins makes six interventions, all of them explicit or implicit interrogatives, while the Greg and Leon exchanges consist almost entirely of affirmation or negations, and this pattern continues in the final sequence of exchanges. It is a little difficult to accept Labov's interpretation that 'we have two boys who have so much to say that they keep interrupting each other and who seem to have no difficulty in using the English language to express themselves'. These conclusions are based upon criteria which are inappropriate to the context and in an important respect are patronizing. Further, Labov's local interpretation of the exchanges seems on analysis to be unwarranted. Yet these examples of interchange (or rather the interpretations) are repeatedly quoted and virtually sacrosanct.

The view here is that we have neither expressive speech nor a rich (*sic*) array of grammar in one context and that we have severely reduced speech in another. What we have are interchanges which are embedded in different social bases and thus founded upon different rules and competences. It has little to do with asymmetry. Robins maintains an interrogative mode in all contexts, and his questions press from the outside, whereas Greg's and Leon's affirmations, negations, and interrogatives are generated from within the age and gender rules they both share. I agree only with Labov's conclusion: 'We see no connection between verbal skill in the speech events characteristic of the street culture and success in the school'. However, what is required is less *ad hoc* ideology and interpretation and a more systematic, general understanding of the social basis of modalities of communication and their distributive principles and differential outcomes.

The meeting of such a requirement invites an analysis of the distribution of power and principles of control which regulate and distribute, unequally, communicative performance principles which differentially position speakers with respect to interactional power and context management. This is the focus of study of the code thesis. In essence the deficit position states that there is an absence of attributes (cognitive, linguistic, cultural) in one group and the presence of such attributes in another which lead to educational failure on the part of one group and success on the part of the other. One of the effects of the deficit position is to displace responsibility for failure (and presumably for success) from the school to the family/community.

In essence, the language variety/difference position is that any meaning can be expressed in any language, so that for each linguistic utterance in A there is a corresponding utterance in B (where A and B represent styles, standards, dialects, or functional varieties) which conveys the same semantic information (Gordon, 1981: 95). Although Gordon adds that the proposition is untestable for our purposes, it is crucial to examine the central assertion that any meaning can be expressed in any language. From the point of view of the code thesis this is not the issue. What is at issue is the social distribution of privilege and privileging meanings, or, more explicitly, the social distribution of dominant and dominated principles for the exploration, construction, and exchange of legitimate meanings, their contextual management, and their relation to each other. With respect to the deficit position the code theory does not support the view that the sole origin of educational failure and success lies in the presence or absence of attributes of the student, family, community. Success or failure is a function of the school's dominant curriculum, which acts selectively upon those who can acquire it. The dominant code modality of the school regulates its communicative relations, demands, evaluations, and positioning of the family and of its students. The code theory asserts that there is a social class-regulated unequal distribution of privileging principles of communication, their generative interactional practices, and material base with respect to primary agencies of socialization (e.g. the family) and that social class, indirectly, affects the classification and framing of the elaborated code transmitted by the school so as to facilitate and perpetuate its unequal acquisition. Thus the code theory accepts neither a deficit nor a difference position but draws attention to the relations between macro power relations and micro practices of transmission, acquisition, and evaluation and the positioning and oppositioning to which these practices give rise.

Criticism (specific)

We shall take Stubbs (1983) as a source of major criticism. In this critique, as in many others, a major paper (Bernstein, 1981) is ignored, as also is research by members of the Sociological Research Unit (e.g. Adlam *et al.*, 1977; Cook-Gumperz, 1973), although selective reference is made to papers more conducive to Stubbs's position.

Relations between codes and grammar

All share common linguistic competences but codes act selectively on how, when, where, and why these common competences are differentially realized in specialized contexts. Further, codes are essentially semantic (indeed, semiotic) principles which regulate grammatical/lexical exploration. But the latter in turn feedbacks upon the semantic specialization created by the code, serving to project clarity, objectifies the semantic and leads to an exploration of the messages of the code, including possibly the limitations of the code itself.

Codes and grammatical choice

This relation will vary with the context. The same grammatical form, 'if . . . then', may be a feature of a restricted variant as an imperative delivered in a regulative context, or a feature of an elaborated variant in an instructional context. Thus similar grammatical forms have different code significations in different contexts; code markers are context-specific (Bernstein, 1971a, 1973). Further, whilst it is the case that anything can be said in simple sentences – that is, there is no necessary relation between grammatical form and cognitive function – it is unlikely that everything can be said with equal facility and felicity. It would be possible to translate this paper into simple sentences but it would be a long and arduous task and would be possible only on the basis of an elaborated code, as would the condition of existence of the paper in the first place.

Codes and frequency counts

The criticism here is that counting the relative frequency of isolated units of language can establish only a continuum, never a qualitative difference. Nothing can be reliably inferred from differential frequencies. Clearly, frequency counts of isolated units are not the best means of inferring underlying structures. It is preferable to distinguish texts on the basis of their internal rules of distinctive cohesion and collocation. However, linguistics was then, and perhaps is now, stronger on description below than above the level of the sentence. Frequency counts can still be of service; the service depends upon what is counted, and this in turn depends upon the problem and the discourse in which the problem is constituted. What is trivial or significant is given by the discourse to which the phenomenon is referred.

In our case, if we distinguish in terms of our previous family types, then positional, restricted, and personal elaborated variants of the regulative contexts certainly will not realize absolute differences in units. Indeed, the same unit – for example, an imperative – will appear in positional and personal modes of control, but it will appear in a different position in the *sequence* of control. However, there is no question of the qualitative differences in those modalities of control at the semantic level, or of their qualitative difference, from the point of view of those applying and receiving such control. And this holds for instructional contexts. If we are comparing relative frequencies within a context, we have been forced to use statistical significance differences in frequencies as our criterion for inferring qualitative differences in patterning arising out of differences in relevances. A more text-wide principle is to be preferred, and this has been attempted in the creation of networks for the regulative context. Trudghill's statement (1983) that after sixteen years all we have is differences in the use of pronouns between groups of children is a sign only of what this linguist has failed to read rather than a comment on the research.

Codes and theory

It is argued that no predictions can be made from the theory, and therefore the thesis is not scientific. The examples often given are the relations between family types and codes. In the first place, we have empirical evidence of the existence of such family types; second, we have evidence that, certainly within the middle class, these are associated with the expected differences of occupational function (Wells, 1985; Aggleton, 1984); third, there is evidence that, within the working class, positional families are associated with children who produce narrative in instructional contests (Adlam *et al.*, 1977). However, because positional and personal families can be found in both middle and working classes, it is argued that no predictions of language use can be made. Within the middle class differences between family types are differences *within* an elaborated code essentially creating differences in the modality of realization. The modal family type expected within the lower working class is positional and the coding orientation restricted because of its class occupational function and relations. We have interview data that such is the case (see earlier references).

However, in the lower working class, if the coding orientations of the children were elaborated, we would expect the family to be of the personal type. Indeed, the conditions (whether these are true or false is beside the point for the purposes of this discussion) for the emergence of such families within the working class were given in Bernstein (1973). The models of family types in no way create the situation argued by Stubbs, that elaborated variants in socialization may be realized by either elaborated or restricted codes. Indeed, it can readily be inferred that we regarded person-oriented lower working-class families as the site for code changes (Bernstein, 1970a, 1973).

It is also clear that Stubbs makes the mistake of assuming that elaborated variants will not have a reduced range of syntactic alternatives and a narrow range of lexes (see earlier discussion of instructional discourse). The linguistic realization of a variant is a function of the meanings relevant to the context. The type of variant is defined by those meanings. Further, it is argued (Gordon, 1981) that the models of family types (and by implication other models derived from the thesis) are tautological in the sense that roles, practices, meanings, speech are not defined independently of each other and thus the entailed relationships are logically necessary. However, the model exhibits the processes whereby boundary procedures, categories of function punctuate and shape a specific semantic, which in turn selectively constrains principles generating speech in contexts. Thus, from the point of view of the socializer, roles regulate codes, but from the point of view of the socialized the acquisition of codes regulates role acquisition. There is no contradiction, as Gordon (1981) asserts in his repetition of Jackson's critique (1974). See also later discussion.

In empirical research the different levels of the model are examined independently of each other in order to test their interrelation. Finally, Stubbs, like others, constantly shifts from issues of performance to issues of competence, as in 'What has to be explained is why working-class children do not frequently *use* linguistic forms they quite clearly know (and which tend to be valued by the teachers)' (1983: 63). The issue is not the linguistic form but the relationship between power, social positioning, privileging practices, and meanings. Codes are carried by linguistic forms but have their origin outside such forms.

Codes and their recontextualizing

Stubbs (1983: 54), commenting upon Bernstein (1973), states that:

> for reasons which are not known middle-class children are more successful [i.e. do what teachers and experimenters want] in both such settings. One obvious conclusion to draw from this, however, is that it is schools which should change, not children. (Bernstein does not draw this conclusion.)

It is precisely this unwarranted aside which slyly turns the reader away from the many analyses which have been undertaken of school transmissions. Yet in the same paper that Stubbs criticizes (Bernstein, 1973: 241) the following appears:

> It has always been very clear to me that the class structure affected access to elaborated codes through its influence upon initial socialization into the family *and* through its fundamental shaping of both the organizational structure and contents of education. [Italics in original]

Again on page 241, 'Whether such codes [elaborated] perform the above function [alienation of the working class] depends more and more in industrialized societies upon the classification and frames which control their transmission in formal education.' Stubbs and others in this respect overlook:

> Even more can be done to ensure that the teacher's core responsibility, the transfer of skills and sensitivities, can be effectively carried out. For in the final count it is *what* goes on and *how* it goes on in the *school* that matters. Educational visitors, teacher/ social workers, although highly relevant, are no substitute for constant appraisal of both the methods we are using and the culture and organisation of the school. [Bernstein, 1970c; italics in original]

In a sense the opposition between home background and school in the search for the origins of differential educational achievement is not helpful. Clearly, ineffective schools where students often spend over five hours a day for ten or more years of their pedagogic life are likely to reduce the achievements of all children. And it is self-evident that the hypothesis 'differences [between schools] are related to methods and styles of management at the level of the school and subject department' (Smith and Tomlinson, 1989: 302) is likely in general to be true. But what methods, what styles of management go with what achievements? However, it does seem a little premature to claim that 'the same child would get a CSE grade 3 in English at one school but an O level grade B in English at another' (Smith and Tomlinson, 1989: 301) on the measures used in this otherwise outstanding study to evaluate the social, economic, and pedagogic background of the child. It is clear that more refined analysis of variations within nominal social class/ethnic group membership is required before we can begin to construct 'the same child'.

Brandis and Bernstein (1974) were able to show that indices of familial–child communication *within* nominal social class position (education and occupation) were more highly correlated with the child's 'IQ' than social class position, and these indices were highly correlated with teachers' general and specific evaluations and expectations of the child. Bakker *et al.* (1989) present results pertinent to these issues. However, it is abundantly clear that the crucial lever of formal pedagogic change must be the school, and education will continue to fail to compensate for society to the extent that schools fail to meet the potential of their effectiveness through lack of resources, methods, management, or parental/community *rapport*.

Edwards (1987 and elsewhere) recycles other critics' (e.g. Gordon, 1981) positioning of the theory which disengages the two halves of the theory, leaving only the focus on family transmissions, despite the papers from 1964 onwards reprinted in *Class, Codes and Control* vol. 3. Edwards (1987) shows that teachers hold positions of deficit, and believe in the linguistic deformity of working-class speech, etc., and uses these findings to charge the theory with legitimizing if not creating those notions, even when the teachers do not mention the theory or its author. Yet Edwards does not ask where these teachers obtained their views of the theory. Where also do they obtain their notions of Piaget, of Marx, of Freud? Presumably from their training. There is no direct line from the theory to teachers, only a process of mediation, of recontextualizing. It is this process which requires sociological analysis (Bernstein, 1986). This repositioning of the theory operates both positively and negatively to construct the issue in terms of deficit/difference, and this in turn serves to mask the fundamental problematic. Marx refers to the lumpenproletariat in terms which would leave no doubt of a deficit position, yet it would be ludicrous to disconnect such a description from the problematic of his fundamental analysis.

Finally, we shall examine criticisms which are not concerned with the more narrowly defined sociolinguistic features of the theory, which have formed the substance of the criticisms we have previously considered, but which are more concerned with the sociological concepts, the relationships they specify, and their empirical relevance. It clearly is not possible to consider all the comments to which the concepts and the models have given rise. We shall select two critics, King and Gibson, who have been particularly concerned with the theory who, although focusing upon different aspects, share a similar objection to its structuralist perspective.

King (1978, 1979) maintains that the concept of an invisible pedagogy is vacuous and misleading because he could find no evidence of this pedagogic practice in the primary schools he studied. It does seem a little strange that on this local basis he dismisses the analysis of that practice, its generating rules and its social and ideological base. Jenkins (1989) found in her analysis of the origins of progressive education and its social class base that the model of an invisible pedagogy closely described the pedagogic practice in part created and sponsored by the New Education Fellowship and that the social and ideological base was as predicted. Daniels (1988) selected a school in his sample *because* it used an invisible pedagogy. Daniels (1989) compared the drawings produced by children taught by an invisible pedagogic practice with the drawings produced by children taught by a visible pedagogic practice and found that the images were as predicted by the theory. *Dialog-pedagogike* in Sweden in the 1970s fitted the model of an invisible pedagogy (Kallos, 1978). King (1976, 1981a, b) tested empirically earlier work on schools where I had used an open/closed instrumental/expressive model. King argued that his data, based on seventy-two schools in his first study, and on forty-five schools in the follow-up study, revealed no or little sign of schools showing systematic tendencies in line with the model.

Tyler (1988: 162) considers that the simple correlation technique used by King was inappropriate to reveal underlying patterns:

> By taking the patterns of correlation as evidence of the existence of codes, he [King] appears to have missed the whole point of the structuralist approach, that it is not the size of the correlation that matters but its position within a patterned field of such relations.

Tyler (1984) used canonical correlation analysis in his study of a number of data sets (work organizations and Canadian post-secondary colleges) and found strong evidence for the existence of coding principles (classification and framing). Grannis (1972) in his New York study of open classrooms used the classification and framing analysis and found that classification and framing could vary independently of each other. 'What we have found is indeed the larger array of combinations that Bernstein argued was possible at the same time that the strongest association was those we expected' (pp. 2–105). It seems that King is somewhat over-zealous in his strident criticisms, uses too local a base for his evidence, and employs inappropriate statistical descriptions.

A number of criticisms have been made of the classification and framing concepts, but few of their integration into the definition of code as set out in the paper 'Codes, modalities and the process of cultural reproduction' (Bernstein, 1981). Gibson has conveniently included a number of criticisms in his sustained and detailed critique, which attacks the theory for its structuralist perspective, 'spurious precision', 'elasticity of concepts', 'reifications', 'tautologies', 'contradictions', and 'invalid use of the concept of code'. In the same way as Stubbs has been used as a paradigm focus of sociolinguistic criticism, so Gibson will be taken as a paradigm form of a more conceptual critique.

We shall outline here in some detail a critique of Gibson's which is given in his book *Structuralism and Education* (1984). I shall spend some time on it for a similar reason he gives for his own critique, that is, it is important and representative of a certain kind of error. In his book (ch. 7) Gibson identifies two major sources of error, one of which he calls 'conventional structuralism'; the other he identifies as 'Bernstein's structuralism'. 'Conventional structuralism' refers to theories, concepts which construct aggregates or wholes, that is, structures, e.g. social class (and its subsets), social structure, educational systems and (presumably) culture, language. It would seem here that Gibson is objecting to the language of sociology, particularly with reference to social institutions. However, it appears that the objection is not to the language but, presumably, to its use where causal relations are made between structures, where interactions are dissolved by structures and so lose their power of agency. It seems strange, if not bizarre, to allude to the above as a form of structuralism in which Gibson includes the Parisian varieties.

Gibson purports to show through a series of short quotations from papers (1958–82) that I am guilty of 'conventional structuralism'. However, what he fails to indicate is that the papers (and the empirical research) progressively analyse social relationships within families and schools (conventional structuralism?) which are expected to regulate different forms of socialization, different orientations to the use of language and its exploration, different orientations to meanings. Gibson might care to look at Cook and Bernstein's complex system of choices for empirical analysis of interaction within familial regulative contexts (Cook-Gumperz, 1973) and Pedro's for the classroom (1981), where he would see the variety of possibilities within different forms of control.

Further, because the term 'structure' is used, or logically similar terms, it does not mean that relationships within or between structures are seamless, inevitable, or permanent. Finally, whilst some structures necessarily come before interactions, interactions are shaped by prior structures but in turn structures are shaped by interactions. The abstracted quotations Gibson gives from papers are often summaries anticipating or closing analyses, or they refer to the most general formulations of a hypothesis, to be explored later at logically lower levels of formulation, that is, at the level of interactions. Indeed, the whole thrust of the research has been to show how specific interactional forms and processes within the family and school may act to relay the cultural reproduction of class relations. Implicit in Gibson's charge of 'conventional structuralism' are embedded notions of the 'hidden hand', of invisible structures of reifications and their iron determinism. To these and other issues we will now turn to consider Gibson's critique of 'Bernstein's structuralism'. Gibson offers the following criticisms.[1]

1 The enlargement of concepts and their elasticity make them 'slippery and elusive', while code explains everything and so explains nothing. This is nonsense. The argument in the 1981 publication of 'Codes, modalities, and the process of reproduction', to which the criticisms are directed, proceeds from a general definition of code to the specific conditions for writing specific codes by stating the specific forms which interactions must take if certain meanings are to be selected by participants and certain forms of realization of the meanings offered. This level of specification of the theory (and precision) given in the 1981 paper is applied to the empirical analysis of children's speech given in one of the appendices. Empirical research is the best testimony to the power of the theory and the delicacy of its principles of description.

2 Gibson considers that the basic scheme is tautological and this tautology masquerades as causal relationships. Clearly, formal derivations from definitions are logical. The statements quoted by Gibson as examples to illustrate this point are in fact made to draw attention to crucial empirical issues which follow from the definitions. Thus: 'Any change in the principle of classification will require a change in the degree of insulation' (glossed by Gibson as

'a change in boundary relations produces a change in boundary relations', p. 314). 'The degree of insulation is a crucial regulator of the relation between categories' (pp. 313–14), translated by Gibson as 'Relations between categories regulate relations between categories.' 'The stronger the insulation between categories then the stronger the boundary between one category and another' (p. 313). All the above statements draw attention to the crucial significance of insulation, its role in the analysis and so is basic to its understanding. Gibson's so-called translations, like so many of his other substitutions, not only miss the point but ensure it can never be seen.

3 Concepts are also supposed to be reified and causal. 'The second halves of statements merely become a re-statement of the first half', e.g. 'Where there is strong classification between education and production this creates the condition for the relative autonomy of education' (1987: 313–14).

First of all, reification of concepts. In the paper it is made clear that classification and framing presuppose classifiers and framers, and it is their power and control which create boundaries and forms of communication which attempt to reproduce their dominance. Only a trivial reading could divorce these concepts from agents' interactions, meanings, and communication.

Classification and framing are theoretical concepts which attempt to specify the nature of the rules transmitters and acquirers are expected to learn if they are to produce what count as legitimate meanings, and the legitimate form of their realizations in relevant contexts. We do not have classification and framing in our heads but tacit rules for the recognition and realization of contextually specific meanings and practices.

With respect to the statement above quoted by Gibson as an example of tautology, the condition of strong classification between education and production makes possible many things, but the issue to be then discussed is that of the relative autonomy of education. Is this so difficult to understand?

Gibson selects another example: 'In the same way as relations between categories can be governed by strong and weak classification so principles of communication can be governed by strong or weak framing' (p. 325). This, Gibson states, is tautology, causality, and reification rolled into one. The quotation is torn from its context in the paper, where it is placed after the end of a long discussion on the social division of labour and principles of classification *and* introduces a lengthy discussion of framing and principles of communication. There is no reification, as it is made abundantly clear that what is being described is different forms of interactional practices, and it is these which act selectively on meanings, realizations, and contexts. Tautology is irrelevant. The statement simply summarizes what has been, and what will be discussed.

4 The theory is charged with spurious precision. This criticism can only be met by the usefulness of the theory and its models in creating powerful descriptions and interpretations. There are a number of empirical researches which show the usefulness of the theory in these respects.

5 Gibson recycles criticisms that the theory is 'ungraspable' and suffers from major confusions. After thirty years of research he produces what he takes to be the following contradiction: (*a*) 'The ability to switch codes controls the ability to switch roles' (Bernstein, 1974: 129); (*b*) 'if you cannot manage the role, you can't produce the appropriate speech' (Bernstein, 1974: 177). Now (*a*) comes from an example of how talk, in a social relation, may progress from a ritual opening to a more individualized form, to a more collective form, and then possibly return to a ritual closure. Thus the perspective is that of the participant's *talk* and how the ability to switch across forms of talk regulates the taking up of different *roles* in the encounter.

The second quotation, (*b*), follows an analysis of an example of another context in which it is clear that the talk can be characterized as an elaborated variant (a discussion of a film fictitiously taking place at the home of Jonathan Miller). Here the analysis in the original text does not focus upon the form of the talk but upon the *social position* of the speaker in the production of the talk. The statements before (*b*) are:

> Thus each member of the group is on his own as he offers his interpretation. Elaborated variants of this kind involve the speakers in particular role relationships, and *if you cannot manage the role, you can't produce the appropriate speech*. For as the speaker proceeds to individualize his meanings, he is differentiated from others like a figure from its ground.

Here the example of a formal discussion brings out the importance of being able to cope with a particular role which may receive weak collective support in the realizing of appropriate speech.

There is no contradiction between the quotations. Having a repertory of different forms of talk regulates the roles you can take up, and some roles, for some forms of talk, receive less collective support. The second example, (*b*), was followed by a discussion of 'communalized' as opposed to 'individualized' roles and speech variants. If anything, the second quotation and its preceding example *extend* the understanding of the speech/role relation. It does not contradict it. This shows how critics (recontextualizers) suppress the original contexts of their quotations in order to make a text conform to their own recontextualizing principles, not to its original coherence.

6 Gibson states that it is a crucial error to assume that codes are fundamentally different from 'principles', and argues that for Bernstein the codes are *behind* principles, whereas for Gibson codes *are* the principles or rules, syntax, or grammar or modality. This is perhaps a more interesting point than others which Gibson raises. But different codes regulate different recognition and realization rules which in turn are the principles for distinguishing between contexts and for the creation and production of the specialized relationships within a context. In this sense codes are behind recognition and realization rules. Recognition rules and realization rules, however, are not codes, as Gibson maintains; they are specialized by codes. Codes are the principle of selection of the recognition and the realization rules. Thus different codes regulate different recognition and realization rules. The theory is concerned to distinguish different codes, their modalities, and their different social bases. The structuralist enterprise here does not mislead; the misleading is provided by Gibson.

7 Finally, Gibson argues that 'codes make people mere tools or puppets in the hands of absent structures which create and govern them'. In the first place, all theories deal with 'invisibles', so that is not the problem; the problem for Gibson must be the determinism of 'invisible' structures which makes puppets of us all. Now in the first place, when Gibson presents his exposition of the theory before his criticism, he omits to give that part of the theory concerned with change – a part which is intrinsic to and inseparable from the theory. The model he refers to has three levels: reproducing, acquiring, and transforming. This Gibson does not refer to. In the same paper (Bernstein, 1981) he is criticizing it is made absolutely clear that at the same time as one is positioned within order the possibilities of disordering are tacitly present. Ordering and disordering, being arranged and rearranging, reproduction and transformation, the voice of others and one's own 'yet to be voiced' are intrinsic to socialization, according to the theory. It is also made clear that, in the relation between structure and interaction, interaction is not simply the medium of, and relay for, structure translated into communication but is the means of its change. However, critics see what they need to see. In terms of the theory 'message' can lead to a change of 'voice'.

In the 1981 paper which Gibson draws upon, a long example is given of how effective resistance can be offered by pupils to a particular pedagogic regime. This analysis also shows that forms of pedagogic resistance may have implications for the production of countervailing strategies at work (see chapter 1 of this volume).

The social unit of the theory is not an isolated individual but *interaction* between transmitters and acquirers and their controls. Indeed, 'acquirer' was chosen because the term points to activity rather than passivity. Gibson's claim that the theory is 'highly deterministic, rigid and inhuman' is as much a consequence of his determinism and rigidity as it is of my alleged inhumanity. Finally, Gibson believes that 'any explanatory scheme which loses sight of human competence and creativity (and capacity for resistance and stubbornness) loses its power'. But the fundamental issues are the realizations of human competence. Competence for what? The realizations of what counts as human creativity. Creativity of whom? For what? Stubbornness and resistance to whom, when, how, and for what reason? To ask these questions (even better, to answer them) is the beginning of an understanding of human potential and the constraints on its actualization.

Note

1 The page references refer to:

> 1974 *Class, Codes and Control*, vol. 1, *Theoretical Studies towards a Sociology of Language*, second edition, London: Routledge.
>
> 1977 *Class, Codes and Control*, vol. 3, *Towards a Theory of Educational Transmissions*, second edition, London: Routledge.
>
> 1982 'Codes, modalities and the process of cultural reproduction: a model', in M.W. Apple (ed.) *Cultural and Economic Reproduction in Education*, pp. 308–55, reprinted from *Language and Society* 10 (1981): 327–63.

Not all quotations selected by Gibson have been taken up, or this already lengthy discussion would necessarily have been much longer. A misinterpretation can take one line but its correction can take many.

Part II

On pedagogic discourse

Chapter 4

Education, symbolic control, and social practices

In this lecture[1] I intend to share some thoughts about education and symbolic control. I shall start with the following hypothesis, which I will then attempt to ground. Even if the hypothesis fails the view may still be interesting. *The more abstract the principles of the forces of production the simpler its social division of labour but the more complex the social division of labour of symbolic control.* The hypothesis requires me initially to describe the two social divisions of labour their relation to each other, and what generates both, that is, education. Second, I shall need to show how each relates to education and the consequences. As we all have an idea of the social basis of the mode of production and the economic field it generates and changes, I shall say very little about that field.

However, the notion of a social division of labour of symbolic control may not be so well known, although I think we all have an idea of what it refers to: the new professions which regulate mind, body, social relations, their special contexts and temporal projections. I will spend most of the first half of this lecture describing, analysing, and creating a language to talk about this.

I will define symbolic control, the field of symbolic control, its agents and their functions. Next I will show this field's difference from the cultural field. I shall then be in a position to test the hypothesis, which will require a somewhat brutal and swift drive through a period of about 700 years and on to the future. If the hypothesis is useful it certainly won't be useful to you, or your children, but possibly to their children.

I shall start with a very rapid glance at major ideas about the relation of the economic and the cultural. Marx opened the game with his epitaph on idealism: existence determines consciousness. The well known metaphor of the 'material base' and the 'superstructure' focused discussion for the next hundred years on the relation between the economic and cultural fields. It is, of course, a matter of great interest that the analysis by Marx of the economic field and its social base and contradictions is far more systematic and historically located than his analysis of the cultural field and its shaping of consciousness.

Certainly since the late '50s these ideas have been subject to considerable revision. Gramsci's analysis of civil society, hegemony, intellectuals, and cultural transformation has been powerfully influential. Althusser based his arguments very much on Gramsci in his analysis of ideology and the State apparatus, whilst his student, Poulantzas, carried out a much more delicate analysis of class groups, ideology, and the specializations of consciousness. However, despite the focus on ideology and consciousness in neo-Marxism, there is still a very weak and, to my mind, inadequate specification of the relation between the discourses, social relations, division of labour, and transmission systems which create the relation between ideology and consciousness.

From a completely different and opposed perspective, Foucault's analysis of power, knowledge, and discourse is a mighty attempt to show the new forms of the discursive positioning of the subject. Yet, surprisingly, there is no substantive analysis of the complex of agencies, agents, social relations through which power, knowledge, and discourse are brought into play as regulative devices; nor any discussion of the modalities of control. In a way it is discourse without social relations. Further, Foucault ignores almost completely any systematic analysis of the common denominator of all discourses, education and the modalities of its transmission. For a theorist interested in normalization,[2] produced by the new discourses of power, to ignore education is one thing, but to ignore religious discourse is even stranger. Let us be quite clear: this lecture is in no sense an attempt to fill this gap, but perhaps to outline no more than a possibility.

Symbolic control, field, agents, discourses

I shall start at the beginning. Symbolic control: essentially and briefly, symbolic control is the means whereby consciousness is given a specialized form and distributed through forms of communication which relay a given distribution of power and dominant cultural categories. Symbolic control translates power relations into discourse and discourse into power relations. I may add, it can also transform those very power relations. A tricky device. I shall briefly describe the field of symbolic control and its activity in contrast to the field of activity of production.

By 'the field of symbolic control' I refer to a set of agencies and agents that specialize in discursive codes which they dominate.

These codes of discourse, ways of relating, thinking, and feeling, specialize and distribute forms of consciousness, social relations, and dispositions. Whereas the dominant agents of the economic field regulate the means, contexts, and possibilities of physical resources, the dominant agents of the field of symbolic control regulate the means, contexts, and possibilities of discursive resources. Thus in the economic field, production codes; in symbolic control, discursive codes. We can make some comments about these two fields.

1 In the case of the economic field there is an explicit inter-dependence of its specialized functions and agencies. In the case of the field of symbolic control the agencies and functions are likely to be seen as discrete, and specialized, and their underlying ideologies as less transparent.
2 The dominant agents of the economic field are likely to share common interests and a common ideology, whereas in the field of symbolic control there is no necessarily shared ideology among its dominant agents, and this field is likely to be constituted by opposing positions, depending upon the field's autonomy from the State.
3 The complexity of the division of labour in one field does not determine the complexity of another. The fields can vary independently of each other.

Agents of dominant discourses: production and symbolic control

We shall start first by distinguishing between different categories of agents who specialize in dominant discursive codes increasingly made available by the higher reaches of education. These discursive codes can have a direct relation to physical resources, in which case these agents become dominant agents (but not necessarily ruling agents) of the field of production (the economic field) and are responsible for managerial, technological, administrative, financial functions. However, discursive codes can have a direct relation not to physical resources but to discursive resources.[3] In that case their agents become agents of symbolic control, and are responsible for a range of specialized functions – priests, doctors, scientists, social workers, personnel officers (see later classification). Agents of symbolic control may function in the field of production (scientists, doctors, architects, psychologists, administrators) or they may function in agencies specializing in symbolic control. In the same way, agents of production may function in specialized sectors in the field of production or they may function in agencies specializing in symbolic control. But, wherever these agents of production are located, their practices are directly related to the means, contexts, and possibilities of physical resources.

We can make further divisions. An agent may be located in the field of production or in that of symbolic control, but the function may be carried out in either the public or the private sector. Thus the function may be a part of State control or part of private enterprise. Figure 4.1 is a diagrammatic presentation of the distinctions.

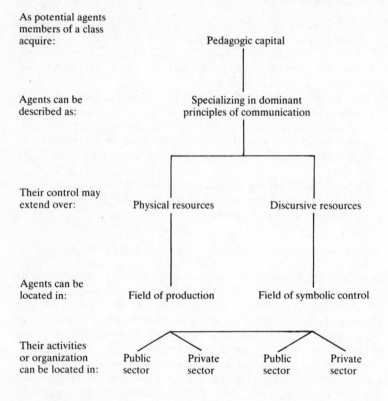

Figure 4.1

Problems arise when we consider agencies in the field of production which have clear and explicit symbolic control functions but, as we shall see, are not considered specialized agencies of symbolic control functioning in the field of control. We are thinking here of theatres, private art galleries, films, television (operating in the private sector), publishing houses, newspapers, etc. Now what marks off these agencies which have symbolic control functions from agencies in the field of symbolic control? We consider that two features distinguish these agencies which operate in the economic field from those which operate in the field of symbolic control. The first feature refers to their *internal organization*, whilst the second refers to a difference in *function*.

We must first distinguish between two different practices carried out by agents of symbolic control who operate in the private sector (Figure 4.2).

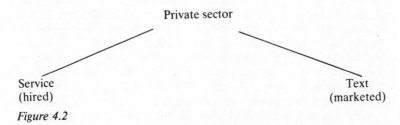

Service (hired)   Text (marketed)

Figure 4.2

Service. Agents of symbolic control operating in the private sector may offer a service which can be hired, similar to agents of production (accountants). The former agents may practise in private clinics, as lawyers, as psychotherapists, etc., in which case they are hired and function rather like one-person businesses, as entrepreneurs. Whether one wants to include these activities as entrepreneurial practices within the field of symbolic control or specialized outside it will be related to the research and its problems. However, the distinction is important to keep in mind, for reasons which will become clearer later.

Text. Agents of symbolic control may not offer a service to be hired but instead create a *text* to be marketed. We are thinking here of journalists, designers, editors, actors, directors, etc., who function essentially in agencies in the field of production but who themselves are agents of symbolic control. In these agencies these agents create the text but they do not have power over the text. Those who *market* the text have the power. Those who produce it may be said to have control over its expected realizations. Thus, where we have an agency concerned with marketing a text, it will be an agency drawing upon two classes of agents, one from production, holding power, the other from symbolic control, holding control over the limited text.

It is clear that these agencies which market texts (theatre, films, publishing, the mass media, private galleries, television, etc.) carry intrinsic tensions arising out of the meeting of two differently specialized agents – one the production of physical resources, the other the production of discursive resources.

We are now in a position to distinguish between agencies with symbolic control functions operating in the economic field and agencies specializing in symbolic control operating in the field of symbolic control.

Differences in internal organization. Agencies in the economic field with symbolic control functions market a text, and the marketeer(s) has power over the text, power over its form, content, context, possibilities, distribution. Specialized agencies in the field of symbolic control are, of course, subject to policy and the economy and constraint, usually by the State, but in societies with party systems and regular voting procedures the policy, economy, and constraint are subject to popular evaluation and change, which the agents of symbolic control serving in the field can influence.

Difference in general function. There is a major difference in general function between symbolic control functions in the field of production and in the field of symbolic control. Agencies which operate in the field of symbolic control have, in Foucault's term, *explicit normalizing functions.* That is, they produce general norms for law, health (physical, mental, and social), administration, education, and for the legitimate production and reproduction of discourse itself.

Thus we can distinguish between agencies in the field of symbolic control and in the field of production in terms of differences in internal organization and differences in general function. It should then be possible to distinguish different practices and realizations of agents of symbolic control according to whether they operate in the field of symbolic control or in the field of production (the economic field). If they operate in agencies marketing a text – publishers, theatres, films, television, cosmetic houses, fashion houses – we could say that they are operating in the cultural field.[4] In this way it would be possible to distinguish the field of symbolic control, the field of production, and the cultural field. We would then be concerned with the relationships within and between these fields and their relationship to the State.

Division of labour of agents of symbolic control

Some of these agents may function in agencies within the field of symbolic control, production, or culture.

Regulators. These are agencies and agents whose function is to define, monitor, and maintain the limits of persons and activities. This would include the legal system and religious agencies. We would include the police and prison service with respect to what could be considered the pedagogic practices of their overall function.[5]

Repairers. These are the agencies and agents whose function is to diagnose, prevent, repair, isolate what count as breakdowns in body, mind, social relationships. At different times some repairers may well act as regulators. At other times some repairers will be in conflict with regulators. Specialized services here would be, for example, medical, psychiatric, and social services.

Reproducers. Teachers.

Diffusers. Mass and specialized media agents.

Shapers. Creators of what count as developments within or change of symbolic forms within the arts, crafts, and sciences.

Executors. These are agents whose function is administrative (the civil service, local government), but they will be found in all agencies in all fields.

Specialized agencies in the field of symbolic control

Examples:

Regulators. Religious, legal.

Repairers. Medicine, psychiatric, social services, counselling/ advice bureaux, child guidance clinics.

Reproducers. Education (the school system).

Diffusers. Media agencies of the State and national theatre, opera, ballet, music, galleries.

Shapers. Universities, research centres, higher education agencies, research councils, private foundations.

Executors. The civil service, central and local government.

These agencies may or may not be directly controlled by the State, although it is clear that some, by definition, must be. The crucial issue is always their degree of autonomy from or dependence on the State, and in particular the degree, range, and location of autonomy or dependence. All these agencies/agents are concerned with the maintenance and change of order by discursive means, and all are concerned with aspects of normalization. The titles given to agents/agencies must be seen against the background of their general function of order and processes of normalization.

Thus agencies in the field of symbolic control regulate specialized discourses of communication. They operate dominant discursive codes regulating social relations, consciousness, and disposition. These agencies may be either public or private and, if public, directly or indirectly subject to the State. In most contemporary societies there has been a gradual extension of State control, both directly or indirectly, over the field of symbolic control and a replacement of agents of symbolic control by agents of production as managers of these agencies.

Ideology and agents of symbolic control

If we are concerned with the ideological orientation of agents of symbolic control, this analysis would lead to the following. The ideological orientation of these agents would be a function of their field location. Doctors, psychologists, personnel officers, architects, researchers, administrators functioning in the field of production are likely to have different interests and identifications from similar agents functioning in the field of symbolic control. A common professional identity may be less significant than field location and position.[6]

There may well be an opposition between agents in the field of symbolic control and agents in the field of production. On the whole, the agents in the field of symbolic control have a strong interest in the extension of public expenditure, for this creates positions, and increases the range of applications and influence, whereas agents in the field of production have an interest in restricting public expenditure. Thus there is likely to be opposition between similar agents in the two fields over the role of the State and opposition over the relation of the State to the two fields. This opposition represents an opposition between fractions within the new middle class, not only about the role of the State but also about modalities of symbolic control (Bernstein 1977d, 1988).

Fields, ideology, and social class

On the basis of the distinctions in function we have outlined, it should be possible to gain a more sensitive understanding of the relation between ideology and social class if we produce a more delicate occupational grid in which we would consider for any one member:

1 Discursive function: production/symbolic control.
2 Field location: production/symbolic control.
3 Position: hierarchical location.

It may well be that similar manual and control practices may generate different relations between ideology and social class according to field location (see Holland, 1986).

Finally, we would like to draw attention to the role of education in constructing the consciousness of agents in the fields of symbolic control and of production.

Fields, class, and the formation of consciousness

We shall expand here a formulation initially developed in 'Aspects of the relation between education and production' (Bernstein, 1977a). In that paper we distinguished between three class agents:

1 *Ruling class:* those agents who have decisive power over decisions with respect to the means, contexts, and possibilities of physical resources and so ultimately over production codes.
2 *Symbolic control:* those agents who control the means, contexts, and possibilities of discursive resources (discursive codes) in agencies in the field of symbolic control.
3 *Working class:* those agents who are initially, but not necessarily passively, dominated by production and discursive codes.

We shall be concerned in this analysis essentially with agents of symbolic control who function in the educational system. In the case of all the three agents we shall ask whether the field of education or the field of production (the economy) is the primary influence upon the formation of consciousness under the condition of a strong classification between the two fields; the modal European relation. Where there is a strong classification, production and education have separate organizing principles particular to each field. In the case of weak classification the two fields are integrated by a common organizing principle, e.g. China during the Cultural Revolution.

In Figure 4.3 the minus sign (–) indicates that the corresponding field is only a relatively weak influence on consciousness, whereas the plus sign (+) indicates that the corresponding field is a relatively strong influence on consciousness. To sharpen this distinction we have placed an R next to the minus sign and a C next to the plus sign. R indicates that the field is a regulator, that is, affects manner, style, whereas C indicates that the field constitutes consciousness, that is, the field is the primary site of interests, social relations, orientations. The two diagonals issuing from symbolic control show the expected relations between these agents and those of the ruling class and working class (opposition, suspicion, resistance), whereas the curve connecting the ruling class and working class shows the expected relation of opposition.

If we now ask of each group what is the most probable site, education or production, for the formation of consciousness under conditions of strong classification, we suggest the following answers.

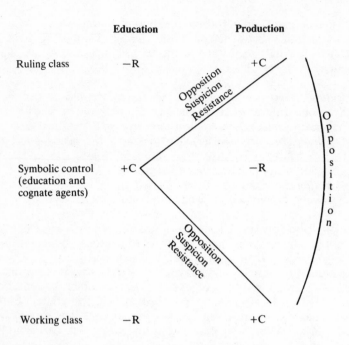

Figure 4.3

Ruling class

We consider that production is more likely to be the crucial site for the constitution (C) of consciousness, whereas the modality of education is more likely to regulate (R) the manner or style of expression. For this group their own personal involvement in their education – in the sense of the significance and penetration of its discourses – is likely to be relatively reduced, and success in school examinations, degree choice, and level of success are not likely to be highly salient motivators. Their objective relation to education is more likely to be realized in a concern for its output, a disciplined, appropriately trained work force.

Working class

Here, as in the case of the ruling class, production is more likely to be the site for the constitution (C) of their consciousness, and again, as with the ruling class, education will be seen as an attempt to regulate the manner or expression. This is not to say that selected members of this group are not concerned to gain certificates, examinations, and training helpful to positions within the economic field. It is, however, to say that for many it is less likely to be the case, and as a consequence the effects of education are likely to be attempts to influence conduct, character, and manner. Although the plus and minus signs are the same for both ruling class and working class, the relations are likely to be those of opposition.

Symbolic control (education and cognate agents)

Here we can see that the proposed signs (+ −) are reversed with respect to both the ruling and the working class. Thus for this group it is proposed that the members' consciousness is directly constituted by the modality of education and indirectly regulated (R) by production. If we look at Figure 4.3 it becomes clear that the difference in the constituting sites of consciousness between the agents of symbolic control as teachers, etc., and the working class can lead to suspicion, mutual failures in understanding, if not, under certain conditions, opposition or pedagogic resistance on the part of some working-class pupils. Similarly, the difference in the constituting sites of consciousness between agents of symbolic control (here education and cognate agents) and the ruling class is likely to lead to mutual failures, suspicion and opposition, resistance. We thus have an image of structural marginalization and isolation of education and cognate agents on the one hand, and of the specialization of their strongly classified consciousness on the other. And this is likely to be reproduced by these agents in the forming of the consciousness *of controlling agents specializing in the field of symbolic control*. We shall see in the next section the origins of this specialization of consciousness.

We are now in a position to test the hypothesis, a prior condition of which was to distinguish between two social divisions of labour, that of production and that of symbolic control, to define and locate agencies and agents specialized in each field; and, finally, to show the contemporary relation between education and production with respect to different classes and social groups. The hypothesis is that *the more abstract the principle of the forces of production the simpler its social division of labour but the more complex the social division of labour of symbolic control, both relatively and absolutely*.

If we consider the principle of the forces of production in the nineteenth century, then we are concerned with the steam engine. Over the next century the principles have become increasingly abstract and today give rise to self-regulating communication

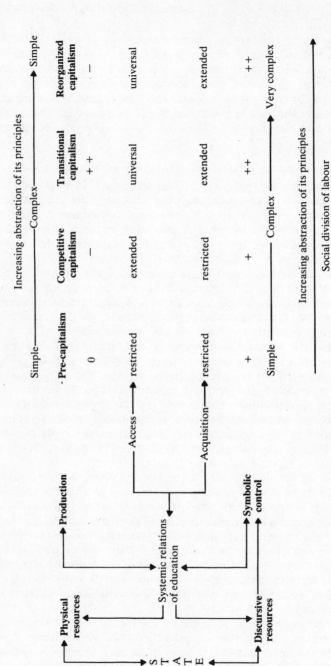

Figure 4.4

systems with complex powers of control. To explore the hypothesis of an inverse relation between the division of labour of production and symbolic control we shall embark on a simplified analysis of the relation between those two divisions of labour since the medieval period and their relation to education and in the later period to the State.

Education and the division of labour

The model (Figure 4.4) sets out the relationships to be considered and the changes in their different strengths. We shall first describe the four historical periods and the elements of the model.

There is clearly a problem regarding the terms to be given to the four periods. Whereas there is likely to be agreement on the terms for the first two periods, this is less likely for the third and even less likely for the fourth. The third period sees, at its beginning, mass-production techniques, the collectivizing and homogenizing of labour, later the development of multinationals, corporate capitalism, and, finally, post-Ford production systems dominated by consumer individualism. The term to cover the whole of this period is unlikely to exist. The term given, reorganizing (or *transitional*) capitalism, should be placed in the context of the above elaboration. The overlapping fourth period we shall call reorganized capitalism. It would be expected that multinational movements and mergers should continue; at the same time, small-scale entrepreneurial functions might well coexist with person-servicing functions. On the one hand we may see a combination of controls entailing, perhaps, greater centralization in some areas, symbolic control, and devolution in others (the economy), and on the other a greater flexibility in working hours and locations (Torstendahl, 1984; Jessop *et al.*, 1987). It might be relevant to add that changes in forces, divisions of labour, social relations, and the consumer demand of the economic field which leads to reorganized capitalism may well also be responsible for a reorganized socialism.

In summary, the changes brought about during transitional capitalism (reorganizing capitalism) would provide the basis for the 'new individualism'. Similar changes in socialist societies (and socialist theory) are likely to provide the basis of the 'new collectivism' or the new principles of socialist solidarity (Figure 4.5). Thus we would have movements in reorganized capitalism and reorganized socialism stemming from the same source (changes in the forces, divisions, and social relations of production) where the 'new individualism' and the 'new collectivism' (?) confront each other's similarities and differences.

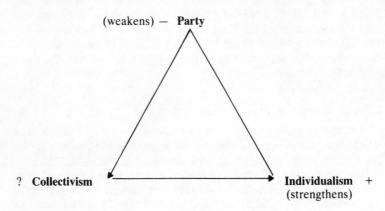

Figure 4.5

Four historical periods are broadly distinguished as:

1 *Pre-capitalism*, the medieval period.
2 *Competitive capitalism*, essentially the nineteenth century.
3 *Transitional capitalism:* twentieth-century reorganizing capitalism.
4 *Reorganized capitalism.* a hypothetical projection into the twenty-first century.

In Figure 4.4 two social divisions of labour, one based on physical resources, production, the other based on discursive resources, symbolic control, are mapped on to the punctuations in the time periods showing the nature of each division on the Durkheimian scale simple–complex.

The role of the systemic relations of education with respect to their contribution to the field of production and symbolic control is indicated in terms of the two outputs of education. Physical resources can enter into production and discursive resources can enter into symbolic control. Of course, we are aware that the outputs of education are always discursive. We are here indicating that one output can provide principles/skills for the field of production and that another can provide principles/skills for the field of symbolic control. Further, the role of the State with respect to education and its outputs and with respect to the social division of labour for each of the four periods may be examined.

We are also able to assess *access* and *acquisition* for each historical period on a scale restricted–extended–universal. 'Access' here refers to levels of education up to university. 'Acquisition' refers to acquisition of the dominant privileged pedagogic code on a scale of restricted–extended–universal. Thus, if acquisition is universal, then all pupils acquire the privileged and dominant pedagogic code of the secondary school as measured by public examinations. We can see that whilst access eventually becomes universal, across the historical period acquisition achieves no more than a relative extension across the last hundred years, and according to the model this is projected in the future.

Finally, 0, – , + refer to the linkage of education to the creation of physical resources (production) and to the creation of discursive resources (symbolic control). Thus 0 indicates no linkage, – indicates a weak linkage, and + indicates a strong linkage.

We shall now give no more than a synopsis of the linkage between education and production and symbolic control, together with the relative strength of their social division of labour, for the four periods. Where appropriate, we shall also add the role of the State to this necessarily synoptic and simplified analysis.

Pre-capitalism (medieval)

Production

We see that the linkage between education and production and so its social division of labour is indicated by 0, that is, there is no linkage. Indeed, we have to wait until the twentieth century before we see a + , that is, a strong linkage. The reason for the 0 in the medieval period is clearly that the relay for the production and reproduction of physical resources – that is, the relay for the production and reproduction of manual practices – lay outside education. The relay operated in the family and the guilds. That is, it was invisible to education and invisible to those who operated a mental practice. It is probably for this reason that, whereas we know something about the transmission and acquisition of mental practices, we know very little about the transmission and acquisition of manual practices. For the latter is not part of the consciousness entailed in the formation of mental practices, or, if it is, it is not likely to be formed by education. Thus originally the relays for manual and mental practice were invisible to each other and operated in discrete and differently specialized fields. The exception to this strong field classification was certain orders of the medieval monastery, and it may well be that developments in science took place here because of the integration of practices. We had to wait until the mid-twentieth century kibbutz for the next

Compare this with:

> By contrast the Koran is the result of a unique event, the 'descent' into worldiness of a text whose language and form are thereafter to be viewed as stable, complete, unchanging: the language of the text is Arabic, therefore a greatly privileged language and its vessel the messenger Mohammed similarly privileged. Such a text is absolute and cannot be referred back to any particular interpreter or interpretation although this is clearly what the Babinites tried to do (perhaps, it is suggested, under the influence of Judeo-Christian exegetical techniques).
>
> [Said, 1980: 168]

Organization

If we now look briefly at the organization of knowledge in the medieval university, basing our view on that of Durkheim's examination of the University of Paris, we find the first fracturing, dislocation, classification of official discourse in the distinction between the Trivium and the Quadrivium. The subjects of the Trivium were logic, grammar, and rhetoric, the emphasis changing with the rise of social groups in the Renaissance. The subjects of the Quadrivium were arithmetic (number), geometry (space), astronomy (motion), and music (time). Durkheim sees the Trivium as essentially the exploration of the word, and the word is God, whereas the Quadrivium he sees as the exploration of the world, initially an *abstract* world. The Trivium was studied first, the Quadrivium second. Word before world.

The first classification/dislocation of discourse was integrated by

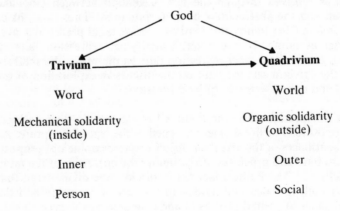

Figure 4.6

150

God and the word was embedded in the world. What Durkheim did not do was link these insights with earlier concepts. Thus it might be argued that the Trivium provided the integrated discursive basis for *mechanical* solidarity, whereas the differently specialized and discrete discourses of the Quadrivium pointed to the discursive base of *organic* solidarity. From our point of view this means that the initial form of socialization of agents specializing in symbolic control made instructional discourse about the abstract phenomenal world subordinate to regulative discourse: an explicit recognition of the function of these agents, and an explicit, perhaps unique, recognition of language as the source of the disguise and revelation of the mind.

We might ask how the classification between the Trivium and the Quadrivium came about. At one level the Durkheimian answer of no world without the word is satisfying. Yet it may also be misleading. Whilst it conceptualizes the different social bases of the Trivium and the Quadrivium, it does not account for the dislocation. Is it possible that the dislocation Trivium/Quadrivium is a metaphor for another signifier? The Trivium explores and celebrates and sets limits to discourse and expresses at a deep level the relation between the person and Christ (word as relation), whereas the Quadrivium appears to be a celebration and leads to an exploration of the material world. But both may be more than that. The Quadrivium is not simply an exploration of an abstract world; it points to an exploration of ways of acting upon the world. In this sense the Quadrivium is not about the person but about what lies *outside* the person. Thus the Quadrivium signifies the *outer*. The Trivium is about the inner, the discursive constitution of the inner. Trivium: inner–person–sacred; Quadrivium: outer–social–profane. The profane enters into the sacred by the formation of Christian inwardness and is then regulated by it. In Islam and biblical Judaism there is no split between inner and outer, person and social. They are mutually embedded in the holiness of God made manifest in lived ritual and law. The dislocation Trivium/Quadrivium may well be intrinsic to Christianity as a metaphor signifying the dislocation between inner and outer, person and society, and the new relation between the two that Christianity makes possible. And this dislocation has preoccupied the intellectual field, facilitated by the Church's selective recontextualizing of Greek thought. The problematic arising out of this dislocation has preoccupied the West ever since. From this point of view the Trivium/Quadrivium dislocation is a metaphor of the deep grammar of Christianity and produced by it.

In summary we find in the pre-capitalism period:

1 No link between education and production, and production has its own specialized invisible relay in the family and guilds, but a strong link between education and symbolic control. Thus there is an inversion of the strength of the linkage between education and symbolic control and education and production.
2 Education is abstract in orientation, with dislocated discourses privileging the Trivium as the fundamental regulative discourse.
3 *The division of labour of production is simple and so is that of symbolic control, as it is essentially coterminous with the Church, and its agents integrate a number of functions.*

Competitive capitalism (mid-nineteenth century)

Production

Here we can begin to see a linkage between education and production. It is very doubtful whether this linkage is based upon the relationship between the instructional discourse of the denominational schools (and later of compulsory education) and skills relevant to production; rather it is based upon a view of education as a means of creating a docile, sober, work force, socialized in the new factory morality. As Glass put it euphemistically, 'an education for gentling the masses'. In other words, the dominant discourse and practice of the school were regulative. Entrance to skills was through apprenticeships. It is likely that elementary education played an important future role in the creation of the developing clerical function and the rise of the white-collar worker. Until the reform of the universities and the opening of the great northern universities, science and invention existed more outside the universities than within them.

Throughout the century there is an increasing move towards a complex social division of labour of production.

Symbolic control

Throughout the century there is an increase in the complexity of the social division of labour. The Churches were responsible for the development of denominational schools, training colleges for teachers, and voluntary societies were active among the poor. The State intervened more and more: child labour regulation, health, factory inspectors, the poor law and, after 1870, public education. By 1902, with the development of selective secondary schools, the modern educational system was in place, the traditional universities had been reformed, the University of London[8] and the northern universities were more geared to the requirements of industry and commerce. The social division of labour of symbolic control is developing, as the social division of labour of production, from simple to complex. The linkage between education and production is indicated as − but the linkage between symbolic control and education is +. Education as yet offers little specialized training for the new agents of symbolic control. This becomes the distinguishing feature of eduction in the next century, essentially towards the latter half.

Transitional capitalism: the twentieth century

Production

It is only in this period and especially in the latter half that there are strong links between education and production arising out of new techniques of managment and production, and the new forces of production towards the last quarter of the century: electronics, computer control, bio-engineering. The linkage between education and production is strengthened by the ideology of mobility through education, and of education as offering equal opportunity. Yet on the whole (and where this does not happen it is a matter of great interest) education is more likely to act to maintain the structural relations between class groups whilst changing the structural relation between individuals through selective success and failure. Education officially celebrates and ideologizes the individual, whilst in reality it obscures the relations it maintains between social groups. The linkage between education and production fostered by equality ⌐f opportunity and mobility through education is more ideological than real in its effects, especially for minority groups.

In the latter decades of the century, with rising unemployment, the new communications revolution, and increased international competition, the linkage between education and production is seen as crucial, and the failure of the economy to develop is blamed on the failure of education to provide relevant skills. Education is viewed as too abstract, too remote from work, too narcissistic. Education is to be vocationalized and to become more dependent upon the needs of the economic field and more ruled by principles derived from that field.

Thus by the late twentieth century two opposing tendencies can be seen. On the one hand the increased complexity of the social division of labour is weakening, despite the introduction of some new skills, and the line between mental and manual work becomes blurred as journalists type into computer-controlled production processes; on the other hand the vocationalizing of education

153

tightens the linkage between curricula and the economic field at all levels of education.

Symbolic control

We find in this period remarkable developments of the specialized discourses of symbolic control and their application, essentially in the social and behavioural sciences – in medicine, psychiatry and psychoanalysis, and in the new disciplines of semiotics and cognitive science. A whole new range of discourses has become available in higher education to create the discursive basis for both the expansion and the increasing differentiation of agents of symbolic control: agents with different, even opposing interests, depending upon their field location, symbolic control or production. the State, especially after 1945, extends the range of its agencies and agents in the field of symbolic control, e.g. education, health, social services, family support agencies, clinics, and housing.

Initially these agencies are managed, or major decisions are taken, by dominant agents within the field of symbolic control with respect to the planning, principles, and practice of these agencies. The field to a great extent manages itself. Its agents have a vested interest in an expansionist State committed to a high level of public expenditure. With expansion in the number of positions, there is less control of selection, which, together with the 'progressivism' of the 1960s, gives rise to an expert/professional bias towards a collectivism of the left.

Towards the end of the century, starting from the late '70s, a failing economy, inflation, and rising unemployment shift the political balance to the right, that is, to a new right, based not upon land, nor upon managerialism/corporativism but upon the market. The ideology of the market is celebrated, the myth of its powers of social, individual, and economic redemption is used to undermine the old collectivism and as a defence against future forms. Agents of symbolic control become ideologically suspect because of their support of collectivism and/or public expenditure, especially those within the educational system. The State withdraws from the economic field but provides support for a small-business entrepreneurial sector and, for the unemployed, paid careers in the new vocationalism of education.

However, the crucial change is the State's increasing control over its own agencies of symbolic control, especially education, at all levels, where dominant agents drawn from the field of production now have crucial management functions. The State field of symbolic control no longer plans or manages itself. The change is a change in State ideology and regulation, but the increase in the complexity of the field of symbolic control across the century is undeniable. What is of interest is the State's indifference, even hostility, to its professional base, that is, to the specialized discursive base of the agents. This we will now examine.

Orientation of knowledge

In the last decades of the twentieth century we are witnessing an extensive weakening of the control of the Trivium, and the Quadrivium's specialized, discrete discourses are undergoing a change in both orientation and organization. This change is a consequence of the rise of the new conservatism of the market and the rise of its agents as managers of the policy and practice of education. Market relevance is the key orientating criterion for selection of discourses, their research, their focus, and their relation to each other. This movement has profound implications, from the primary school to the university. This can be seen in the stress on basic skills at the primary level, vocational courses and specialization at the secondary level, and new instruments of State control over higher education and research.

There is a new concept both of knowledge and of its relation to those who create it, a truly secular concept. Knowledge should flow like money to wherever it can create advantage and profit. Indeed, knowledge is not just like money: it *is* money. Knowledge is divorced from persons, their commitments, their personal dedication, for these become impediments, restrictions on flow, and introduce deformations in the working of the market. Moving knowledge about, or even creating it, should not be more difficult than moving and regulating money. Knowledge, after nearly a thousand years, is divorced from inwardness and is literally dehumanized. Once knowledge is separated from inwardness, commitment and personal dedication, then people may be moved about, substituted for each other, and excluded from the market.

This orientation represents a fundamental break in the relationship between the knower and what is known. In the medieval period the two were necessarily integrated. Knowledge was an outer expression of an inner relationship. The inner relationship was a guarantee of the legitimacy, integrity, worthwhileness of the knowledge, and the special status of the knower. It is not difficult to see embryonically here the basis of the ethic and ideology of the professions. Now we have a *dislocation*, which permits the creation of two independent markets, one of knowledge and another of knowers. The first dislocation between the Trivium and Quadrivium constituted inwardness as a prior condition of knowing; the second, contemporary, dislocation disconnects inner from outer as a precondition for constituting the outer according to the market principles of the new right.

Organization of knowledge

Independent of the change in orientation to knowledge, but not entirely out of sympathy with its requirements, is a change in the relation between disciplines to what we shall call *regions*. A discipline is a specialized, discrete discourse, with its own intellectual field of texts, practices, rules of entry, modes of examination, and principles of distributing success and privileges, e.g. physics, chemistry, mathematics, history, psychology, sociology, economics, linguistics, etc. Disciplines or singulars are on the whole narcissistic, oriented to their own development rather than to applications ouside themselves.

Regions are a recontextualizing of disciplines into larger units which operate both in the intellectual field of disciplines and in the field of practice. Regions are the interface between disciplines and the technologies they make possible. Thus engineering, medicine, architecture, management are regions, and so is cognitive science. What disciplines enter into a region depends upon the recontextualizing principle and its social basis. Sometimes new subjects like computer science take on the characteristics of regions rather than of disciplines, especially when they issue in a new technology.

What we are witnessing, then, is a movement, which started much earlier in the USA, towards the regionalization of knowledge: a good indicator of its technological orientation. We can see this increasing regionalization as a weakening of the strength of the classification of discourses, and with this weakening a formation of less specialized professional identities whose practices are technological.

Clearly, education as a specialized body of knowledge and practice is a region but it can be distinguished, in two respects, both from regions and from singulars (discrete autonomous bodies of knowledge whose agents have appropriated a space for themselves). Education is condition for both regions and singulars. Education constitutes the primary pedagogic habitus for teachers and pupils, whereas all other regions constitute the secondary pedagogic habitus. Education is, of course, the primary agency of symbolic control.

In summary:

1 It is clear that in this period, at least until the end, there has been an increase in the complexity of both the social division of

labour of production and in that of symbolic control.

2 The link between education and both fields is now relatively strong (+ +) and regulated by a State operating an anti-collectivist, market-based ideology. Knowledge is dehumanized and circulates as money drawn to advantage and profit. The field of symbolic control and the economic field celebrate the 'new individualism' under conditions of an increase in national and multinational organization.

3 There has been throughout this period, relative to the previous one, an increase in the level of abstraction of the principles of both production and symbolic control.

Reorganized capitalism: the twenty-first century

We are here looking ahead and extrapolating from the previous period into the next. There are grounds for asserting a revolution in communication control systems begun in the previous period. Bio-engineering, the new control over genetic codes, permits for the first time the suspension of evolution by culture. Cognitive science models intelligence and the mechanism underlying it together with social implications. Computer systems initiate, co-ordinate, plan, model, are reflexive to their own learning, generate problems, and anticipate breakdowns through self-regulating controls.

Production

The revolution in communication control systems will produce major changes in the social division of labour of production. Its complexities and interdependence of specialized functions will now be more and more in the software. The higher-level executive functions and their technological support are likely to remain. From this perspective there will be a simplification in the social division of labour of production. It is the reverse of the first pre-capitalist period, where the simplification lay in the machine-less manual functions. In the case of reorganized capitalism the simplification lies in the presence of a narrow range of executive/technological specialized functions.

However, it may well be the case that a new manual handcraft, artisan industry could emerge, with its own commercial outlets, reviving apprenticeship and even guild-like organizations: a neo-medievalism. It is also possible that there will be an expansion of the cultural field, of its agencies and agents. The expansion of that field may bring together or blur the relationship between the cultural field and the field of symbolic control.

Symbolic control

Will the same process of simplification of the social division of labour affect the field of symbolic control? The answer given here is that it is unlikely. On the contrary, the field may increase both in its internal complexity and in absolute numbers.

Symbolic control is essentially a language, and its rules are acquired rather like a language. In the case of language its rules are not learned by a stimulus–response, reinforcement process. Its rules are acquired through tacit inference of their underlying ordering principles in the context of social interaction, and the speaker is then able to produce and receive novel combinations of the language and recognize them as legitimate. In the case of symbolic control the same process operates. Its surface rules are acquired through tacit inference of their underlying ordering principles, which not only allows generalization to new situations but enables ambiguities and dilemmas intrinsic to the nature of the rules themselves to produce new rules consonant with the underlying ordering principles. These rules cannot be reduced to a software, although programmes could assist acquisition. However, the basis of symbolic control is laid down before reading is possible. In a sense, symbolic control is as much caught as taught. It is realized in special arrangements, temporal orderings, ritual frames, as well as in specialized discourses. But the essence and deep structure of symbolic control lie at another level. Its essence lies in its transformation of the language of feeling and desiring. No software can teach a computer this. Thus symbolic control will continue to be constructed and relayed by human agents operating with specialized discourses made available through the recontextualizing fields of education, which will give to that control its ideological modalities.

It may be that there will be changes in the primary sites for acquisition, regulated by social class and pedagogic selection. The development of computers, networking, and pedagogic software may enable the family to become the primary site of acquisition for some students who will be absolved from the responsibility of continuous school attendance and surveillance. It is to be expected that such students would be pursuing intellectually oriented studies leading to university-type institutions, whereas those destined for manual or artisan occupations and those destined for distribution and servicing may well be expected to attend schools and receive more continuous surveillance and moral regulation. Alternatively, manual/artisan students may follow a regime outlined by deschooling, whereby such students would be attached, apprentice fashion, to 'masters' but would be centrally located in a school and distributed from that centre. Thus the family would retain its primary role in intellectual socialization, whereas the school (or equivalent) would retain its primary role as regulator of artisan/distributive functions. The boundaries between the field of symbolic control and the cultural field may well become blurred, depending upon the degree of autonomy of those fields, the location of autonomy, and the range made available by the State.

The field of symbolic control under the condition of a relative simplification of the social division of labour of production may have now extensive normalizing functions, pointing towards greater internal differentiation of its field, and an expansion of the cultural field and its regulation of leisure practices. On this argument the twenty-first century will witness a relative simplification of the social division of labour of production as a consequence of an increasing abstraction of the principles of its forces, whilst the intrinsic feature of symbolic control, that it is a language of feeling and desiring, will ensure that its constructions and relays will be human. Extensive normalizing activities are likely to increase its differentiation, and thus the complexity of its specialized functions.

However, the story does not end there. Symbolic control which inscribes the legitimate, translates power into discourse, and discourse into modalities of culture may well unwittingly also be the guardian of the possibility of the new. There is a paradox at the heart of symbolic control. Control cannot control itself, any more than discourse can control discourse. Symbolic control, always a condition for someone else's order, carries within itself the potential for transforming the order of the imposing other.

The pedagogic device which produces symbolic control and its modalities, in the very process of its transmissions, makes available principles which both shape and can reshape consciousness. The device itself produces a struggle for power over its realizations. Finally, as we have argued elsewhere, normalizing processes produce norms and their agencies, which are rarely free of the contradictions, cleavages, and dilemmas they are set up to control. Socialization into norms, from this point of view, is then always socialization both into another's voice and into one's own 'yet to be voiced'.[9]

Conclusions

In this paper we have attempted to explore one hypothesis referring to an inverse relationship between the social division of labour of production and that of symbolic control. We have argued that in the period we have called pre-capitalist both divisions of labour were simple, and that over the period towards what we have termed reorganized capitalism the relation between the fields underwent changes. The fields kept in step with each other, both achieving great complexity in the last fifty years of the twentieth century. In its last decade, and in the next period, increases in the level of abstraction of the forces of production produce a simplification in the social division of labour of production. However, increases in the level of abstraction of the principles of symbolic control do not produce a simplification of its social division of labour, for the reasons offered above. Further, it has been argued that the field of symbolic control is likely to become internally more differentiated and extensive as a consequence of more elaborate normalizing functions arising out of the weakening of the discipline of work.

We have also attempted to show the linkage of the two fields with education. We noted the exclusion of manual practice in the first period but strong links with symbolic control (0 production, + symbolic control). Indeed, throughout the whole of the period under discussion, education has a strong linkage with production only under transitional capitalism. In the last period, we have argued, the linkage between education and production is likely to be strong only for the higher levels of education, which create a simplified social division of labour of production. It may well be that in the twenty-first century manual, artisan, craft practices, apprenticeships and guilds may be formed outside the educational system much as in the first period; a neo-medievalism. However, the linkage between State education, symbolic control, and the cultural field is likely to be very strong. Thus over the whole period the linkage between education and symbolic control is increasingly strong and wide-ranging whilst the linkage with production becomes more narrowly specialized. It may well be that class reproducing functions will be maintained, even strengthened through the strong linkage of education, symbolic control, and the cultural field. Finally we have argued that symbolic control, an essentially human relay, carries both order and the possibility of its change; whilst its agencies create a focus for opposition, resistance and challenge.

Appendix 4.1: the discourse of education

We have discussed the Trivium/Quadrivium with reference to the organization of knowledge in the medieval university. However, it is possible to see the organization of knowledge in the training of teachers as a structural homology of the organization of knowledge in the medieval university. This is not as untoward as it may seem, for much of the activity of the medieval university was directed towards study for the priesthood.

If we consider the training of teachers in colleges of education in the United Kingdom, then the generic form of the organization of knowledge entailed a dislocation between two different discourses: a general discourse concerned with a body of knowledge called 'education' and specific discourses called professional subjects. The latter entailed study of the subject(s) the student was expected to teach in school. The content of education varied, as did the discursive base of those who taught it. We can distinguish probably the following stages in England: (1) a situation where the same lecturer covered both 'education' and professional subjects, (2) where lecturers were specialized to one or the other of the two discourses, 'education' and professional subjects, (3) where 'education' itself consists of specialized discourses taught by specialists (philosophy, psychology, sociology, history), (4) when a new body a recontextualized knowledge is inserted between 'education' and professional subjects, 'curriculum studies'. Curriculum studies is in part, but not wholly, technical in focus and probably in aspiration.

We are now moving to a fifth stage where the specialized disciplines which constituted 'education' in stages 3 and 4 are weakened as political, cultural, and academic sites. Such weakening of the disciplines leaves only psychology, which, with curriculum, ensures a dominant technical training of teachers. Finally, there is every sign that we shall be entering a sixth stage where professional training will be, for the first time, the dominant discursive site for the training of teachers carried out almost wholly in the schools. Thus as we move from stage 1 to stage 6 we move from the integration of education and professional discourses where education is dominant, taught by one college-based lecturer, to the dominance of professional studies sited in the schools and managed by teachers.

In terms of Trivium and Quadrivium we can regard 'education' as representing the Trivium and professional studies as representing the Quadrivium. Thus 'education' as Trivium is concerned with specializing the consciousness of the teacher, whereas professional

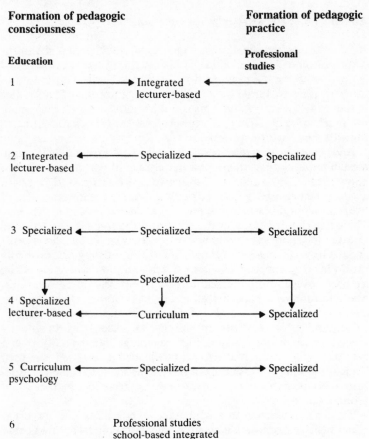

Figure 4.7 Discursive bases of teacher training

studies as Quadrivium are concerned with specializing the performance of teaching the various subjects taught in school. As with the
original organization of knowledge, 'education' as Trivium was
dominant in regulating the theory and setting limits on the practice
in stage 1. Indeed, in this stage one teacher combined both discourses of teacher training, but the technical was embedded in
moral positioning. In stage 2 'education' and professional studies
are separated but 'education' retains its integrated basis. In stage 3
the separation between 'education' and professional studies is very
strongly marked both with respect to discourses and with respect to
their teachers. Stage 3 represents also the period of the most
marked subordination of the Quadrivium of teacher training to its

Trivium (the 1960s). Stage 4 represents the first weakening of the Trivium (the early 1970s), with the rise of curriculum studies as a region inserted between 'education' and professional studies, the beginning of the technologizing of teacher training and the shift to the importance of the Quadrivium of professional studies.

Curriculum studies as a recontextualized body of knowledge and practice had a close relationship with the State at a time when the State began its move towards explicit control over the contents of the schools with the formation of the Schools Council. Stage 3 (the 1980s) represents the final weakening of the Trivium of education and its replacement through the dominance of curriculum studies, together with the rise of the dominance of policy, management, and assessment. The 1980s saw the increasing technologizing of teacher training and a redrawing of its discursive topology. The 1980s represent a major shift towards a secular concept of teacher training as a necessary parallel, if not condition, of the general shift to the regionalization of knowledge. Finally, in the 1990s we can expect this movement to be completed with the dissolution of the Trivium education and the dominance of the Quadrivium as school-based professional training.

Notes

1 This paper is in essence a public lecture given in Santiago in 1988, sponsored by CIDE, to inaugurate the translation and publication of an invited seminar, Poder, Educacion y Coniencia Sociologia de la Transmission Cultural, which I gave at CIDE in 1985. I would like to record my gratitude to Dr Cristian Cox for support, encouragement, and valuable discussions. I am also grateful to Professor Gerald Grace for the criticism he offered.

2 'Normalization becomes one of the great instruments of power at the end of the classical age. For the marks that once indicated status, privilege and affiliation were increasingly replaced – or at least supplemented – by a whole range of degrees of normality indicating membership of a homogeneous social body but also playing a part in classification, hierarchization and the distribution of rank. In a sense, the power of normalization imposes homogeneity; but it individualizes by making it possible to measure gaps, to determine levels, to fix specialities and to render the differences useful by fitting them one to another. It is easy to understand how the power of the norm functions within a system of formal equality, since within a homogeneity that is the rule, the norm introduces, as a useful imperative and as a result of measurement, all the shadings of individual differences.' (Foucault, 1977: 184.) It is a matter of doubt

whether normalizing discourses individualize in the sense that they *bring about individualization*. It could be argued that the social basis of visible power is mechanical solidarity, and the social basis of invisible power is organic solidarity. Thus the social basis for the creation of specialized interdependent *difference* is produced by a mode of solidarity where people face each other as individuals and the value system does not generate a morality which minutely regulates conduct. This represents a prior condition for normalization, for the development of its discourses, and for changes in the modality of symbolic control.

3 As I have said elsewhere, the distinction between physical and discursive resources is a low-level distinction. Clearly, no resource can be realized without discourse.

4 'Culture' cannot be identified with the cultural field, as this is but one modality of its realization.

5 It may be thought unusual to include the police and the prison service under the general category of symbolic control. Attention is drawn here to pedagogic features of their function and to different modes of its realization. For example, variation in the interface between the police and communities, variations in their training, variations in the concept of prison, prisoner, confinement.

6 Holland (1986) carried out empirical research into the conceptions of middle-class and working-class adolescent boys and girls of the domestic and industrial division of labour and of its social relations, using the model outlined here to classify their parents' occupations. Holland found differences in their conceptions according to the field location of parents. Cox (1986) used the same model in his study of the social basis of educational reforms in Chile. Jenkins (1989) applied the model to classify the creators and shapers of progressive education in her study of the New Education Fellowship. Gouldner (1979) provides one of the best theoretical statements of the origins, formations, differentiations, and destiny of what he sees as a new cultural bourgeoisie distinguished as a specialized speech community. Gouldner draws upon Bernstein's sociolinguistic papers but ignores the paper 'Class and pedagogies, visible and invisible', in Bernstein (1975) and its revision in Bernstein (1977), in which the ideas in this paper were initially presented.

7 In the sense of a number of interpretations.

8 See Namie (1989) for the role of the University of London in the formation of educational systems in the then colonies through the University of London Colonial Examinations.

9 See chapter 1.

Chapter 5

The social construction of pedagogic discourse

It is a matter of some interest that the sociology of education has rarely turned its attention to the analysis of the intrinsic features constituting and distinguishing the specialized form of communication realized by the pedagogic discourse of education. Many of the analyses of the sociology of education, especially those carried out by the diverse group of theories of reproduction, assume, take for granted, the very discourse which is subject to their analysis. These theories, in particular, see pedagogic discourse as a medium for other voices: class, gender, race. The discourses of education are analysed for their power to reproduce dominant/dominated relations external to the discourse but which penetrate the social relations, media of transmission, and evaluation of pedagogic discourse. It is often considered that the voice of the working class is the absent voice of pedagogic discourse, but we shall argue here that what is absent from pedagogic discourse is its own voice. If theories of cultural reproduction or transformation of culture formulate ordering or disordering principles, then those principles relate to the message of pedagogic discourse, not to ordering/disordering principles intrinsic to its logic as a specialized discourse.

This paper should be regarded as only a possible step towards the specification of ordering principles intrinsic to the production, reproduction, and change of pedagogic discourse. The basic concepts and ordering rules are developed at length in Bernstein and Diaz (1984). Applications may be found in Diaz (1984), Cox (1984), Moore (1984), and Tyler (1988). The work of Foucault has had an influence upon our approach but we should emphasize that our focus is very different. Indeed, we would consider that the articulation of the specific grammar of the pedagogic device is fundamental to much of Foucault's work. For the relations between Foucault and the approach taken here see Diaz (1984) and Atkinson (1981, 1985). Despite the extensive literature of the sociology of education, if we examine the major texts within this field which give a definition of its range of concerns, and perhaps in particular the most recent and detailed of these, *The Social Sciences in Educational Studies: a Selected Guide to the Literature* (Hartnett, 1982), we do not find any systematic account of the principles of the specialized communicative practice which is the distinguishing feature of the school's central activity, transmission/acquisition.

From *Education, Economy and Society* (Halsey *et al.*, 1961) to *Power and Ideology in Education* (Karabel and Halsey, 1977) we have an important index of the transformation and development of focuses of interest within the sociology of education. Yet the question of the analysis of pedagogic discourse and its regulative practices receives little attention. The editors, however, in their introduction to *Power and Ideology in Education*, noted that Durkheim looked at education in France from the period of the 'Primitive Church' to that of the 'Third Republic', exploring the history of what the French call *les idées pédagogiques*, a concept that includes not only the formal curriculum but also the way in which the knowledge is transmitted and evaluated. Interestingly enough, the 'new sociology of education' (*Knowledge and Control: New Directions in the Sociology of Education*, ed. M.F.D. Young, 1971) took as its focus the problematic nature of knowledge and the manner of its transmission, acquisition, and evaluation in schools. Young states that:

> It is or should be the central task of the sociology of education to relate the principles of selection and organisation that underline curricula to their institutional and interactional settings in schools and class-rooms and to the wider social structure. [1971: 24]

However, this programme, whatever else it produced, did not produce what it called for.

General theories of culture reproduction (see Apple, 1982b) again appear to be more concerned with an analysis of what is reproduced in, and by, education than with an analysis of the medium of reproduction, the nature of the specialized discourse. It is as if the specialized discourse of education is only a voice through which others speak (class, gender, religion, race, region). It is as if pedagogic discourse is itself no more than a relay for power relations external to itself; a relay whose form has no consequences for what is relayed.

The perspective of the Centre for Contemporary Cultural Studies at the University of Birmingham in opposing the determination of French theories of cultural reproduction (Johnson, 1981; Willis,

1977, are two examples) has as yet produced no systematic analysis of the cultural practice intrinsic to the educational process, although this approach has attempted to create an active place and position for the working class in the shaping of this process.

Perhaps the most important attempt to formalize the role of education in the reproduction of class relations has been carried out by Bourdieu and Passeron (1970). Whilst they are concerned with the analysis of the legitimation of structures of culture, principles of transmission/acquisition, communicative practices, and their systems of meanings, together with an analysis of how their arbitrary features disguise the power relations which they transmit (through *méconnaissance* to *la violence symbolique*), there is very little systematic and specific analysis of the principles whereby a specific discourse is constituted or of the principles of its transmission. Bourdieu and Passeron distinguish two forms of communication in very general terms, 'magisterial' (language of the transmitter) and 'popular' (language of the working class). Bourdieu and Passeron are more concerned with the *relation* to pedagogic communication, that is, with differences between acquirers with respect to how they have been positioned in their relations to legitimate pedagogic communication, than with the analysis of the relations *within* pedagogic communication. (See later discussion.)

Finally, if we turn to more specific aspects of the school, we can find a diverse (not to say divergent) literature, from Waller's *Sociology of Teaching* (1932) to the major review of current empirical research by W. Tyler of school organization (1985, 1988). Here is perhaps a bedrock of the field of the sociology of education, empirical studies of the school as an organizational structure and of interactional practice where curriculum, pedagogic practice, and modes of evaluation set the terms for the crucial encounters in the classroom context of teachers and pupils. Perhaps the key new studies here are those of classroom language and the context and practices of its regulation and negotiation (Delamont, 1976; Stubbs, 1975; Cazden *et al.*, 1972; Edwards, 1980). These studies, crucial as they are, presuppose a particular focus, a focus which is less concerned with the question of how the distribution of power and principles of control establish a regulating discourse, but more concerned, and validly so, to articulate the principles of interactional communication and practice within the local context of the classroom. It is of little value to make a derogatory distinction between surface realizations and their underlying principles or grammar of realization, for what is one person's surface is another's underlying principles, and vice versa. The body of work to which we have referred is of major relevance. Indeed, it not only provides us with crucial points of reference and key concepts, but has also formulated the parameters for empirical research.

The problematic and its intellectual context

We shall here develop some of the points made in the introduction in order to focus more clearly on the problematic to be addressed. In so doing it should be possible to show how this problematic itself emerged from the field of research. We shall construct a model (see p. 173) which will allow us to map and position within the map various approaches within and between levels of analysis and disciplines. We shall be concentrating on theories of cultural reproduction, but the major thrust of the analysis should be equally applicable to cultural theories of 'resistance' and to those which put forward a 'critical pedagogy' thesis (Giroux, 1989). We shall be looking critically at these theories but our criticisms should not be read as acts of dismissal. The criticisms are not made and should not be considered as part of a methodology of disposal; a field procedure for the displacement of theories of others. The concern here is to show (eventually) what such theories and approaches presuppose, what is not addressed, and, perhaps inadvertently, what cannot be addressed as a consequence of the form the theories take.

If we look at the way in which education is positioned in theories of the cultural reproduction of class relations, it is quite clear that culture cannot be wholly identified with class relations. Class relations produce a bias in culture, act selectively on the appropriation of features and relations of culture for the purpose of the legitimation and reproduction of class relations. Education is a crucial concentration of, and amplifier for, this bias. The paradigm in which I was working positioned education in this way and contributed towards this view. Indeed, those who worked within this approach were convinced that the rules of the play of education had been revealed. Education had been demystified, its true nature revealed. The power relations had been exposed, and it was shown how these relations underlay and shaped discourse and practice and distributed forms of consciousness. And if the play were to be summed up — what is education?

Education is a relay for power relations external to it. The degree of success of the relay is not here the point. The educational system's pedagogic communication is simply a relay for something other than itself. Pedagogic communication in the school, in the nursery, in the home, is the relay for class relations; the relay for gender relations; the relay for religious relations, for regional

168

relations. Pedagogic communication is a relay for patterns of dominance external to itself. I am certainly not denying that this is the case, that it is not true. But if this is what is relayed, what is the medium which makes the relaying possible? It is as if this medium were somehow bland, neutral as air.

Think of a carrier wave. One can distinguish between the carrier and what is carried. What is carried depends upon the fundamental properties of the wave. Think of hi-fi (assuming you have a hi-fi system). When the tuner is activated what is heard is a function of the system carrying the signal; the system carrying the signal has already regulated the signal. What of pedagogic communication? We know what it relays, but what is the relay? We know what it carries, but what is the structure that allows, enables it to be carried? This is very similar to a distinction between language and speech. It is as if when we study pedagogic communication we study only the surface features, only its message, not that structure which makes the message possible. At the same time, as with others, when I read (but more often when I travelled) it occurred to me that what we have to account for about educational systems, educational practices, is not how different they are from one society to another but their overwhelming similarity. The most outstanding feature of educational principles and practices is their overwhelming and staggering uniformity independent of the dominant ideology.

The question here is, what is it that is generating this stability? This was another question that I began to put to myself. I started by asking such questions. How is it possible to make a distinction between a relay and what is relayed? There are strong hints in Durkheim's writing on education and pedagogic processes. I then started to look differently at theories of cultural reproduction. What I have to say about them applies to all of them, but not necessarily in the same way. It may be helpful to keep the crucial theorist in mind, Bourdieu, as, to highlight particular points, reference will be made to his work as a paradigm case.

We shall not deal with the usual criticisms, which do not illustrate the point I want to make; that is, I am not going to argue, 'These theories of cultural reproduction are morally repugnant because they are so deterministic.' I am not concerned with this criticism. From one point of view for me this is an empirical question. Further, I am not concerned with the criticism that these theorists do not include the state in their analysis, or that their concept of class is inadequate. Nor am I concerned with the criticism that these theories cannot deal with variations within the groups they analyse, that they deal mainly with aggregates rather than with variations within groups. I am more concerned that a theory of cultural reproduction has to be able, in the same theory, to translate micro into macro, and macro into micro, with the same concepts. Such theories have to deal with the problems of translation of levels in the same language. I became interested here because there are few theories, to my mind, that are able to accomplish this. Further, such theories should be able to deal with the production, the transmission, *and* the acquisition of pedagogic culture. Now this is an immense undertaking, and I know of no theory that is able to deal with production, transmission, and acquisition (not to mention change). In fact very few of these theories have an adequate theory of acquisition.

Another criticism is more relevant. Theories of cultural reproduction ought to have within them very strong rules which enable the theorist or the researcher to say, 'This is the same,' 'This is a variation,' 'This is a change.' Surely any theory of cultural reproduction must have strong markers to distinguish the 'same' or 'similar' from 'variation' and 'change'. Very few theories have markers of this kind. Indeed, change is relegated to the millennium. Change occurs when we have accomplished the transformation of the social basis of production. Thus we shall have change in the modality of cultural reproduction when we have changed the social basis of the mode of production. It is not altogether clear what counts as change in the social basis of the mode of production, especially with respect to the new decision-making mechanism and its social basis. From the perspective to be taken here it is possible to produce changes in the social basis of the mode of production without changing the principles of the modality of education. There is no necessary relationship between changing the social basis of relations in the economic field and changing the social basis of the principles of the reproduction of the cultural field.

The next two points are very relevant. Basically, theories of culture reproduction are essentially theories of distorted communication, really theories of what could be called a double distortion of communication. First, such theories argue that pedagogic communication is distorted in the interest of a dominant group, and, second, that there is a distortion of the culture and consciousness of the subordinate group. Basically, theories of culture reproduction are theories of a double distortion. But if there is a theory of distortion there must be, implicit or otherwise, a theory of undistorted communication. More fundamentally, there should be a theory of communication from which one can derive the distorted and the so-called undistorted. Here is an irony: theories of culture reproduction are essentially theories of communication without a theory of communication. The view to be put here is that the inner structure of the pedagogic *is* such a theory of pedagogic communication.

Summarizing so far, theories of cultural reproduction are concerned with messages, the messages of patterns of dominance. We are here referring concretely to what goes on in a school: the talk, the values, the rituals, the codes of conduct are biased in favour of a dominant group. These privilege a dominant group, so such codes of communication are distorted in favour of one group, the dominant group. But there is another distortion at the same time; the culture, the practice, and consciousness of the dominated group are misrepresented, distorted. They are recontextualized as having less value. Thus there is a double distortion. However theories of culture reproduction are essentially theories of communication without an explicit theory of communication.

Our second point entails another irony. Theories of culture reproduction, resistance, and pedagogic critique not only do not have a theory of communication but the concepts that they use are incapable of generating specific *descriptions* of the agencies central to their concern. That is, such theories do not generate specific principles of description of the agencies of their analysis. Consider a theory that puts agency before structure, that shows the way in which groups themselves resist and actively oppose pedagogic communication rather than being positioned by it. Now if we look at the concepts that, for example, Willis (1977) uses, there is no way in which these can describe the distinctive discursive relations, features, and practices which constitute the school. There is no way in which one can analyse a school, or any other agency of cultural reproduction. (A theory of cultural resistance/reproduction, ideally, should handle more than school; it should be able to include hospitals, the relationship between doctor and patient, between social worker and client, probation officer and probationer.) Any theory of cultural reproduction must be able to generate principles of description of its own objects. Consider Bourdieu and Passeron (1970). The only concepts available for the analysis of the form, practices, and contents of educational agencies are concepts such as arbitrary authority, arbitrary communication, pedagogic authority, pedagogic communication, pedagogic work, habitus. There is no way, on the basis of such concepts, that one can generate an empirical description of any specific agency of cultural reproduction. Thus we have theories of cultural reproduction/resistance and pedagogic discourse critique which cannot generate the principles of description of the agencies of their concern. And the answer is clear why they cannot do this.

For those theories and approaches are not really concerned with such description. They are concerned only to understand how external power relations are *carried* by the system, they are not concerned with the description of the carrier, only with a diagnosis of its pathology. Their concepts specify what is to be described, they call for a description, but are unable to provide principles for that description. In a sense the concepts are diagnostic; they refer to the source of a social pathology. In a way these theories specify that the normal is the pathological (an inversion of Durkheim) but the non-pathological form is rarely if ever described in the sense in which description is used here. Indeed, this would be regarded as a sealing-off of future possibilities, as such a description would be seen as excluding future posibilities, the benign form of which has its source only in an on-going dialectic. Bourdieu's analyses preserve a deep scepticism at attempts to euphemize control.

What we shall now do, with the aid of Figure 5.1, is to indicate the fundamental relationships which any theory of cultural reproduction has to deal with, and, for that matter, any theory of pedagogic communication, or, more generally, any theory which attempts to link pedagogic communication with pedagogic consciousness/conscience. We have in Figure 5.1 sets of fundamental relations which will both situate and adumbrate the problematic to be addressed.

Field of research

Figure 5.1 can be read at two levels (macro and micro) and any feature of their interrelation may be considered. The macro is read off the outer terms of the diamond, and the micro relations are the inner terms. It may be asked why class is given as only a micro relation. This is not the case; it is subsumed within – indeed, it is a condition for – the social basis of the macro relations of 'work' and the 'State'. It is possible to consider relations between macro and micro levels for any one feature or set of relations. For example, we can ask what relative autonomy means when considering the economy and the educational system and the State, and/or the relation between that relative autonomy (should it be available) and transmission/acquisition at the level of the classroom.

The basic question to be asked is always with reference to the privileging pedagogic text. Here we can distinguish between relation to and relation within the privileging text. Does a theory or approach focus upon the pedagogic subject's *relation* to this text in terms of his/her social class, gender, race attributes, or *any other discriminating attribute*, or does the theory/approach focus upon

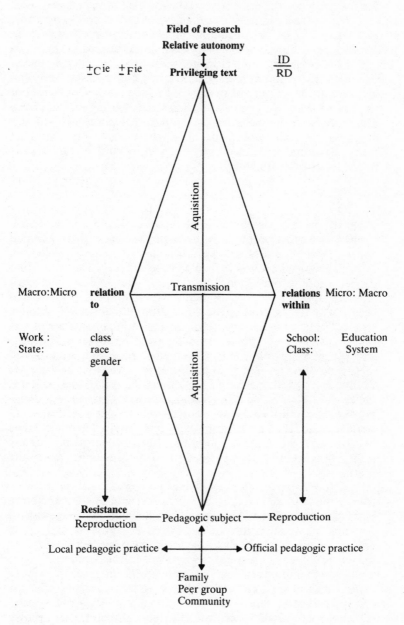

Figure 5.1

the internal constituents of the privileging text in the process of its transmission and acquisition at the level of the classroom or school (at the micro level) or educational systems (at the macro level)? In Figure 5.1 we draw a fundamental distinction between the *positioning* of the pedagogic subject with respect to any privileging text at either macro or micro level (*relations to*) and positioning *within* any privileging text at the micro level of the classroom/school or the macro level of the educational system. We should be able to place theories and approaches on the map of relations in Figure 5.1 in terms both of their focus or emphasis upon 'relation to'/ 'relation within' the privileging text with respect to the macro/ micro levels of analysis.

Features of the field

Basically, all theories of cultural reproduction/resistance necessarily have a concept of relative autonomy (except early Bowles and Gintis). The concept of relative autonomy has to do with relationships between the economic field and the cultural field (education) or between the State and education, or both. The concept of relative autonomy derives originally from Durkheim (1938) but is used essentially by reproduction and cultural theorists to denote a space of relative independence of the educational system which is said to give its agents some autonomy over the contexts, contents, and processes. These contexts, contents, processes, agents, and their procedures have an area of their own discretion; they are not wholly determined by external regulation. Thus the pedagogic text (as given in Figure 5.1) is in some sense free of external determinancy and in some important sense, from this perspective, is an intrinsic product of the educational process itself. There is no time to go into this, but I do not subscribe to such a concept and in many respects I think it is rarely defined so precisely as to be empirically useful.

In a fundamental sense, as pedagogic communication, of both transmitter and acquirer, cannot be programmed (and therefore has some autonomy) and is a specialized language, it is not possible for that communication to be effectively policed and made uniform. Further, the basis of the hierarchy of pedagogic (school/ university) discourse cannot always be derived from class hierarchies or their dominant cultures except with reference to a simple mental/manual division. In these two senses there is a potential discretionary space. However, in Bourdieu and Passeron relative autonomy creates a space whereby the autonomy (the relative independence of the educational system from external regulation) gives the educational system an appearance of neutrality which is the source of the disguising, the bias of the arbitrary nature of the system, its processes, and texts. Such relative autonomy then disguises the class bias of education. The power *rapports* which give rise to the bias create symbolic violence *where the power rapports of pedagogic practice are misrecognized.* Whether we consider Bourdieu and Passeron, or any other cultural theory, relative autonomy at the micro level translates into a biased text, a text whose acquisition is a function of the class position of the acquirer. (We can note in passing that in the theory we have been discussing, if relative autonomy does not hold, then all the relations derived from it do not hold.)

Returning to Figure 5.1, we start at the top with 'relative autonomy', because of its biased and biasing regulation of the privileging pedagogic text. We can read off from the outer left of the horizontal line of the diagram the macro relation, autonomy, from production and/or the State. The 'text' which in the diagram we have called 'privileging' confers class, gender, race privilege directly or indirectly. It is important to understand that we are here using 'text' both in a literal and in an extended sense. It can refer to the dominant curriculum, dominant pedagogic practice, but also to any pedagogic representation, spoken, written, visual, postural, sartorial, spatial.

It is important to broaden the concept of a privileging 'text' to include privileging spatial features. For example, in the homes of the new middle class there is often a rule which constitutes the relationship between objects and their space. There should be an inverse relation between the number of objects and the size of their containing space, and this constructs a particular privileging space. This is not so as to facilitate a walkabout. It is because every object therein shows strong selective rules which delicately and exquisitely exemplify sensibility and distinction. Further, because there are few objects, these can enter into a whole series of different relationships with each other, and so any one set of relationships is a further demonstration of unique taste. Finally, as there are few objects, each is likely to be very costly. In the late nineteenth century the rule was reversed, and many and varied objects completely filled the space. Thus the concept of a 'privileging text' includes the rules whereby the material context is created.

If we now look at the horizontal line of Figure 5.1 we have on the left 'relation to', on the right 'relations within'. 'Relation to' accounts for how the pedagogic subject is positioned with reference to the 'privileging text'. Now, if we look at education (school), the positioning of the child as pupil, the crucial control on such positioning, with respect to the 'privileging text', is essentially a matter of class, race, gender, and age. Thus class, race, gender, and age position the subject with respect to the 'privileging text' but – note – these attributes tell little about how the 'privileging text' itself has been constituted; little of the rules of the constitution of that 'privileging text' except in terms of including/excluding relations. Some have been positioned favourably because of their habitus, and some have been positioned unfavourably because of their different habitus. Here we are basically talking about the positioning of subjects with respect to their relation to the privileging text, and that is a function of their class, race, gender, and age. Now this leads back (looking at the foot of the diagram) to the 'local pedagogic practice'. Below 'pedagogic practice' in Figure 5.1 we have the family; what happens on the street (peer relations), what happens in the community (community relations). This is what is meant by the local pedagogic practice, and it is the *local* pedagogic practice within the family, peer group, and community which initially positions the child or the parents with respect to the 'privileging text'. Some are positioned in a way such that they can appropriate it, some are not. Those who can appropriate the 'privileging text' are likely to have received in the home a version of the 'official pedagogic practice'. Thus we can consider at the level of the family the degree of presence of an 'official pedagogic practice' or its absence.

Now we shall look at the other side of the horizontal line 'relations within'. 'Relations within' refers to the rules whereby the 'privileging text' has been internally constructed. 'Relations within' tells us about the relationship within the 'privileging text', that is, the rules whereby that text has been constituted, which makes the text as it is, which gives it its distinctive features, its distinctive relations, its mode of transmission and contextualization. We shall spend some time illustrating the significance of 'relations within', for it is these relationships which are inadequately specified in theories of cultural reproduction or resistance or transformation. By 'inadequately specified' I mean there is an absence of rules whereby descriptions can be generated of distinctive features of the 'privileging text', *its mode of construction, mode of representation, mode of presentation, and acquisition*. Now Bourdieu, either in Bourdieu and Passeron (1970) or in his book *Distinction* (1986), is essentially concerned with 'relation to' the 'privileging text' rather than with 'relations within'. Indeed, it is the dominant concern with the former ('relation to') which deprives this work of the possibility of adequate description of the 'privileging text', a condition for which *is* a realization of the 'relations within'. This issue can be illustrated by an examination of *Distinction*, a crucial analysis of the complex and subtle process whereby the social basis of the distribution of taste (music, painting, literature, cinema, theatre, table manners, cuisine, etc.) is exposed and demystified. However, Bourdieu is less interested in the distinctive features of the object of the taste that is privileged than concerned to show the legitimation, principles, and processes of its *distribution*.

Let me give an example. In the 1960s if one went into the expensive, careful homes of the new middle class and its upper-class counterpart you were likely to see either originals (in the case of the smart and wealthy) or reproductions (in the case of the socially mobile) of abstract expressionism, basically of the New York paradigm. Narrative/figurative painting would be rare, although produced. Today if one goes into similar houses one will see less abstract expressionism and more metaphysical realism. What has happened is that the *figure* now has an important place in the scene. Not the figure as it was, because practices rarely return to what they were. The same movement can be seen in students' work at art schools. This is not to say that abstract modalities are not painted or sold, only that there has been a relative but important shift of emphasis. This we regard as of significance. There is a difference in learning to look, a difference in the talk, in the gaze, in the social context of the artwork's construction, circulation, and consumption.

Bourdieu is less interested in the process of the development of the dominant code generating abstract expressionism or in the development of the dominant code of the new realism, or the change in the positioning of these two modalities of the visual arts field. In Figure 5.1 these processes are included under 'relations within'. On the whole, theorists of cultural reproduction are less concerned with 'relations within' the 'privileging text'; they are more concerned with the principles conferring legitimacy and distribution, with the subtle forms of representation *within a hierarchy based upon privileged taste/texts*. These theories are more concerned with the surface ideological markings of the text (class, gender, race) than to analyse how the text has been put together, the rules of its construction, circulation, contextualization, acquisition, and change.

We shall now take our example from education itself. 'Relations within' at the micro level of the school would refer to the 'privileging text' (depending upon what we were here taking as its representation) in the context of the process of its transmission/acquisition/evaluation in the classroom. At the micro level of agency, we might be referring (again depending up what we are here taking as its representation) to the rules that place the text within the pedagogic discourses of the school within a course, within a curriculum, together with the organizational practice, that is, the rules regulating the relations between agents and contexts. At a relatively more macro level we would be referring to the rules regulating the construction of those discourses from which the initial 'privileging text' was derived, to the power positions within relevant pedagogic recontextualizing fields and to the direct or indirect control by the State.

Briefly, theories of cultural reproduction, resistance, or transformation offer relatively strong analyses of 'relation to', that is, of the consequences of class, gender, race in the unequal and invidious positioning of pedagogic subjects with respect to the 'privileging text', but they are relatively weak on analyses of 'relations within' (perhaps with some exceptions, e.g. U. Lundgren). Now if a theory is weak at analysing 'relations within' it is not possible to derive from that theory, nor can that theory realize, strong rules for the description of the agencies/processes of its concerns. Nor can such theories generate an explicit theory of pedagogic communication. On this argument, if we are to understand *transmission* (the horizontal line in Figure 5.1), then we must be able to understand the relation of 'relation to' and 'relation within', both at macro and micro levels, and this is also the case for acquisition (the vertical line of the diagram). Indeed, with respect to the latter, 'acquisition', if we are unable to specify the rules regulating the construction, representation, and contextualizing of the 'privileging text' – that is, specifying 'relations within' – then we cannot know what has been acquired, either positively or negatively. And if we do not know this, how can we know the relationship between the 'privileging text' and the consciousness of the pedagogic subject? And if we do not know that, then in what sense can we talk about reproduction, resistance, transformation?

We can in the same diagram examine macro relationships, micro relationships, and the relationships between macro and micro. The micro relationships of 'relation to' (class, gender, race) are given on the inner left of the horizontal line in the diagram and the micro context of 'relations within' is given by the inner right-hand side of the diagram (school/class). The macro relationships of 'relation to' are indicated on the outer left of the horizontal (State/work), whereas the macro relationships of 'relations within' are indicated on the outer right-hand side (the education system). It is possible, then, to place any theory with respect to macro/micro relationships in terms of what are and what are not its concerns.

Finally, if we wish to examine the influence of the family and community on their contribution to the transformation of their children as pedagogic subjects we should look at the foot of the diagram. Here we have simplified and shown only two orientations of the pedagogic subject as regulated by the family/peer group/ community. We distinguish between families with respect to the extent to which the 'local pedagogic practice' is embedded in an 'official pedagogic practice'. The latter refers to that practice which facilitates the acquisition of the privileging text(s) of the school. Now at extremes we have families where the 'local pedagogic practice' dominates the 'official pedagogic practice' because the latter is absent as a practice, or is excluded, or is present only in a weak form; and families where the 'official pedagogic practice' dominates the 'local pedagogic practice'. We consider that where the 'local pedagogic' dominates at the level of family, peer group or community, this is likely to be a function of the class/gender/race position of the family, and the acquirer here is more likely to be unequally positioned with respect to the acquisition of the 'privileging text' or be positioned in opposition/resistance to it. We regard such positions as having the potential to generate a 'resisting' pedagogic subject. On the other hand, where the 'official pedagogic practice' dominates the 'local pedagogic practice' the children will be positioned as 'reproducing' pedagogic subjects, but not necessarily reproducing *political* subjects. We repeat: this is a simplification. It would be inappropriate to believe that these are the only two positions or necessary outcomes.

We have included the peer-group relation of the acquirer between the family and the community at the foot of the diagram but have not incorporated this crucial pedagogic site in our discussion and can here make only a brief comment. The peer group is a set of relations and practices which is a potential threat, from the point of view of 'official pedagogic practice', or a site of potential independence, alternative, 'resistance' from the perspective of the acquirer. In so far as 'official pedagogic practice' within the school/family is dominant as a control over the peer group, those relations and practices support reproduction. The relationship between 'official pedagogic practice', 'local pedagogic practice', and peer-group pedagogic practice may interact to produce a variety of outcomes.

If I were to position my own research within this field, then it would seem that the work on the family and the school drew attention to both contents and different positioning with respect to those contents. That is, the early work up to Bernstein (1971b) focused essentially upon micro features of 'relation to' and 'relations within'. Later work has attempted to build out towards more macro considerations of the constitution and regulation of elaborated codes and their modality.

I have outlined what I take to be the complex of agencies, relations, and practices necessary for the analysis of cultural reproduction, resistance, and transformation at both micro and macro levels. It is possible to consider the differential emphases of different approaches and of different theories, and in this way see both the continuities and the discontinuities in this intellectual field. We can see that even where 'relations within' are subject to analysis, whether at the level of classroom practice (interactional and sociolinguistic research) or at the level of the school (ethnographic studies), or at the level of the curriculum or of critical pedagogy, there is no fundamental analysis of the internal logic (in the sense of regulating principles) of the pedagogic relay nor of its relation to what is relayed.[1] And it is this problematic we shall now address.

The pedagogic device

Our analysis will first outline what we take to be the internal orderings of the pedagogic device which we consider is the condition for the production, reproduction, and transformation of culture. We consider that this device provides the intrinsic grammar of pedagogic discourse through *distributive rules, recontextualizing rules, and rules of evaluation.* These rules are themselves hierarchically related in the sense that the nature of the distributive rules regulates the recontextualizing rules, which in turn regulate the rules of evaluation. These distributive rules regulate the fundamental relation between power, social groups, forms of consciousness and practice, and their reproductions and productions. The recontextualizing rules regulate the constitution of specific pedagogic discourse. The rules of evaluation are constituted in pedagogic practice. The pedagogic device generates a symbolic ruler of consciousness. The question becomes: whose ruler, what consciousness? The second section of the paper attempts to construct a general model for the answering of such questions.

Distributive rules

We shall start with a consideration of the means whereby a relation is constructed between power, social groups, and forms of consciousness. We consider that this relationship is established through the controls on the specialization and distribution of different orders of meanings. These different orders/orderings of meanings can be said to create different knowledges/practices. The controls over the differential specialization and distribution of principles for the ordering of meaning attempt to effect specialization and distribution of forms of consciousness and practice. From this point of view, if we wish to understand the production, reproduction, and transformation of forms of consciousness and practice, we need to understand the social basis of a given distribution of power and principles of control which differentially position, reposition, and opposition forms of consciousness and practice. We shall postulate that between power and knowledge, and knowledge and forms of consciousness, is always the *pedagogic device* (PD). We shall define the pedagogic device as the distributive, recontextualizing, and evaluative rules for specializing forms of consciousness.

Fundamental distributive rules mark and specialize the thinkable and the unthinkable and their entailed practices to different groups through the mediation of differently specialized pedagogic practices.

In all societies there are at least two basic classes of knowledge, the esoteric and the mundane; knowledge of the other and the otherness of knowledge, of how it is, the possible, as against the possibility of the impossible. We are well aware that the line between these two classes of knowledge/practices is relative to any given period, and that the principles generating both classes are also relative to a given period. In small-scale, non-literate societies with a simple division of labour – societies, until fairly recently, particularly studied by social anthropologists – the division between the 'thinkable' and the 'unthinkable', the practice of its management, were effected by the religious system, its agents, and their practices. Today the controls on the 'unthinkable' lie essentially, but not wholly, directly or indirectly in the upper reaches of the educational system, in that part concerned with the production rather than the reproduction of discourse; whereas the 'thinkable' is a different power-regulated recontextualizing, in the lower reaches of the educational systems – that is, in its reproductive rather than its productive levels. In both 'simple' and complex societies a structurally similar distribution of forms of consciousness is to be found, differently specialized through different agencies and produced by differently specialized pedagogic discourses. The similarity is more profound; the system of meanings is structurally similar. We are here referring not to any similarity between magic and science or, for example, to the sharing of powers of complex navigation, but to the sharing of a *particular order* of meaning which establishes the particular relation between the material and the immaterial, so relating one world to another, the mundane to the transcendental. This relation always, by definition, transcends the local and discrete. It is not that this order of relation is abstract; it is more a question of the form taken by the abstraction. It is a form whereby there is an indirect relation between meanings and a specific material base (a given social division of labour and its social relations). Under these conditions there is a potential discursive 'gap', a 'space' which can become the site of alternative possibilities, for alternative realizations of the relation between the material and the immaterial. This potential 'gap', 'space', the site of the 'unthinkable', the 'impossible', can be beneficial and dangerous at one and the same time. It is the meeting point of order and disorder, of coherence and incoherence; it is the crucial site of the 'yet to be thought'. In a fundamental sense this potentiality is a potentiality of language itself. Any distribution of power attempts to regulate the realization of that potential, in the interests of the social ordering it creates, maintains, and legitimates. In 'simple' societies this regulation is effected by the religious system and by the cosmologies to which it gives access and controls.

In the language of codes (Bernstein, 1981) we should draw a distinction between elaborated orientations and an elaborated code. If the code is elaborated, then the principles regulating the realizations of the code are themselves the object of explicit principles of analysis *and such a code is the cultural/pedagogic relay*. From this point of view the cosmologies of 'simple' societies are the product not of elaborated codes but of *elaborated orientations* which create the relations between the mundane and the transcendental. Here the principles of the transcendental realizations are not themselves subject to further principles of exploration.[2] In complex societies, certainly in Europe, the institutionalizing of elaborate codes in specialized agencies and agents was accomplished in the medieval period with the development of the ancient universities and monastic schools.

We are arguing that elaborated orientations and, even more, elaborated codes are the media for thinking the 'unthinkable', the 'impossible', because the meanings they give rise to go beyond local space, time, context and embed and relate the latter to a transcendental space, time, context. A potential of such meanings is disorder, incoherence; a new order, a new coherence. We are suggesting that the relationship between power, knowledge, and forms of consciousness and practice is accomplished by the distributive rules of the pedagogic device. The pedagogic device provides distributive rules which regulate the different specialization of consciousness to different groups. We see this historically in terms of the guardians and transmitters of the realization of elaborate orientations in simple societies and later in complex societies, of legitimate elaborated codes, and their modalities which transmit pedagogic discourses and their practices. Through its distributive rules the pedagogic device is both the control on the 'unthinkable' and the control on those who may think it. We shall see later that intrinsic to such a device are both the imposition of order and the means of its transformation.

Recontextualizing[3] rules: pedagogic discourse

If the distributive rules mark and distribute who may transmit what to whom, and under what conditions, and in so doing attempt to set the outer and inner limits of legitimate discourse, then pedagogic discourse is the rules of specialized communication through which pedagogic subjects are selectively created. We shall define pedagogic discourse as the rules for embedding and relating two discourses. It will be remembered that the distributive rules attempt to control the embedding and relating of the material in the immaterial, the mundane in the transcendental, and the distribution of such meanings. Pedagogic discourse is the specialized communication whereby differential transmission/acquisition is effected. We commence with the question 'What discourse is embedded in what discourse?'

We shall define pedagogic discourse as the rule which embeds a discourse of competence (skills of various kinds) into a discourse of social order in such a way that the latter always dominates the former. We shall call the discourse transmitting specialized competences and their relation to each other *instructional* discourse, and the discourse creating specialized order, relation, and identity *regulative* discourse (appendix 5.1). To show visually the distinctive feature of pedagogic discourse we shall write it as:

ID/RD

where the oblique means embedded. The rules constituting pedagogic discourse are not derived from the rules regulating the internal characteristics of the competences to be transmitted. In an important sense, pedagogic discourse, from this point of view, is a discourse without a specific discourse. It has no discourse of its own. *Pedagogic discourse is a principle for appropriating other discourses and bringing them into a special relation with each other*

183

for the purposes of their selective transmission and acquisition. Pedagogic discourse, then, is a principle which removes (delocates) a discourse from its substantive practice and context, and relocates that discourse according to its own principle of selective reordering and focusing. In this process of the delocation and the relocation of the original discourse the social basis of its practice, including its power relations, is removed. In the process of the de- and relocation the original discourse is subject to a transformation which transforms it from an actual practice to a virtual or imaginary practice. Pedagogic discourse creates imaginary subjects. We must sharpen our concept of this principle which constitutes pedagogic discourse. It is a *recontextualizing* principle which selectively appropriates, relocates, refocuses, and relates other discourses to constitute its own order and orderings. In this sense, pedagogic discourse cannot be identified with any of the discourses it has recontextualized. In this sense it has no discourse of its own, other than a recontextualizing discourse. We have now made the move from the distributive rules to the recontextualizing rules, the rules which constitute pedagogic discourse.

The dominance of regulative discourse

From the above discussion it can be seen that, as pedagogic discourse is a recontextualizing principle, which transforms the actual into the virtual or imaginary, then any recontextualized discourse becomes a signifier for *something other than* itself. What this 'other' is, the *principles of the principles* of the recontextualizing which regulates what principle of recontextualizing is selected – or, perhaps more accurately, the principle which regulates the range of alternative principles available for selection – varies according to the dominant principles of a given society (see later discussion). In this sense regulative discourse is itself the precondition for any pedagogic discourse. It is of course obvious that all pedagogic discourse creates a moral regulation of the social relations of transmission/acquisition, that is, rules of order, relation, and identity, and that such a moral order is prior to, and a condition for, the transmission of competences. This moral order is in turn subject to a recontextualizing principle, and thus this order is a signifier for *something other than itself*. It is perhaps less obvious how regulative discourse creates order, relation, and identity in instructional discourse. That is, in the intrinsic orderings of the competence to be acquired. We shall take as an example the acquisition of physics in the secondary school.

First of all, such physics is a recontextualized discourse. It is the result of recontextualizing principles which have selected and declocated what counts as physics from what we could call the primary context of the production of discourse[4] and relocated, refocused physics in the secondary context of the reproduction of discourse. In this process physics undergoes a complex transformation from an original to a virtual/imaginary discourse.[5] The rules of relation, selection, sequencing, and pacing (the rate of expected acquisition of the sequencing rules) cannot themselves be derived from some logic internal to physics nor from the practices of those who produce physics. The rules of the reproduction of physics are social, not logical, facts. The recontextualizing rules regulate not only selection, sequence, pace, and relations with other subjects, but also the theory of instruction from which the transmission rules are derived (appendix 5.2). The strength of the classification and framing of recontextualized physics is itself ultimately a feature of regulative discourse. In this way, order, relation, and identity in the transmission of instructional discourse are themselves embedded in the principles of order, relation, and identity of regulative discourse. Pedagogic discourse is then a recontextualizing principle/discourse which embeds competence in order and order in competence or, more generally, consciousness in conscience and conscience in consciousness (Figure 5.2). We shall take up later the question of whose order, what competence.

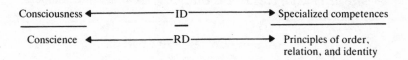

Figure 5.2

Evaluation rules: pedagogic practice

We shall be here be concerned to show the fundamental ordering principles of any pedagogic discourse. At the most abstract level the recontextualizing principle which selectively creates ID/RD produces a specialization of time, text (or its metaphoric equivalent), and space and the conditions of the interrelation (Figure 5.3).

185

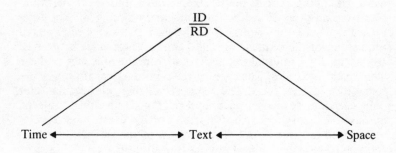

(i)

Figure 5.3

We can at a lower level of abstraction transform Time into Age. Thus the practice of any ID/RD leads to a punctuation in age, to dislocation of ages sequentially related. The degree of delicacy of the punctuation of time and the span of life appropriated by pedagogic time (in principle from pre-procreation to post-resurrection) is a matter of a given historical context but specialization of, and differentiation within, time are integral to pedagogic discourse. The text is always transformed into a special age-related content. Pedagogic practice creates a licence to speak in its own temporal punctuations. Thus:

(ii)   Age ⟷ Content ⟷ Context

Finally we can transform (ii) into the level of the social relations of pedagogic practice and the crucial features of the communication. *Age is transformed into acquisition. Content is transformed into evaluation. Context is transformed into transmission.* Thus:

(iii)   Acquisition ⟷ Evaluation ⟷ Transmission

We can see that the key to pedagogic practice is *continous evaluation*. If we place the horizontal and vertical relations together we obtain the view of pedagogic practice shown in Figure 5.4. See appendix 5.3.

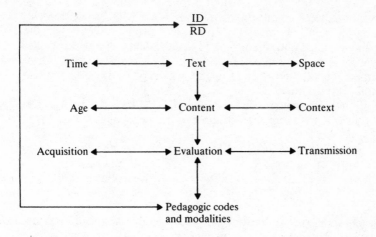

Figure 5.4

The code condenses in its grammar the orderings within and between distributive rules, recontextualizing rules, and evaluation rules. However, there may well be contradictions, cleavages, and dilemmas created by these rules, so that pedagogic practice does not necessarily reproduce pedagogic discourse and what is acquired is not necessarily what is transmitted. The power relations which constitute, legitimate, and maintain the classification of the code (paradigmatic features) and the control relations which constitute, legitimate the framing of communicative relations (syntagmatic features) are themselves the producing product of on-going contradictions, cleavages, and dilemmas of social relations. The set of rules of the pedagogic device is condensed in the code of transmission/acquisition.

We have so far postulated distributive rules which are the official regulation of the degree of classification of the distinction between the 'thinkable/practices' and the 'unthinkable/practices' and so upon the degree of insulation between groups, practices, and contexts and between differently specialized principles of communication. The pedagogic device reproduces but does not create this distinction between the 'unthinkable' and the 'thinkable'. It attempts to regulate the distribution. The distributive rules are a basic classificatory principle regulating the relationship between the distribution of power, the distribution of knowledge, and the distribution of forms of consciousness. We know that in general those who *reproduce* legitimate knowledge institutionalize the 'thinkable' whilst those who *produce* legitimate knowledge institutionalize the 'unthinkable' and that we find these are two strongly classified groups within the legitimate fields of the production and reproduction of education. What is 'the thinkable' and what is 'the unthinkable', the form of the regulation, the social composition of the different agents will vary from one historical situation to another.

Following Weber, we can see a parallel between the positions in the religious field and the positions in the pedagogic field:

Religious field	*Pedagogic field*
Prophet	Producers
Priest	Reproducers
Laity	Acquirers

In general the rule is that one can occupy only one position at any one time. However, in the pedagogic field, at the level of the university or equivalent institution those who produce the new knowledge are also their own recontextualizers. It is a matter of interest that, at the level of the university, there is increasing differentiation of research from teaching, e.g. discussion of the stratification of institutions with respect to research postgraduate, undergraduate institutions.

We have said that pedagogic discourse is the rules for embedding an instructional discourse in a regulative discourse. Instructional discourse regulates the rules which constitute the legitimate variety, internal and relational features of specialized competences. This discourse is embedded in a regulative discourse, the rules of which regulate what counts as legitimate order between and within transmitters, acquirers, competences, and contexts. At the most abstract level it provides and legitimizes the official rules regulating order, relation, and identity. The tendency is to separate these discourses as moral and instructional discourses, or to see them as ideologically penetrated rather than to regard them as one embedded discourse producing one embedded inseparable text. The grammar of pedagogic discourse (the underlying ordering principle) condenses competence into order and order into competence. We have argued that this grammar which produces the internal orderings of pedagogic discourse is not a grammar for specializing a specific discourse, creating its own rules of demarcation and internal order, but a principle of delocating, relocating, and refocusing other specialized discourses, bringing them into a new relation with each other and introducing a new temporal, internal ordering. Pedagogic discourse is constituted by what we shall call a recontextualizing grammar.

This grammar necessarily transforms, in the process of constituting its new orderings, the appropriated discourses into imaginary discourses and thus creates a *space for the play of ideology*. This recontextualizing grammar, the grammar of appropriation, is linked to the levels of pedagogic practice by realization rules. These realization rules are derived from theories of instruction (implicit or explicit).

These theories of instruction are themselves necessary to form ID/RD and are themselves constituted by recontextualizing principles which regulate the internal orderings, temporal and contextual realizations of the discourses of pedagogic practice. The theory of instruction is a crucial recontextualized discourse, as it regulates the orderings of pedagogic practice, constructs the model of the pedagogic subject (the acquirer), the model of the transmitter, the model of the pedagogic context, and the model of communicative pedagogic competence. Changes in the theory of instruction can thus have consequences for the ordering of pedagogic discourse and for the ordering of pedagogic practice. We can distinguish two modalities of theories of instruction, one oriented to the logic of transmission and one oriented to the logic of acquisition. The former will privilege graded *performances* of the pedagogic discourse, the latter will privilege shared competences of the acquirer. (See appendix 5.2.)

We can now summarize the order and orderings of the pedagogic device as a grammar regulating the relations within and between three levels. The degree of determination – that is, the outer boundaries and inner possibilities of each level – is a matter of the historical and ideological context of the device. The pedagogic device is thus a *symbolic ruler of consciousness* in its selective creation, positioning, and oppositioning of pedagogic subjects. It is the condition for the production, reproduction, and transformation of culture. The question is: whose ruler, what consciousness?

The effectiveness of the device is limited by two different features, one internal to the device and one external to it.

Internal. As we will develop later, the very discourse which is subject to control contains within itself the possibilities of the transformation of its own principles. For it is not possible to control the 'thinkable' without the shadow of the 'unthinkable'. The principles which are reproduced carry orders of possibility other than the set to be reproduced.

External. The distribution of power which speaks through the device itself creates potential sites for challenge and oppostion to its principle and legitimacy. Thus the device may well become, and

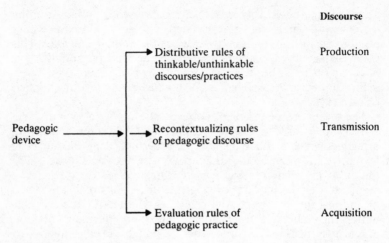

Figure 5.5

usually is, a crucial arena of struggle for control, as it is a condition for the productions/reproductions of culture *and* of their inter-relations.

Before we turn to consider the question 'Whose ruler, what consciousness?' we should draw attention to our original problem. Studies in the sociology of education on the whole take for granted (perhaps with the exception of Durkheim, 1938) the analysis of the intrinsic distinguishing features of specialized pedagogic communicative practices. In our language studies are concerned only with the analysis of the 'message' of pedagogy (class, gender, race, region, nation, religion), not with its 'voice'. In such studies the 'voice' of pedagogy is a 'voice' that is never heard, only its realizations; that is, its messages. The 'voice' is constituted by the pedagogic device. A more appropriate metaphor may be that the pedagogic discourse device is a grammar for producing specialized messages, realizations, a grammar which regulates what it processes: a grammar which orders and positions and yet contains the potential of its own transformation. Any sociology of education should have a theory of the pedagogic device. Indeed, such a theory could well be its necessary foundation and provide the fundamental theoretical object of the discipline.

Contexts, fields and definitions

Primary, recontextualizing, and secondary contexts

In the model which follows reference is made to the fields of symbolic control and the field of production. In the previous chapter there has been extensive discussion of how these fields have been conceived and their relation to the State. This discussion should be borne in mind in the context of the analysis which follows. In this section, as a preparation for the next, we shall discuss the relationships between the rules of the pedagogic device and the fields for the production, recontextualizing, and reproduction of pedagogic discourse. This is followed by formal definitions of official and local pedagogic discourse and the systemic and classificatory relations of education.

We shall outline the three fundamental contexts of educational systems and show their relation to the rules which constitute the pedagogic device.

Primary context: production of discourse

We shall distinguish three crucial, interdependent contexts of educational discourse, practice, and organization. The first of these we shall call the *primary* context. The process whereby a text is developed and positioned in this context we shall call *primary contextualization*. The latter refers to the process whereby 'new' ideas are selectively created, modified, and changed and where specialized discourses are developed, modified, or changed. This context creates the 'intellectual field' of the educational system. This field and its history are created by the positions, relations, and practices arising out of the *production* rather than the reproduction of educational discourse and its practices. Its texts, today, are dependent partly, but by no means wholly on the circulation of private and State funding to research groups and individuals.

Secondary context: reproduction of discourse

This context, with its various levels, agencies, positions, and practices, refers to the selective reproduction of educational discourse. We shall distinguish four levels, tertiary, secondary, primary, and pre-school. Within each level there may be some degree of specialization of agencies. We shall call these levels and their interrelations, together with any specialization of agencies within a level, the *secondary* context of the production of pedagogic discourse. This context structures the *field of reproduction*. We can ask here questions referreing to the classificatory and framing principles regulating the relations between and within levels and regulating the circulation and location of codes and their modalities.

Recontextualizing context: relocation of discourse

From these two fundamental contexts and the fields they structure we shall distinguish a third context which structures a field or sub-set of fields, whose positions, agents, and practices are concerned with the movements of texts/practices from the primary context of discursive production to the secondary context of discursive reproduction. The function of the positions, agents, and practices within this field and its sub-sets is to regulate the circulation of texts between the primary and secondary contexts. Accordingly, we shall call the field and the sub-set structured by this context the *recontextualizing fields*.

Official pedagogic recontextualizing field

1 This will include specialized departments and sub-agencies of the State and local educational authorities together with their research and system of inspectors.

Pedagogic recontextualizing field (see later discussion)

1 This will include university and polytechnic departments of education, colleges of education together with their research, and private foundations.
2 It will include specialized media of education, weeklies, journals, etc., and publishing houses together with their readers and advisers.
3 It may extend to fields not specialized in educational discourse and its practices, but which are able to exert influence both on the State and its various arrangements and/or upon special sites, agents and practices within education.

When a text is appropriated by recontextualizing agents, operating in positions of this field, the text usually undergoes a transformation prior to its relocation. The form of this transformation is regulated by a principle of *decontextualizing*. This process refers to the change in the text as it is first delocated and relocated. This process ensures that the text is no longer the same text:

1 The text has changed its position in relation to other texts, practices, and position.
2 The text itself has been modified by selection, simplification, condensation, and elaboration.
3 The text has been repositioned and refocused.

The decontextualizing principle regulates the new ideological positioning of the text in its process of relocation in one or more of the levels of the field of reproduction. Once in that field, the text undergoes a further transformation or repositioning as it becomes active in the pedagogic process within a level. It is crucial to distinguish between, and analyse, the relations between the two transformations, at least, of a text. The first is the transformation of the text within the recontextualizing field, and the second is the transformation of the transformed text in the pedagogic process as it becomes active in the process of the reproduction of acquirers. *It is the recontextualizing field which generates the positions of pedagogic theory, research, and practice.* It is a matter of some importance to analyse the role of departments of the State in the relations and movements within and between the various contexts and their structuring fields.

To be complete we should state that the major activities of recontextualizing fields are creating, maintaining, changing, and legitimizing discourse, transmission, and organizational practices which regulate the internal orderings of pedagogic discourse. We can show a relationship between the internal rules of the pedagogic device and the three fundamental contexts of European educational systems. Distributing rules relate to the primary context, recontextualizing rules relate to the recontextualizing context, and evaluative rules relate, in this case, to the secondary context. We have been careful here to refer to the primary context for the production of pedagogic discourse *within* the educational system. It is clear that there are primary contexts and sites for the production of pedagogic discourse external to the educational system.

We have here attempted to provide a background for the model which follows in the final section. This model has been developed to provide the description required to answer the question raised in the analysis of the pedagogic device: whose ruler, what consciousness?

Definitions

We shall give here definitions of official State pedagogic discourse together with other relevant definitions.

Official pedagogic discourse (OPD)   Official rules regulating the production, distribution, reproduction, interrelation, and change of legitimate pedagogic texts (discourse), their social relations of transmission and acquistion (practice), and the organization of their contexts (organization). Official pedagogic discourse is an embedded discourse and is the realization of the interrelations between two differently specialized discourses: instructional discourse and regulative discourse.

Specific instructional discourse (SID) regulates the rules which constitute the legitimate variety, internal and relational features of specialized competences in any one agency.

Specific regulative discourse (SRD): the rules which regulate in any one agency what counts as legitimate order between and within transmitters, acquirers, competences, and the organizational context. At the most abstract level SRD provides and legitimizes the official rules regulating order, relation, and identity.

Pedagogic text: a text produced/reproduced and evaluated in, or through, and always for the social relations of transmission/acquisition. A text is a distinctive realization of pedagogic discourse and is a specific selection, integration, and contextualizing of 'pedagogemes'.

Pedagogeme: the smallest distinctive unit of practice or disposition which can be a candidate for evaluation.

We can distinguish between *official* pedagogic discourse (OPD) and *local* pedagogic discourse (LPD). The latter regulates the process of cultural reproduction at the level of the initial contextualizing of culture, essentially in the family and in peer-group relations. There may well be oppositions, resistances, or correspondences and support, dependences, and independences in the positioning relations between official and local pedagogic discourse. The basic model we propose can, we believe, apply to local pedagogic discourse, although it is likely here that its principles will be embedded in tacit practice.

External relations of education   The educational system is considered to have two qualitatively different types of external relations, which regulate it in different ways and to different degrees. These external relations we shall call *systemic* relations. These are the relations between the educational system and the production and reproduction of resources – physical (production) and discursive (symbolic control). This distinction between physical and discursive resources must be seen as a low-level description, for it is always the case that there can be no physical resource without a prior discursive resource.

Physical resources. The education system *may* have an output which can serve as a potential or actual resource for agencies of production, distribution, and circulation of capital with respect to their division of labour and social relations.

Discursive resources. The education system always has an output which serves as a potential or actual resource for the agencies of symbolic control, their social division of labour, and social relations. Such an output is defined as a discursive resource.

The systemic relations of education with respect to discursive resources pre-date the systemic relations with respect to physical resources, are relatively tighter, and, in the future, are likely to be more enduring, complex, and State-regulated.

Classificatory relation   This refers to the relations between education and production where these relations are viewed as categories of function. If the relation between these two categories is strongly classified, then there is strong insulation between the categories, which creates a space in which each category can differently specialize its generative principles and practices. If there is weak classification between the category of education and the category of production, then there is low insulation between the categories and both will share a common generative principle and practice. In other words, in the case of weak classification there is an integration of generative principles, whereas in the case of strong classification the principles are kept apart and are differently specialized. In Europe the modal relation is one of strong classification; only in China for a short period, 1966–76, was there a limited attempt to weaken the classificatory relation between education and production. The *systemic* relation (where it is strong) translates at the level of the acquirer into his/her motivation and aspiration. This does not mean to say that all acquirers accept their positioning within such a translation. The *classificatory* relation translates into the features of the privileging texts to be acquired. The stronger the classification between education and production, the more likely that the privileging text will be a realization of a pedagogic code, whose values are likely to be $+C^{ie}+F^{ie}$ (strong classification, strong framing for both internal and external values). In this context, the text will be both highly abstract and abstracted from relationships other than its own.

Realization of the device

Whose ruler? What consciousness? A model

We shall confine discussion of our model to the production and reproduction of official pedagogic discourse in contemporary developed societies.[6] Official pedagogic discourse regulates the rules of the production, distribution, reproduction, and inter-relations of transmission and acquisition (practice) and the organization of their contexts (organization).[7] We must first distinguish what we have called in the model 'dominant principles' of the society. These create an arena of challenge, conflict, and dilemma, but at any one time specify basic principles of order, relation, and identity, setting at least their outer boundaries and in certain contexts their inner limits. We can regard these dominant principles as an expression of the dominant political party of the State or, rather, an expression of the relations between the various parties or interest groups. The dominant principles are regulated by the distribution of power and principles of control which determine the means, contexts, distribution, possibilities, and social relations of physical and discursive resources.

We are here concerned only with the relation between the dominant principles and the constitution of positions, agents, and practices in the official recontextualizing field which is responsible for creating, maintaining, and changing official pedagogic discourse. This field will usually have a core of officials drawn from official pedagogic agencies of the State and consultants, advisers, etc., drawn from the educational system and from the economic field and the field of symbolic control. In this way official pedagogic discourse is always a recontextualizing of texts, and of their generating social relations, from dominant positions within the economic field and the field of symbolic control.

We distinguish in our model two recontextualizing fields. One we have already described as the official recontextualizing field (ORF), regulated directly by the State, politically through the legislature, administratively through the civil service. There may be more than one Ministry active in this recontextualizing field. Today in the UK we must note the Department of Employment. The official recontextualizing field may incorporate, selectively, specialized services from agents/agencies external to it, which in turn alter the position of these agents in their respective fields.

The major activity of recontextualizing fields is constituting the 'what' and 'how' of pedagogic discourse. The 'what' refers to the categories, contents, and relationships to be transmitted, that is their *classification*, and the 'how' refers to the manner of their transmission, essentially to their *framing*. The 'what' entails recontextualizing from intellectual fields (physics, English, history, etc.), expressive fields (the arts), manual fields (crafts), whereas the 'how' refers to the recontextualizing of theories from social science, usually psychology. The recontextualizing field brings together discourses from fields which are usually strongly classified, but rarely brings together the agents. On the whole, although there are exceptions, those who produce the original discourse, the

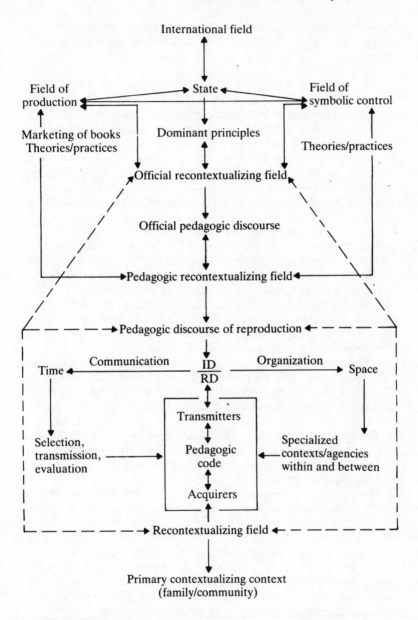

Figure 5.6

effectors of the discourse to be recontextualized, are not agents of its recontextualization. It is important to study those cases where the producers or effectors of the discourse are also its recontextualizers.

We can define the relative autonomy of pedagogic discourse to the extent that pedagogic recontextualizing fields (PRF) are permitted to exist and affect official pedagogic practice.[8] Pedagogic recontextualizing fields, as in the case of the official field, are concerned with the principles and practices regulating the circulation of theories and texts, from the context of their production or existence to the contexts of their reproduction. The pedagogic recontextualizing field may have, as its core, positions/agents/ practices drawn from university departments of education, colleges of education, schools, together with foundations, specialized media, journals, weeklies, and publishing houses.

The pedagogic recontextualizing field may be strongly classified internally, producing sub-fields specialized to levels of the educational system, curricula, groups of pupils. It is useful to distinguish agencies of pedagogic reproduction which, within broad limits, can determine their own recontextualizing independent of the State (the private sector) and agencies which although funded by the State may have a relatively larger measure of control over their own recontextualizing (until recently the universities).

Both recontextualizing fields, the official and the pedagogic, are affected by the fields of production (the economy) and symbolic control. There is a double relation between recontextualizing fields and the fields of production and symbolic control:

1 The theories, practices, social relations within these fields will exert an influence upon the discourse to be transmitted and on how they are transmitted; upon both the 'what' and the 'how' of pedagogic discourse.[9]
2 The training requirements of agents (especially dominant agents within the field of symbolic control) will influence the 'what' and 'how'.

However, as we have argued that pedagogic discourse creates *imaginary subjects*, we should not overestimate the fit between pedagogic discourse and any practice external to it. Indeed, on our argument the 'fit' is essentially an imaginary practice which may well be differently ideologically positioned by the activities of different agencies, e.g. education/production/symbolic control.

The pedagogic discourse of reproduction which is inserted in the contexts of reproduction (*which* school contexts depends upon the relative autonomy given to levels or agencies at different levels of the educational system) is then constituted by a complex set of relations between recontextualizing fields and positions within such fields. In our model of the pedagogic device we gave only a very general abstract formulation of pedagogic practice. We showed only how a given ID/RD creates specific communicative practices (time) and organizational practices (space) to constitute the code to be acquired. Any pedagogic practice of reproduction is given by ID/RD where the unit of analysis may be a level of the education system, an agency, a curriculum, a unit of the curriculum, or a context of transmission.[10] (For the coding rules of ID/RD see Bernstein and Diaz, 1984.)

However, what is reproduced in schools may itself be subject to recontextualizing principles arising out of the specific context of a given school and the effectiveness of external control over the reproduction of official pedagogic discourse. Further, what is reproduced may be affected by the power relationships of the recontextualizing field between the school and the primary cultural context of the acquirer (family/community/peer relations). The school may include as part of its practice recontextualized discourses from the family/community/peer relations of the acquirer for purposes of social control, in order to make its own regulative discourse more effective. Conversely, the family/community/peer relations can exert their own influence upon the recontextualizing field of the school and in this way affect the latter's practice.

We have not drawn attention in our model to the differential and invidious positioning of acquirers with respect to the distribution of pedagogic capital, moral significance, and respect. Such is not our intention in this paper. The model allows for considerable internal dynamics in the production, distribution, reproduction, and change of pedagogic discourse.

1 Dominant principles themselves refer to an arena of conflict rather than to a stable set of relations.
2 There is a potential or actual source of conflict, resistance, and inertia between the political and administrative agents of the official recontextualizing field.
3 There is a potential or actual source of conflict, resistance, and inertia between the positions within the pedagogic recontextualizing field, and between it and the official recontextualizing field.
4 There is a potential or actual source of conflict, resistance, and inertia between the primary cultural context of the acquirer (family/community/peer relations) and the recontextualizing principles and practices of the school.

5 Transmitters may find themselves unable or unwilling to reproduce the expected code of transmission.

It becomes a matter of considerable interest to know where, when, and why the circulation of principles and practices realized in pedagogic discourse is innovated from below or imposed from above.

From this brief description of the levels of the model and their interrelation it is possible to see the complex relations between power, pedagogic discourse of reproduction, and the distribution of forms of consciousness. Because every discourse is a recontextualized discourse, every discourse and its subsequent texts are ideologically repositioned in its transformation from the original field of its production or existence to the field of its reproduction. The model attempts to explicate at least formally what it means to say that pedagogic discourse is a recontextualized discourse. Finally, the model shows how complex is the process between the initial movement (circulation) of a discourse and the effect of that discourse upon the consciousness and specific positioning of an acquirer.

Comments upon the model

A distinguishing feature of the institutionalizing and realization of the European pedagogic device is the stability of the realizations of its distributive, recontextualizing, and evaluative rules irrespective of the dominant principles of the society. The dominant modality of this pedagogic device entails a strong classification between education and production. We mean by a strong classification that there is a strong insulation between education and production which creates a specialized space for education to develop its own generative discourse and practice. Where there is a weak classification between education and production there is a low insulation between these categories and both are more willing to share similar generative principles. An example of such a weakening of the classification occurred in China until 1976 for a limited period and with limited effect.

The origin of the strong classification between education and production can be traced to the medieval period, where we find that the official pedagogic device excluded manual practice from its recontextualizing rules. Manual practice was acquired through local pedagogic devices within the family and guild. Thus mental and manual practice was historically strongly classified, and this has left its mark on the European pedagogic device. It means that the consciousness of agents of symbolic control is more likely to be positioned and specialized by the modality of education than by the mode of production, and this has many implications which cannot be pursued here. (See chapter 4.) So far we can see that the modal European pedagogic device produced a strong classification between mental and manual practice. Its recontextualizing rules positioned its discourse in highly abstract knowledge and its pedagogic practice (evaluation rules) in an intensely subjective experience (see chapter 4). Durkheim argues that Christianity necessarily points to both *abstraction* and *inner experience*. 'Its God must be believed in and thought about.' An excellent discussion of these issues is to be found in Alexander (1982). Concentration of pupils/students/teachers in one agency facilitates moral intensity and the disciplining of feeling/belief, whilst the initial abstract orientation was facilitated by the recontextualizing of Greek thought.

It is perhaps understandable why manual practice was excluded from the recontextualizing rules. Further, we can note that the distributive rules of the European pedagogic device produced *within* pedagogic discourse an equivalent of the manual/mental dislocation; a strong classification between those who produce the discourse (who by legitimate criticism and discovery generate new principles, forms, and techniques) and those who reproduce the discourse. Only at the university or its equivalent is this classification weakened, but even here there is a tendency to separate producing and reproducing functions institutionally and to reward them differently. We have, then, a second dislocation generated by the distributive rules of the pedagogic device between *producers* and *reproducers* of knowledge. It is because of this dislocation that particular recontextualizing fields have developed which specialize and position agents, practices, and texts, with their own principles of orthodox/heterodox and conditions of entry. These fields are not necessarily parasitic on the fields of production of intellectual discourse or manual/expressive practice. The activation of texts, relocated according to dominant positions in the recontextualizing field, their transformation within that field into pedagogic texts or principles, their dissemination through pedagogic practice, may well have important repercussions on the position of the recontextualized text in its field of origin (e.g. Piaget).

It is important to distinguish societies in terms of the relative autonomy of pedagogic recontextualizing fields from the official fields. Where there is only one field (the official one) it is likely that pedagogic agencies of the State will control the publication of manuals, textbooks, etc. In the latter case, changes in the political discourse of the State will be marked by changes in the dominance of positions within the official recontextualizing field. Where pedagogic recontextualizing fields exist, are effective, and enjoy relative autonomy, then it is possible for activities within this field to recontextualize texts which *in their own right* may be considered illegitimate, oppositional, originating in counter-hegemonic sites of the production of discourse (Holland, 1985). Such texts are likely to be defused, refocused in their recontextualizing and thus made safe (e.g. Freire). The degree of autonomy of the pedagogic recontextualizing field can profoundly affect the pedagogic discourse reproduced in schools, essentially through the initial and in-service training of teachers and through the books/textbooks which issue from the pedagogic recontextualizing field. However, more direct control over schools by the State through highly centralized curricula and systems of assessment and inspection can severely limit the influence of the pedagogic recontextualizing fields. Control by the State over the funding, topics, and focus of research further limits the influence of the pedagogic recontextualizing field.

It is important to point out that the model describes recontextualizing fields within the *official* education system. Here the field of production of discourse refers to the development of discourse arising out of the research and critical functions of the universities, special institutes, and polytechnics. This is not to say that such production does not occur in any other contexts of the education system, only that the agencies mentioned specialize, as part of their function, in the production rather than the reproduction of discourse. The theories and practices of this field of the production of discourse are selectively recontextualized not only at lower levels of the education system but also in the field of production and symbolic control. It is also important to make clear that the production of discourse takes place outside the educational system's own field. Indeed, such production is selectively recontextualized within education. It is the case, however, that such production is influenced by official pedagogic discourse.

We have commented on some basic dislocations produced by the modal European pedagogic device irrespective of the dominant principles of society.[11] These dislocations may be expressed as follows:

Physical resources   *Discursive resources*

Manual : Manual : : Production : Reproduction

We can formulate a more general model on the basis of our previous argument (Figure 5.7). This general model describes the sets of relation created by official elaborated codes and their modalities. These codes are in the first place reproduced through official pedagogic discourse which presupposes:

1 *Distributive rules* which specialize the *production* of intellectual discourse to a particular field/context, with its own agents, positions, practice, and evaluations; the *reproduction* of pedagogic discourse to its own field/context; and specializes manual discourse to its own field.
2 *Recontextualizing rules* regulate the transformation of discourse within the field of the production of discourse into the field of its reproduction and exclude manual discourse from its dominant modalities.
3 *Evaluation rules* of the dominant pedagogic practice then differentially evaluate discourses generated by manual practices, together with the effectors of such practices and the social groups they presuppose.
4 The *realizations* of such a device will maintain and reproduce a power–knowledge–consciousness distribution, irrespective of whether the dominant principles of a given society celebrate capitalist, collectivist, or dictatorship ideologies.

We suggest that the above interrelations represent the ordering principles (internal grammar) of the realizations of the European modal pedagogic device as institutionalized through State-controlled education systems, and that this internal grammar is common to societies with different dominant principles (capitalist, dictatorship, or collectivist societies of the common form). This internal grammar, essentially based upon strong classification, is not an inevitable realization of the inner logic of the pedagogic device but is a dominant historical and contemporary modality and produces fundamental similarities between educational systems in ideologically differently focused societies and, within broad limits, similar outcomes.

It could be argued against this view that we are now witnessing a new preoccupation with the relation between education and work. This preoccupation is the result of massive changes in, and redefinitions of, the division of labour in the economic field, themselves a consequence of the 'communications revolution'. Severe problems of unemployment, especially among the young, have had a direct effect upon the school, where various forms of skill training and

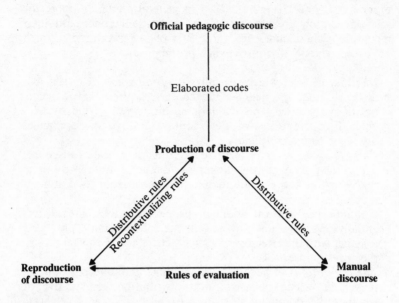

Figure 5.7

vocational emphasis have been promoted and funded by new pedagogic agencies of the State (e.g. the Manpower Services Commission in the UK). However, they are likely to create no more than a
pedagogizing of lower-level skills and social discipline as a basis for
careers. At most we are witnessing the insertion of an 'imaginary
apprenticeship' system within sections of the school.

In terms of our model, this and similar movements (e.g. President
Mitterrand's recent suggestion that schools should be linked to
industrial enterprises) do not affect the *classificatory* relation
between education and production, only the *systemic* relation. The
systemic relation refers to the relationships between the output of
schools in terms of skills/dispositions of various kinds and the
supposed requirements of work. We have argued that it is essential
to distinguish the classificatory from the systemic relations of
education. Strengthening or weakening the systemic relations are
movements independent of changes in the classificatory values.
Thus strong classification can realize apparently opposing
modalities of pedagogic types (the cultivated, the vocational, the
leisured, the professional).

Summary

We have attempted, in outline, to form the possible beginnings for an analysis of the internal grammar of pedagogic discourse and for the analysis of the principles governing its realization, when these are institutionalized as official pedagogic discourse and pedagogic practice. The internal grammar provides for the hierarchical ordering of distributive, recontextualizing, and evaluative rules which produce an embedded discourse of the form ID/RD which at the level of pedagogic practice controls discourse, transmission/acquisition, and organizational practices. We argued that the link between power, knowledge, and consciousness is established by the pedagogic device, which is a symbolic ruler of the construction and distribution of forms of the specializing of subjects and is thus the precondition for the production and reproduction of culture. We regard the pedagogic device as providing the internal grammar of symbolic control, or, from a more traditional perspective, of socialization.

Although this paper has been essentially concerned with the official pedagogic device and thus always with official control over elaborated codes and their modalities, the question arises whether the model is applicable to non-official pedagogic discourse.[12] At this stage it is difficult to provide an answer, as the model has not been subjected to such explorations. However, it is expected to hold for all reproductions of elaborated code discourse and wherever that discourse is presupposed. If it is the case that the internal grammar applies to all such discourse, then the question arises of the relation between this grammar and its realizations. The pedagogic device is essentially a device for translating power relations into discourses of symbolic control and for translating discourses of symbolic control into power relations. In as much as the pedagogic device translates power relations into discourses of symbolic control, then the power relations within the discourse regulate or attempt to regulate the 'yet to be thought', which is a potential of the discourse realized by the device itself. The 'yet to be thought' is a fundamental possibility because language carries the potential of producing the orders of meaning the device is attempting to control and distribute.

The device attempts to control the 'unthinkable' in official discourse in order to maintain a given distribution of power. It does this through its distributive rules, which regulate those who have access to the sites where the 'unthinkable' may be legitimately thought, through recontextualizing rules which construct the 'thinkable', through its agents, and through evaluative rules which shape the acquirer. However, orientations to alternative orders of meaning, and the principles upon which such meanings rest, are themselves made available by the device. Thus, from a purely formal perspective, the pedagogic device cannot but be an instrument of order and of transformation of that order. From a substantive perspective – that is, from the perspective of the realizations of the device – these give rise to tensions, oppositions, and contradictions between social groups who have been specialized and positioned by the realizations of the device. Finally, the device itself creates an arena of struggle for control over its realizations.

Symbolic control made possible by the pedagogic device cannot be computerized, as such control issues always as a discourse to be transmitted and acquired, creating a language whose rules are tacitly absorbed, enabling speakers to create and recognize the legitimate potential of orthodox and heterodox texts without apparent explicit external regulation. Although the regulation of the exploitation of physical resources will become increasingly subject to information control chains, computer-regulated, with built-in self-correcting feedback loops, the regulation of discursive resources cannot be so organized. In as much as it is not possible to specialize a given biology to a given discursive range, there can only be discursive control on discourse itself. And we have seen the contradictions which lie at the heart of such control. We might hypothesize that the more abstract the technological principles for the exploitation of physical resources, the simpler the social division of labour, but the more complex and extensive the social division of labour of symbolic control. There are, it seems, always openings for priests, if not for prophets. Under these conditions the pedagogic device may become the crucial focus of struggle. Finally, we turn from a discussion of the pedagogic device to consider constraints upon its output.

There may well be fundamental oppositions internal to the potential outputs of the pedagogic device. We shall suggest that the device has only two possible outputs, and that these are essentially in opposition to each other. These outputs in contemporary education systems may be distributed according to the age of the pupil or according to the pedagogic status of the pupil. The outputs can be either shared competences or graded specialized performances (and sometimes combinations with different emphases). If we consider societies which are non-literate, segmented, with a simple division of labour, then it is not unusual to find in such societies pedagogic agencies in the form of age-group socialization. After a specified

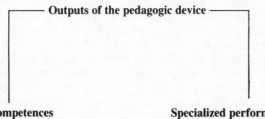

Shared competences
Similar to
Simple division of labour
Mechanical
Solidarity

Specialized performances
Different from
Complex division of labour
Organic
Solidarity

Figure 5.8

period in the age group, exit from it is regulated through rituals of transition, which serve as initiation rites into a new age status as adult. Now in accounts of such rites (evaluation procedures) it is rare to read of individuals who have failed the rite. The reason is that failure is not expected. It is true – for example, in Papua, New Guinea – that occasionally it has been known for an initiate to die, but failure is not intrinsic to the pedagogic agency.

What is intrinsic to such an agency? We suggest that what is intrinsic is not the creation of individual specialized differences but, on the contrary, the creation of *shared competences*. The agency is not designed to facilitate individual differences; rather it is designed to ensure that all have the same range of competences/ practices. It is not designed to promote explicitly, as part of its rules, specialized performances. This is not to say that some individuals will not, in fact, be more effective in performances based upon these shared competences, only that the pedagogic agency is not explicitly concerned to bring it about. If the agency is producing a range of shared competences, then the social relations created are relations of 'similar to'. Relations of 'similar to', where ranges of competences are shared, are relations of relatively low levels of specialization, creating a simple division of labour, celebrating, and controlled by, mechanical solidarity. Here the weight of the society's classification is not upon the work context but upon the kinship system.

Opposed to the above output is the output of a pedagogic agency, which is not shared competences but specialized performances. Such a pedagogic agency is concerned to bring about specialized differences between individuals: differences in their performances. Such an output points to gradings, not only within but also between specialisms. Such an agency is not designed to produce 'similar to' but *different from* relations, and points to a complex division of labour, that is, to organic solidarity and its various modalities, e.g. capitalist, socialist. It would seem, then, that the two potential outputs of the device – shared competences, specialized performances – may well presuppose opposing social bases. Shared competences, a simple division of labour, reduction in the strength of stratification based upon work; specialized performances, complex division of labour, relatively strong stratification based upon work. Thus the potential outputs of the device seem to be relays for weak or strong classification based upon work, weak or strong emphasis upon technological development, low or high levels of differentiated consumption. Which output of the device is selected, and for whom, is a matter of the dominant principles of the society. But it may be that, as the complexity of the social division of labour weakens, as a consequence of the 'communication revolution' which gathered momentum at the close of the twentieth century, then there may well be an enlargement of the pedagogic space which could relay shared competences.

In summary, we have argued that pedagogic discourse is constituted by the *interaction* of at least three fields. That these fields entail positions, agents, and agency specific to each field. That these fields are the result of a relatively strong classification (insulation) between producers and reproducers of discourse. That this separation, insulation, specialization, necessitates the development of recontextualizing fields and their arenas of positions. That the specialization of positions, agents, and agencies to each field by no means rules out the influence of the recontextualizing field upon the field of the production of knowledge. That these fields, internal to the construction of official pedagogic discourse, are themselves constrained by, and in turn regulate, the field of symbolic control and the economic field. That the State, through its several pedagogic agencies, including its inspectorate, procedures of assessment, control of research funding and focus, advisory boards, creates the official recontextualizing field. That the crucial dependence/independence is between the official recontextualizing field and the pedagogic recontextualizing field. The construction of pedagogic discourse creates an arena of struggle which can in principle create interactions from the official recontextualizing field to the recontextualizing interface between the school and its communities.

It would seem that once the emphasis is placed upon specialized performance as the dominant output of the pedagogic device, as a consequence of the requirements of a complex division of labour, then educational systems, irrespective of the dominant ideologies of different societies, become strikingly similar. Differences between societies then may be found in the degree of relative autonomy of the pedagogic recontextualizing field, *and* the field of the production of discourse, from the State. Clearly, a crucial difference between societies is the absence or presence of an effective pedagogic recontextualizing field. We are witnessing in the UK increasing State regulation of this field as part of a policy of State symbolic control.

In the paper the concept of relative autonomy plays an important role in defining the space available to agents, and agencies in recontextualizing fields, and so a crucial role in the construction and relaying of pedagogic discourse. Relative autonomy here is less the basis for disguising the arbitrary nature of power and communication in eduation, so facilitating the illusion of the neutrality of education; rather the concept points to *all* pedagogic discourse as an arena of conflict, a site of struggle and appropriation. Relative autonomy refers to the constraints on the realizations of the pedagogic device as symbolic ruler. Whose ruler, what consciousness, is revealed by the discourses' privileging texts and the procedures of evaluation such texts presuppose.

Conclusion

We have proposed that a pedagogic device can be considered as a set of hierarchical rules, distributive, recontextualizing, evaluative, which constitute its internal grammar. We consider that the realization of these rules with respect to any pedagogic practice can be described in terms of classification and framing values, which establish the pedagogic codes and their modalities. The pedagogic device makes possible the transformation of power (that is, its basis in social relations and their generating sites) into differently specialized consciousness (subjects) through the device's regulation and distribution of 'knowledges' and of the discourses such knowledges presuppose.

In this sense the pedagogic device is the condition for culture, its productions, reproductions, and the modalities of their inter-relations. We believe (but this is clearly subject to further explora-tion) that the internal ordering proposed is common to all peda-gogic devices.[13] In this paper we have restricted our analysis to the official realizations of the pedagogic device and to the power and control relations legitimized and maintained by such realizations. To this end, we constructed a model for generating a description of the *processes* involved in State-regulated realizations of the device, that is, official pedagogic discourse and pedagogic practice. We have argued that, despite differences, there are fundamental similarities and stabilities created by the realizations of the official European pedagogic device.

We were not able, within the limits of this paper, to do more than create formal descriptions and derived relations with respect to pedagogic practice, but we have indicated in the references where more detailed and substantive analyses may be found. 'Individual minds cannot come into contact and communicate with each other except by coming out of themselves,' according to Durkheim, and 'they communicate only by means of signs which express their internal states.' The official pedagogic device politicizes the sign.

Finally, it has been argued:

1 That the pedagogic device at one and the same time constitutes a symbolic ruler and is the means of its transformation, and
2 That the realizations of the device carry the contradictions, cleavages, and dilemmas generated by the power relations positioning the realizations.

Change, then, is a consequence of the inner potential of the device and the arena of conflict which is the social base of its realizations.

Appendix 5.1:
The concepts of instructional and regulative discourse

The distinction between instructional and regulative discourse clearly has its origin in Parsons's distinction between instrumental and expressive. Parsons states: 'Indeed, it is in relation to the differ-entiation of the relational contexts, both of instrumental and of expressive activities, that the most fundamental regulative problems of the social system arise and that regulative institutions are primarily focused' (1951: 79). For Parsons, instrumentalities have their origin in economic theory, particularly Adam Smith's 'division of labour': 'The starting point is the conception of a given actor's ego as instrumentally orientated to the attainment of a goal, a goal which may be of any desired specificity or generality' (1951: 70).

Expressive activities, on the other hand, are fundamental to instrumental ones and are organized 'in terms of a cultural pattern of value orientations' (p. 75). Expressive activities are concerned with relations to ordering principles, to solidarity with and loyalty and commitment to these principles. Parsons (1959), although not explicitly using concepts of instrumental and expressive activities, distinguishes between two axes, an axis of integration at the level of collective values (expressive) and an axis of achievement (instrumental). In Parsons, Bales, *et al.* (1955) Parsons distinguishes between instrumental and expressive roles and indicates that these may well be specialized to gender. The instrumental roles regulate (mediate) practices between systems (male) and the expressive roles regulate values, orientations internal to a system (female). We are not concerned here with the usefulness or otherwise of these distinctions but only to show their relation. We first used these terms in Bernstein (1966), where we distinguished not between roles or activities, but between instrumental and expressive cultures (later, orders) within the school. The former is concerned with 'facts, procedures and judgements involved in the acquisition of specific skills' and the latter with standards of 'conduct, character and manner'. The tensions and conflicts between these cultures/orders are further analysed in Bernstein *et al.* (1966). In the more specific sociolinguistic work we distinguished between four generalized contexts of socialization, of which two major contexts are *regulative* context, concerned with 'authority relationships where the child is made aware of the rules of the moral order and their various backings', and the *instructional* context, 'where the child learns about the objective nature of objects, persons, and acquires skills of various kinds' (1974: 181). However, it is only in Pedro (1981), who took over our model, where *instructional discourse* is defined in terms of 'the principles of the specific discourse to be transmitted and acquired' and regulative discourse as 'the principles whereby the social relations of transmission and acquisition are constituted, maintained, reproduced and legitimated' (p. 207). Thus instructional discourse is concerned with the transmission/acquistion of specific competences, and regulative discourse is concerned with the transmission of principles of order, relation, and identity.

However, behind these distinctions can be found concepts of mechanical and organic solidarity. The former is concerned with the principles of 'similar to' and the latter refers to the principles of 'different from'.

From Durkheim (1938) we interpret the Trivium (logic, grammar, and rhetoric) as constituting the discursive principles of mechanical solidarity, subject to shifts of internal emphasis and conflicts arising out of the developing bourgeoisie; and the Quadrivium, its specialized, separated discourses, astronomy, arithmetic, geometry, and music, pointing to the development of the historically much later organic solidarity. Durkheim (1925), a set of lectures for schoolteachers, is concerned essentially with the regulative discourse of the school. Durkheim (1938), a set of lectures for aggregation candidates, analyses the history and development between disciplines, practices, and moralities of education, and their external regulations. Durkheim concerned himself, in these lectures, with two fundamental questions: 'How the institution of the school came to be formed and how these schools came to be differentiated from the Church.' However, the context Durkheim created for himself in answering these questions was nothing less than an institutional history of the forms and content of education.

Alexander (1982: 285) considers that 'Although Durkheim devoted a great deal of time to the discussion of the relative value of different educational ideas *per se*, his sociological analysis of the evolution of the educational content is less systematic than his history of educational structure'. We can trace the conceptualizing of pedagogic discourse back to Durkheim, and, like him, we are concerned to show the interrelations between dominant power relations and principles of control in the constitution, transmission, and evaluation of pedagogic discourse.

Appendix 5.2: Theories of instruction

Theories of instruction, behavioural or biological (of the inheritance type), take as their reference what is to be evaluated, that is, an acquirer's graded performance of the pedagogic discourse, and these theories presuppose expected differences between acquirers. The social unit of evaluation here is the individual acquirer, and the graded relation *between* acquirers. On the other hand, there are theories of instruction which privilege not the evaluation of the discourse and so transmission, but privilege universal, general, processes internal to acquirers; that is, what is shared. Such theories point to the interactional nature of the acquisition of shared competences and so to a social unit of acquisition involving interactional relations between acquirers. Thus such theories (Piaget, Chomsky, Gestalt) focus upon the development of common competences within acquirers, rather than upon graded performances of a discourse to be acquired.

These two groups of theories may well be translations of two possibilities of the potential output of the pedagogic device itself.

In non-literate societies with a simple division of labour, the relay of pedagogic discourse may well be concerned to position acquirers in the reproduction of common, shared skills rather than in individually differentiated graded performances. We should point out that the skills here do not refer to internal ordering principles, as in Chomsky or Piaget, but to a variety of shared cultural skills. In these societies it is unusual to read of any member failing an initiation test, however demanding, although occasionally a death is reported. The standard European pedagogic device appears to have as its dominant realization a graded individual performance – and this long before the onset of most State-regulated education and capitalistic modes of production. These realizations of the pedagogic device, graded individual performances and shared competences, are today the site of pedagogic struggle between conservative and 'progressive' positions within recontextualizing fields.

It may be possible to draw up a matrix of theories of instruction on the basis of two intersecting dimensions. The vertical dimension would indicate whether the theory of instruction privileged relations internal to the individual, where the focus would be *intra-individual*, or whether the theory of instruction privileged not relations within the individual but relations *between* social groups (inter-group). In the first case, intra-individual, the theory would be concerned to explain the conditions for changes within the individual, whereas in the second the theory would be concerned to explain the conditions for changes in the relation between social groups. The horizontal dimension would indicate whether the

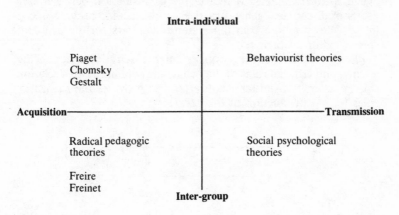

Figure 5.9

theory articulated a pedagogic practice emphasizing a logic of acquisition or one emphasizing a logic of transmission. In the case of a logic of acquisition the focus is upon the development of shared competences in which the acquirer is active in regulating an *implicit* facilitating practice. In the case of a logic of transmission the emphasis is upon the *explicit* effective ordering of the discourse to be acquired by the transmitter. We can now draw up the matrix and place in the various quadrants appropriate exemplars of theories of instructions (Figure 5.9). It is possible to translate these theories of instruction into *codes* of pedagogic practice through the language of classification and framing.

Appendix 5.3: Code: general

Code is defined as a regulative principle, tacitly acquired, which selects and integrates relevant meanings, forms of their realization, and evoking contexts.

Micro		*Macro*
Interactional		*Institutional* (schools)
Meaning	→	Discourse practices
Realization	→	Transmission practices
Contexts	→	Organizational practices

Specific codes modalities. These are constituted by the specific classification and framing values where:

Classification refers to the degree of insulation between categories of discourse, agents, practices, contexts, and provides recognition rules for both transmitters and acquirers for the degree of specialization of their texts.

Framing refers to the controls on the selection, sequencing, pacing, and criterial rules of the pedagogic communicative relationship between transmitter/acquirer(s) and provides the realization rules for the production of their text.

$$\frac{O}{\pm C \qquad\qquad F \pm^{i/e}}{C}$$

where O refers to orientation to meanings, elaborated/restricted (privileged/privileging referential relations); C refers to the principle of classification; F refers to the principle of framing; ± refers to the values of C and F with respect to strength, weak/ strong; i refers to the internal values of F within a communicative context (e.g. family, school, and work); e refers to the external values of F, that is, the regulation on communicative relations between communicative contexts (e.g. family/community and school; school and work); the lines signal that what is above the line is embedded in what is below; C below the lower line is the fundamental C and refers to the basic classification, the basic principle of exclusion, insulation, of the analysis. C could refer to the dominant principles of the society in terms of its class relations and period, e.g. entrepreneurial capitalism, corporate capitalism, etc. Weakening of C here would refer to dominant principles, where attempts were being made or had been made to change class relations. In other analyses the C could refer to the strength of the classification between education and production, which we consider to be the fundamental classificatory relation of education.

Notes

1 An exception here is the systematic studies of Ulf Lundgren and the group of researchers associated with him at the Stockholm Institute of Education of the University of Stockholm, published as monographs under the title Studies in Curriculum Theory and Cultural Reproduction.
2 I think this point requires further discussion. It is not meant that no elaborate coding occurs – indeed, this must be the case, given the presence of elaborated orientations – only that the exploration of principles, 'productive, elaborating, self-reflexivity', is likely to issue from a specialized position in a particular context, as in the case of the trance-singer (see Biesele, 1974). I am grateful for a personal communication from Dr R. Hewitt, SRU, Department of Sociology of Education, Institute of Education, University of London, for both the reference and the discussion. The essential point is that the code of cultural transmission, *the relay itself*, is not an elaborated code.
3 This concept and the model of which it is a part was introduced in Bernstein (1975, 1981). Since completing this paper I have seen Landsheere (1982), where on p. 89 the author draws attention to Bourdieu and Passeron's use of the term 'recontextualization', which Landsheere glosses as the 'the insertion and reformulation of a kind of knowledge or a new technology in the special situation – with its entire historical background – where they are supposed to develop in harmony with the systems of values and attitudes of the person concerned'. No reference is given; quotation as written.

4   Usually the universities or equivalent agencies.

5   A further example can be given of the recontextualizing process, this time with reference to a manual practice. In secondary schools there used to be a large room in which wooden benches were arranged in rows. On display in racks or cupboards there would be an array of tools: saws, chisels, planes, hardware. What we have here is a transformation of a manual practice, carpentry, into pedagogical woodwork. The original practice is abstracted from its own regulative discourse, that is, the power relations of its social context, and its specialized skills are transformed by the school's ID/RD. In general the recontextualizing process governing the movements of discourse from the site of its production or effectivity to its position within pedagogic discourse neutralizes, by abstracting the power relations of, the original social context. It becomes a matter of interest to speculate whether the pedagogic device can do no other than generate symbolic violence, whatever form its realization takes.

6   We have added a level to the model 'international field', which, although relevant to all societies, is often particularly crucial to the official pedagogic discourse of developing societies, as dominant positions in the recontextualizing fields of such societies are often specified by the terms of international funding agencies (Diaz, 1984; Cox, 1984; Domingos, 1984).

7   The regulation of official pedagogic discourse depends upon the relative autonomy of pedagogic recontextualizing fields and contexts other than the official field and context. It is a matter of analysis to determine the location, conditions, and range of such relative autonomy.

8   Public examinations taken at secondary levels of education, often indirectly or directly linked to the university, have a crucial influence upon the practices of pedagogic recontextualizing fields with reference to the provision of textbooks and teaching routines. At the same time, the practices of the recontextualizing field can influence the form and context of public examinations. It is not unusual for members of such boards to be drawn from the pedagogic recontextualizing field, where they act as agents of different functions.

9   Publishing houses create what can be called an industry of texts which have a direct effect upon positions within the recontextualizing field.

10 SID/SRDs may well be strongly classified and so specialized to different social groups within a school and such SID/SRDs may well be arranged on a scale of differential worth. Indeed, it may well be that certain groups are positioned only within SRD, receiving moral regulation rather than instruction in specialized competences.

11 The degree of the dislocation may vary; for example, in France it is much less with respect to discursive resources, for until recently there was a circulation of staff between the *lycée* and the university. We know also that much of the development of science in England took place initially outside the university.

12 Within families, local pedagogic practices are to different degrees embedded in official pedagogic practices. However, we know little about the local pedagogic practices of youth cultural forms and the pedagogic device the reproductions of those forms and their modalities presuppose.

13 We have proposed that the pedagogic device is the fundamental grammar of any pedagogic discourse. It might be worth while testing this proposition to see whether it is capable of application to very different pedagogic discourses. We shall consider here two forms of such discourse, both transmitted outside official pedagogic discourse of the European modality.

Charismatic education. Weber compared charismatic with legal-rational education. Charismatic education takes the form of a series of tests which appear, from the point of view of the initiate, to be unrelated to each other, which are arbitrary in content and time, and which are the means of discovering those who possess the vital charisma of leadership. Here the pedagogic discourse takes the form of providing those contexts and contents which will enable the potential charismatic to show what he/she already possesses. The search is to discover what already exists but is not known to the initiate and can be recognized only by the searcher. This modality is structurally similar to an invisible pedagogy in that the initiate is not aware of the meaning of his/her signs. These can be read only by the searcher who has the theory of reading. Sequencing and pacing criteria rules are implicit. The searcher is the arranger of contents and contexts, created to reveal a unique charismatic competence. Charismatic education can be considered to be a radical form of the invisible pedagogy, where the potential charismatic, once placed in the practice, is constrained by that practice until the diagnosis has been made. The potential charismatic controls the discourse in as much as he/she chooses to remain within it or not.

The *distributive* rules control the 'unthinkable' by selecting the indicators of charisma, and so those who show the signs and those who do not. The *recontextualizing* rules select those tests which perhaps tradition has shown have been successfully passed, or structurally similar tests are designed. Here the producers of the pedagogic discourse are past charismatics. The *evaluative* rules create the specific pedagogic practice of tests and contexts.

Charismatic education is a form where there is no transmitter of the competence, for the competence can only be shown, not acquired. The transmitter is replaced by an identifier with procedural recognition rules and tests. After identification more customary forms of pedagogic discourse may follow.

Manual pedagogic discourse. The analysis in the text is wholly of pedagogic discourse dedicated to mental practice. We shall now see whether the model applies to the transmission of manual practice. We shall take, as an example of the transmission of manual practice, guild-regulated acquisition of manual skills. The progression of this acquisition can be understood as apprentice−journeyman−master, perhaps structurally equivalent to the chivalric progression page−squire−knight. The mystery of the skill is the site of the 'unthinkable', that is, the alternative possibilities which inhere in the skill. The distributive rules distribute those who may or may not have access to this site and who produce the discourse. The distributive rules select those who produce the discourse and who regulate the 'unthinkable'. In the case of manual practice, as in the case of university practice, those who produce the discourse are also the recontextualizers who control the pedagogic discourse of transmission and regulate the content and stages of apprenticeship and journeyman. They also regulate the *evaluation* rules and so the pedagogic practice. The university and guild of the medieval period are based upon the rules of the pedagogic device.

References

Adlam, D.S., with Turner, G.J., and Lineker, L. (1977) *Code in Context*, London: Routledge.

Aggleton, P. (1984) 'Reproductive Resistances: a Study of Origins and the Effects of Youth Sub-cultural Style amongst a Group of new Middle-class Students in a College of Further Education', Ph.D. thesis, University of London.

—— (1987) *Rebels without a Cause? Middle-class Youth and the Transition from School to Work*, Lewes: Falmer Press.

—— and Whitty, G. (1985) 'Rebels without a cause? Socialization and subcultural style among children of the new middle classes', *Sociology of Education* 58, 1: 60–72.

Alexander, J.C. (1982) *Theoretical Logic in Sociology*, II, *The Antinomies of Classical Thought: Marx and Durkheim*, London: Routledge.

Althusser, L. (1971) 'Ideology and the ideological State apparatus', in *Lenin and Philosophy*, trans. B. Brewster, New York: New Left Books.

Apple, M.W. (1982a) 'Curricular form and the logic of technical control', in Apple, M.W. (ed.) *Cultural and Economic Reproduction and Education*, London: Routledge.

—— ed. (1982b) *Cultural and Economic Reproduction in Education*, London: Routledge.

Atkinson, P. (1981) 'Bernstein's structuralism', *Educational Analysis* 3, 1: 85–95.

—— (1985) *Language, Structure and Reproduction: an Introduction to the Sociology of Basil Bernstein*, London: Methuen.

Bakker, B.F.M., Dronkers, J., and Meijnen, G.W. (1989) *Educational Opportunities in the Welfare State*, Nijmegen: Instituut voor Toegepaste Sociale Weten Schapen.

Bernstein, B. (1959) 'Some sociological determinants of perception', *British Journal of Sociology* 9: 159–74.

—— (1960) 'Language and social class', *British Journal of Sociology* 11: 271–6.

References

—— (1962) 'Linguistic codes, hestitation phenomena and intelligence', *Language and Speech* 5: 31–46.

—— (1966) 'Sources of consensus and disaffection in education', *Journal of the Association of Assistant Mistresses* 17: 4–11; longer version in *Class, Codes and Control* 3, revised edition 1977.

—— (1967) 'Open schools, open society?' *New Society*, 14 September.

—— (1969) 'Critique of the concept of compensatory education', paper given at the Work Conference of the Teachers' College, Columbia University, New York; reprinted in *Class, Codes and Control* 1, London: Routledge.

—— (1970a) 'A sociolinguistic approach to socialization: with some reference to educability', in F. Williams (ed.) *Language and Poverty: Perspectives on a Theme*, 25–61, Chicago: Markham; based upon 1963 manuscript, Sociological Research Unit, Institute of Education, University of London.

—— (1970b) 'Introduction' to W. Brandis and D. Henderson (eds) *Social Class, Language and Communication*, London: Routledge.

—— (1970c) 'Social class differences in communication and control', in W. Brandis and D. Henderson (eds) *Social Class, Language and Communication*, London: Routledge.

—— (1971a) 'Social class, language and socialization', in *Class, Codes and Control* 1: 170–89, London: Routledge.

—— (1971b) 'On the classification and framing of knowledge', in *Class, Codes and Control* 1: 202–36, London: Routledge.

—— (1971c) *Class, Codes and Control* 1, *Theoretical Studies towards a Sociology of Language*, London: Routledge.

—— (1973) 'Postscript: a brief account of the theory of codes', in *Social Relationships and Language*, block 3 of the Educational Studies second-level course *Language and Learning*, Milton Keynes: Open University; reprinted in *Class, Codes and Control* 1: 237–56, London: Routledge, 1974.

—— (1974) *Class, Codes and Control* 1, *Theoretical Studies towards a Sociology of Language*, second (revised) edition, London: Routledge.

—— (1975) 'Class and pedagogies: visible and invisible', in *Class, Codes and Control* 3: 116–56, London: Routledge; revised in the second edition, 1977.

—— (1977a) 'Aspects of the relation between education and production', in *Class, Codes and Control* 3, second (revised) edition, 174–200, London: Routledge.

—— (1977b) 'Class and the acquisition of educational codes', note A in *Class, Codes and Control* 3, second (revised) edition, 193–6, London: Routledge.

—— (1977c) 'Foreword' to D.S. Adlam, G.H. Turner, and L. Lineker (eds) *Code in Context*, London: Routledge.

—— (1977d) *Class, Codes and Control* 3, second (revised) edition, London: Routledge.

—— (1981) 'Codes, modalities and the process of cultural reproduction: a model', *Language and Society* 10: 327–63; reprinted in M.W. Apple (ed.) *Cultural and Economic Reproduction in Education: Essays on Class, Ideology and the State*, London: Routledge, 1982, revised version in *C.O.R.E.* 12, 1 (1988); further revised in the present volume.

—— (1986) 'On pedagogic discourse', J.G. Richardson (ed.) *Handbook of Theory and Research for the Sociology of Education*, New York: Greenwood.

—— (1987) 'On pedagogic discourse: revised 1987', *C.O.R.E.* 12, 1.

—— (1988) 'Social Class and Pedagogic Practice', available from the Department of the Sociology of Education, Institute of Education, University of London.

—— and Cook-Gumperz, J. (1973) 'The coding grid: theory and operations', in J. Cook-Gumperz (ed.) *Social Control and Socialization: a Study of Class Differences in the Language of Maternal Control*, 48–72, London: Routledge.

—— and Diaz, M. (1984) 'Towards a theory of pedagogic discourse', *C.O.R.E.* 8, 3: 1–212.

—— Elvin, L., and Peters, R. (1966) 'Ritual in education', *Philosophical Transactions of the Royal Society of London*, series B, 251, No. 772; reprinted in *Class, Codes and Control* 3, second (revised) edition, 1977.

Biesele, M. (1974) 'Folklore and Ritual of Kung Hunter Gatherers' II, 'Song Texts of the Masters of Tricks', Ph.D. thesis, Harvard University.

Bliss, J., Monk, L., and Ogburn, J., (eds) (1983) *Qualitative Data Analysis for Educational Research: a Guide to Users of Systemic Networks*, London: Croom Helm.

Blyth, W.A.L. (1966) *English Primary Education*, two volumes, London: Routledge.

Boltanski, L. (1969) *Prime éducation et morale de classe*, Paris and The Hague: Mouton.

Bourdieu, P. (1986) *Distinction: a Social Critique of Judgement of Taste*, trans. R. Rice, London: Routledge.

—— (1988) *Questions de sociologie*, Paris: Minuit, trans. *Questions of Sociology*, Middletown, Conn.: Wesleyan University Press.

—— and Boltanski, L. (1978) 'Changes in social structure and changes in the demand for education', in S. Giner and M. Scotford-Archer (eds) *Contemporary Europe: Social Structures and Cultural Patterns*, London: Routledge.

—— and Passeron, J.C. (1970) *La Réproduction: élements pour une théorie du système d'enseignement*, Paris: Minuit; trans. R. Nice as *Reproduction in Education, Society and Culture*, Beverly Hills, Cal.: Sage, 1977.

Brandis, W., and Bernstein, B. (1974) *Selection and Control: Teachers' Ratings of Children in the Infant School*, London: Routledge.

—— and Henderson, D. (1970) *Social Class, Language and Communication*, London: Routledge.

Broadfoot, P. (1986) 'Whatever happened to inequality? Assessment policy and inequality: the UK experience', *British Journal of the Sociology of Education* 7, 2: 205–24.

Cazden, C.B., John, V.P., and Hymes, D. (eds) (1972) *Functions of Language in the Classroom*, New York: Teachers' College Press.

Chamborédon, J.-C., and Prévot, J.Y. (1973) 'Le Métier d'enfant: définition sociale de la prime enfance et fonctions différentielles de l'école maternelle', basic paper, Centre de Sociologie Européenne.

Cohen, G. (1981) 'Culture and educational achievement', *Harvard Educational Review* 51, 2: 270–85.

Cook-Gumperz, J., (ed.) (1973) *Social Control and Socialization: a Study of Class Differences in the Language of Maternal Control*, London: Routledge.

Cooper, B. (1976) 'Bernstein's Codes: a Classroom Study', Education Area Occasional Paper No. 8, Brighton: University of Sussex.

Cox, C.D. (1984) 'Continuity, Conflict and Change in State Education in Chile: a Study of the Pedagogic Projects of the Christian Democrat and Popular Unity Governments', Ph.D. thesis, University of London; also in *C.O.R.E.* 10, 2 (1986).

Cremin, L. (1961) *The Transformation of the School*, New York: Knopf.

Dahlberg, G. (1985) *Context and the Child's Orientation to Meaning*, Lund: Liber Laromedel.

Daniels, H.R.J. (1988) 'An enquiry into different forms of special school organization, pedagogic practice and pupil discrimination', *C.O.R.E.* 12, 2.

—— (1989) 'Visual displays as tacit relays of the structure of pedagogic practice', *British Journal of the Sociology of Education* 10, 2: 123–40.

Delamont, S. (1976) *Interaction in the Classroom*, second edition 1983, London: Methuen.

Diaz, M. (1984) 'A Model of Pedagogic Discourse with Special Application to the Colombian Primary Level', Ph.D. thesis, University of London.

Domingos, A.M. (1984) 'Social Class, Pedagogic Practice and Achievement in Science: a Study of Secondary Schools in Portugal' I, Ph.D. thesis, University of London; also in *C.O.R.E.* 11, 2 (1987).

Douglas, M. (1973) *Natural Symbols*, revised edition, London: Allen Lane.

Dreeban, R. (1968) *On what is Learned in School*, Reading, Mass,: Addison-Wesley.

Dreyfus, H.L., and Rabinow, P., (eds) (1982) *Michel Foucault: Beyond Structuralism and Hermeneutics*, Brighton: Harvester.

Durkheim, E. (1893) *De la division du travail social: étude sur l'organisation des sociétés supérieures*, Paris, trans. G. Simpson as *The Division of Labour in Society*, New York: Macmillan, 1933.

—— (1922) *Education et sociologie*, Paris, trans. D.F. Pocock as *Education and Sociology*, London: Cohen & West, 1956.

—— (1925) *L'Education morale*, Paris: Alcan, trans. E.K. Wilson and H. Schnurer as *Moral Education: a Study in the Theory and Application of the Sociology of Education*, New York: Free Press, 1973.

—— (1938) *L'Evolution pédagogique en France*, Paris: Alcan; trans. P. Collins as *The Evolution of Educational Thought: Lectures on the Formation and Development of Secondary Education in France*, London: Routledge, 1977.

Edwards, A. (1980) 'Patterns of power and authority in classroom talk', in P. Woods (ed.) *Teacher Strategies*, London: Croom Helm.

Edwards, J. (1987) 'Elaborated and restricted codes', in U. Ammon, N. Dittmar, K. Mattheier, and W. de Gruyter (eds) *Sociolinguistics: an International Handbook of the Science of Language and Society* I, Berlin: Section.

Eggleston, J. (1977) *The Sociology of the School Curriculum*, London: Routledge.

Faria, M.I. (1984) 'Para a analise de voriacao socio-semantica' I, Ph.D. thesis, Faculdade de Letras, University of Lisbon.

Foucault, M. (1969) *L'Archéologie du savoir*, Paris: Gallimard, trans. A.M. Sheridan as *The Archaeology of Knowledge*, London: Tavistock, 1972.

—— (1975) *Surveiller et punir: naissance de la prison*, trans. A.M. Sheridan as *Discipline and Punish: the Birth of the Prison*, London: Allen Lane, 1977; Harmondsworth: Penguin, 1979.

—— (1982) 'The subject and power', in H.L. Dreyfus and P. Rabinow (eds) *Michel Foucault: Beyond Structuralism and Hermeneutics*, Brighton: Harvester.

Gardener, E. (1973) *The Public Schools*, London: Hamish Hamilton.

Gibson, R. (1984) *Structuralism and Education*, London: Methuen.

Giroux, H.A. (1989) *Schooling for Democracy*, London: Routledge.

Goldthorpe, J., and Lockwood, D. (1963) 'Affluence and class structure', *Sociological Review* XI: 233–63.

References

Gordon, J.C.B. (1981) *Verbal Deficit: a Critique*, London: Croom Helm.

Gouldner, A. (1979) *The Future of Intellectuals and the Rise of the new Class*, London: Macmillan.

Grannis, J.C. (1972) *Columbia Classroom Environment Project: Fifth Progress Report*, New York: Teachers' College, Columbia University.

Green, A.G. (1972) 'Theory and Practice in Infant Education: a Sociological Approach and Case Study', M.Sc. dissertation, Institute of Education, University of London.

Halliday, M.A.K. (1973) *Exploration in the Function of Language*, London: Edward Arnold.

—— (1978) *Language as a Social Semiotic*, London: Longman

Halsey, A.H., Floud, J., and Anderson, C.A. (1961) *Education, Economy and Society: a Reader in the Sociology of Education*, New York: Free Press of Glencoe.

Halsey, A.H., and Sylva, K.D. (eds) (1987) 'Plowden twenty years on', *Oxford Review of Education* 13, 1.

Hartnett, A. (ed.) (1982) *The Social Sciences in Educational Studies*, London: Heinemann.

Hasan, R. (1988) 'Language in the process of socialisation: home and school', in L. Gerot, J. Oldenburg, and T. van Leeuwen (eds) *Language and Socialisation: Home and School*, Proceedings from the Working Conference on Language and Education, 36–96, Sydney: Macquarie University.

—— and Cloran, C. (1989) 'A sociolinguistic interpretation of everyday talk between mothers and children', in M.A.K. Halliday, J. Gibbons, and H. Nicholas (eds) *Learning, Keeping and Using Language: Selected Papers from the Eighth World Congress of Applied Linguistics*, Amsterdam: Benjamins.

Henderson, D. (1971) 'Contextual specificity, discretion and cognitive socialization, with special reference to language', *Sociology* 4, 3; reprinted in B. Bernstein (ed.), *Class, Codes and Control* 2, London: Routledge, 1973.

Holland, J. (1981) 'Social class and changes in orientations to meanings', *Sociology* 15, 1: 1–18.

—— (1983) 'Social struktur och ideologi ungdomars syn pa olika aspektu au den sociala arbetsdelningen', in B. Bernstein and U.P. Lundgren (eds) *Makt, knotroll och pedagogik*, 66–86, Lund: Liber Forlag.

—— (1985) 'Gender and Class: Adolescent Conceptions of Aspects of the Division of Labour', Ph.D. thesis, University of London; also in *C.O.R.E.* 10, 2 (1986).

—— (1986) 'Social class differences in adolescents' conception of the domestic and industrial division of labour', *C.O.R.E.* 10, 1.

Houdle, L. (1968) 'An Enquiry into the Social Factors affecting the Orientation of English Infant Education since the early Nineteenth Century', M.A. dissertation, Institute of Education, University of London (excellent bibliography).

Hymes, D., Cazden, C., and John, V. (1971) *The Function of Language in the Classroom*, New York: Teachers' College Press.

Jackson, L.A. (1974) 'The myth of elaborated and restricted codes', *Higher Education Review* 6, 2: 65–81.

Jenkins, C. (1989) 'The Professional Middle Class and the Origins of Progressivism: a Case Study of the New Education Fellowship, 1920–50', Ph.D. thesis, University of London.

Jessop, B., Bonnett, K., Bromley, S., and Ling, T. (1987) 'Popular capitalism, flexible accumulation and left strategy', *New Left Review* (September–October) 165: 104–22.

Johnson, R. (1981) *Unpopular Education: Schooling and Social Democracy in England since 1944*, London: Hutchinson.

Kallos, D. (1978) *Den nya pedagogiken: en analys av den s k dialog-pedagogiken som svenskt samhallsfenomen*, Stockholm: Wahlstrom & Widstrand.

Karabel, J., and Halsey, A.H. (eds) (1977) *Power and Ideology in Education*, New York: Oxford University Press.

King, R. (1976) 'Bernstein's sociology of the school: some propositions tested', *British Journal of Sociology* 27: 430–43.

—— (1978) *All Things Bright and Beautiful? A Sociological Study of Infants' Classrooms*, Chichester: Wiley.

—— (1979) 'The search for the "invisible" pedagogy', *Sociology* 13: 445–8.

—— (1981a) 'Bernstein's sociology of the school: a further testing', *British Journal of Sociology* 32: 259–65.

—— (1981b) 'Secondary schools: some changes of a decade', *Educational Research* 23: 173–6.

Labov, W. (1969) 'The logic of non-standard English', in J.E. Alacis (ed.) *Report of the Twentieth Round Table Meeting on Linguistics and Language Studies*, Georgetown Monograph Series in Language and Linguistics No. 22, Washington, D.C.: Georgetown University Press, 1970, 1–29.

Landsheere, G. de (1982) *Empirical Research in Education*, Paris: UNESCO for the International Bureau of Education.

Moore, R. (1984) 'Education and Production: a Generative Model', Ph.D. thesis, University of London.

Morrison, K.F. (1983) 'Incentives for studying the liberal arts', in D.L. Wagner (ed.) *The Seven Liberal Arts in the Middle Ages*, Bloomington, Ind.: Indiana University Press.

References

Namie, Y. (1989) 'The Role of the University of London Colonial Examination between 1900 and 1939', Ph.D. thesis, University of London.

Parsons, T. (1949) 'The school class as a social system: some of its functions in American society', *Harvard Educational Review* 29: 297–318.

—— (1951) *The Social System*, London: Routledge.

—— and Bales, F., *et al.* (1955) *Family, Socialization and Interaction Process*, Glencoe, Ill.: Free Press.

Pedroe, E.R. (1981) *Social Stratification and Classroom Discourse: a Sociolinguistic Analysis of Classroom Practice*, Lund: Liber Laromedel.

Plowden report (1967) *Children and their Primary Schools*, report of the Central Advisory Council for Education (England), London: HMSO.

Robinson, W.P. (1973) 'Where do children's answers come from?', in B. Bernstein (ed.) *Class, Codes and Control* 2: 202–34, London: Routledge.

Said, E.W. (1980) 'The text, the world, the critic', in J.V. Harari (ed.) *Textual Strategies: Perspectives in Post-structuralist Criticism*, London: Methuen.

Sharp, R., and Green, A. (1979) *Education and Social Control*, London: Routledge.

Shulman, L.S., and Kreislar, E.R. (eds) (1966) *Learning by Discovery: a Critical Appraisal*, Chicago: Rand McNally.

Silverman, D., and Torode, B. (1980) *The Material Word*, London: Routledge.

Simon, B. (ed.) (1972) *The Radical Tradition in Education in Britain*, London: Lawrence & Wishart.

Smith, D.J., and Tomlinson, S. (1989) *The School Effect: a Study of Multicultural Comprehensives*, London: Policy Studies Institute.

Stewart, W.A.C., and McCann, W.P. (1967) *The Educational Innovators*, London: Macmillan.

Stubbs, M. (1975) 'Teaching and talking: a sociolinguistic approach to classroom interaction', in G. Chanan and S. Delamount (eds) *Frontiers of Classroom Research*, Slough: NFER.

—— (1983) *Language, Schools and Classrooms*, second edition, London: Methuen.

—— and Delamont, S. (eds) (1976) *Explorations in Classroom Observation*, London: Wiley.

Torstendahl, R. (1984) 'Technology in the development of society, 1950–80', *History and Technology* 11: 157–74.

Trudgehill, P. (1983) *Sociolinguistics: an Introduction to Language and Society*, revised edition, Harmondsworth: Penguin.

Turner, G.J. (1973) 'Social class and children's language of control at age five and age seven', in B. Bernstein (ed.) *Class, Codes and Control* 2: 135–201, London: Routledge.

—— (1977) 'The expression of uncertainty and descriptive, instructional and regulative speech', in D. Adlam, G.J. Turner, and L. Lineker (eds) *Code and Context*, 230–44, London: Routledge.

—— and Pickvance, R.E. (1973) 'Social class differences in the expression of uncertainty in five-year-old children', in B. Bernstein (ed.) *Class, Codes and Control* 2: 93–119, London: Routledge.

Tyler, W. (1984) 'Organisations, Factors and Codes: a Methodological Enquiry into Bernstein's Theory of Educational Transmission', Ph.D. thesis, University of Kent at Canterbury.

—— (1985) 'The organisational structure of the school', *Annual Review of Sociology* 15: 49–73.

—— (1988) *School Organisation: a Sociological Perspective*, London: Croom Helm.

Waller, W. (1932) *The Sociology of Teaching*, New York: Wiley.

Wells, G. (1985) *Language Development in the Pre-school Years*, Cambridge: Cambridge University Press.

Willis, P.E. (1977) *Learning to Labour: how Working-class Kids get Working-class Jobs*, Farnborough: Saxon House.

Young, M.F.D. (ed.) (1971) *Knowledge and Control: New Directions in the Sociology of Education*, London: Collier.

Index

abstract expressionism 177
access to education 146–7, 152
achievement, educational 122–3
acquisition 4, 170; classification, voice reproduction and 28–32; education and the division of labour 146–7, 158–9; invisible pedagogies 71; sites of 54, 77, 158–9; transmission and 3, 6–7, 64–5, 65–6; pedagogic practice 186–7, 214; visible pedagogies 54, 77
Adlam, D.S. 4, 119, 121; classification and framing 56, 103, 104, 106
Aggleton, P. 6, 90, 97, 120
Alexander, J.C. 201, 212
Althusser, L. 4, 25, 134
analysis 78
Apple, M.W. 166
assessment 87
Atkinson, P. 165
autonomous visible pedagogies 63, 86–7, 91
autonomy, relative 174–5, 202, 209

Bakker, B.F.M. 123
Bales, F. 211
Bernstein, B. 47, 164, 199, 215; class agents 141; code theory: criticism of 199, 121–30; development of 4, 61, 94–103 passim; modality 109; framing 45; order and change 30;

pedagogic discourse 108, 165, 179–80; instrumental and expressive cultures 211; symbolic control 90, 111; agents 140
bias 79, 168, 175
Biesele, M. 215
Bliss, J. 98
Boltanski, L. 45
Bourdieu, P.: cultural reproduction 167, 169, 171–2, 174–5, 176–7; field 45, 45–6; habitus 3; recontextualization 215; symbolic violence 25
Bowles, S. 174
Brandis, W. 123
Broadfoot, P. 91

capitalism 41, 47, 51–2; education and the division of labour 145–60
Castelnuovo, A. 61
categories 22, 23–4, 32
Cazden, C.B. 167
Centre for Contemporary Cultural Studies 166–7
challenges to framing 39; see also resistance
change, theory of 30, 129, 170
charismatic education 217–18
China 141, 195, 200–1
Chomsky, A.N. 89–90, 212, 213
Christianity 148–9, 151, 201
Church, education's link with 62, 111, 148, 152

class: code theory 3–4, 5–6, 13, 47; change of code 43–4; distribution 109–12, 118–19; elaborated and restricted codes 20, 21, 24–5, 98–9; recognition and realization rules 56–9, 103–6; pedagogic codes 52–4; pedagogic practice 73–86; invisible pedagogies 80–6; visible pedagogies *see* visible pedagogies; symbolic control 140, 141–5

classification: change of code 43; code formula 43, 108, 214–15; code modalities 41, 44; code values 54–5, 58–9; codes of production 49–52; criticism of code theory 125, 126, 127; internal and external values 37; pedagogic device 195, 200, 204–5; power and control 100–1; recognition rules 35, 55–9; 102, 103–7; social basis 18–19; social division of labour 22–8, 99; voice and message 33; voice reproduction and acquisition 28–32

classificatory relation of education 43–4, 195, 200, 204–5, 215

classroom interactions 7

classroom talk 107–8

code values 44, 54–5; definition 101; experimental 55–9

codes 13, 46; class assumption of pedagogic 52–4; competence and 47–8, 113; concept 2–3; criticism of theory 113–30; development of theory 3–4, 94–113; dialect and 48, 113–14; distribution of 20–1; 110–12; elaborated *see* elaborated codes; formula 43, 108, 214–15; frequency counts 120; general 14–15; 214–15; grammar and 119; grammatical choice 119; location of *see* location; modalities 4–5, 41–6, 62, 101, 108–9, 214–15; of production

49–52; recontextualizing 122–30; restricted *see* restricted codes; specific 15–17; modalities 40–6; theory and 120–2; values *see* code values

cognitive messages 80–1

Cohen, G. 90

communicative context 34–5, 54

community 179

competence: code and 47–8, 113; theories of 89–90

competences, shared 71, 189, 207–8, 212–14

competitive capitalism 152–3

complex societies 181, 182

concepts, reification of 127–8

consciousness: formation of 141–5; pedagogic device 180–3, 189

conservative pedagogic practice 73

context: code theory 14, 15, 97, 101–2, 107, 214; communicative 34–5, 54; primary 59–60, 191; recontextualizing 60–1, 192–3; secondary 60, 191–2; sequencing rules 75

control: codes of production 51–2; framing 36; invisible pedagogies 82–6; pedagogic device 189–90; power and *see* power; symbolic *see* symbolic control

conventional structuralism 125–6

Cook-Gumperz, J. 59, 97, 119, 126

Cooper, B. 107

countervailing strategies 39, 130

Cox, C.D. 6, 37, 101, 164, 165, 216

creative replacing 9

criterial rules 53, 54, 66–7, 69–70

critical pedagogy 168, 171–2

criticism 7–9; of code theory 113–30

cultural field 138, 157, 159, 160, 164

cultural relay 63, 64, 65–7

cultural reproduction 6, 166–7, 168–72, 174–9
culture 164; code and competence 47–8, 113; modality of gender and 48–9
curriculum studies 161, 162–3

Dahlberg, G. 101
Daniels, H.R.J. 37, 91; classification and framing 5, 7, 108; implicit criteria 70; invisible pedagogies 124; syntax of generation of meaning 29
decontextualizing 60–1, 192–3
deficit 114, 123; difference and 114–19
Delamont, S. 167
delocation 60–1, 184, 192–3
democratic relations of production 51–2
description: principles of 171–2; speech forms 95–6
dialect 48, 113–14
dialog-pedagogike 91, 124
Diaz, M. 101, 108, 165, 199, 216
difference, deficit and 114–19
diffusers 139
disciplines 156
discourse 21–2; classification principle 26–7; production 59–60, 191; relocation 60–1, 192–3; reproduction 60, 191–2; visible pedagogies 75–6
discursive resources 62, 194–5, 203, 206
discursive rules 66, 70, 71; *see also* criterial rules; pacing rules; sequencing rules
distortion 170–1
distribution of codes 20–1, 110–12
distributive rules 180–3, 187, 193, 206; charismatic education 217; manual pedagogic discourse 218; official pedagogic discourse 201, 203
disturbance of framing 39

division of labour 21–2, 62, 92; classification 22–8, 29; distribution of codes 110; location of codes 20, 109–10; symbolic control 6, 133, 138–40, 143–5, 159–60; education 26–7, 133, 145–59, 160
divisiveness 50
dominance, patterns of 168–9, 171
dominant principles: codes 40–1, 215; pedagogic device 184–5, 196, 199
Domingos, A.M. 37, 77, 107, 216
Durkheim, E. 166, 169, 172, 190, 211–12; Christianity 148, 201; medieval university 148, 150–1, 211–12; pedagogic practice 210; relative autonomy 174; religion and education 62, 111, 148, 212

economic assumptions of invisible pedagogies 80, 81
economic field: dominant agents 92, 112, 135; social division of labour 92; visible and invisible pedagogies 74, 85–6; *see also* production
economy: classification, framing values and 109; pedagogic practice and 91–2
Edwards, A. 123, 167
effectiveness of schools 122–3
elaborated codes 17–32, 62; cultural/pedagogic relay 182, 215; criticism of theory 113–30; development of theory 94–113; official pedagogic discourse 203; specific 40–1; modalities 41–6; suspension 90
elaborated orientations 32, 40, 62, 182–3
embedded pedagogic practices 84, 90–1
entrepreneurial professions 85–6
entrepreneurial service structure 92
evaluation rules 180, 185–7, 193,

206; charismatic education 218;
manual pedagogic discourse 218;
official pedagogic discourse 203
examinations, public 216
exclusion 83
executors 139
expenditure, public 86, 92, 112,
140, 154
explicit normalizing functions 138
expressionism, abstract 177
expressive activities 210–11

family: control 82–3; influence in
pedagogic discourse 179;
invisible pedagogies 80–1;
reorganized capitalism 158–9;
types 96–7, 120–1; visible
pedagogies 77
Faria, M.I. 98, 112
field location 6, 140, 164; *see also*
economic field; symbolic control
food sorting experiment 18–19,
54–5, 103
formal language use 96; *see also*
restricted codes
Foucault, M. 134, 138, 163, 165
fragmentation 50
framing 36–9, 89; code formula
43, 108, 214–15; code
modalities 41, 43, 45; code
values 54–5; codes of
production 49–52; criticism of
code theory 125, 127; power and
control 100, 101, 106–7;
realization rules 38–9, 55–9,
102, 103–7; regulative and
instructional discourse 107–8;
visible pedagogies 54
France 166, 217
Freire, P. 73, 202
frequency counts 120
Freud, S. 69

gender 25, 48–9
Gestalt theory 69, 212
Gibson, R. 124, 125–30
Gintis, H. 174
Giroux, H.A. 73, 168

Glass, D. 152
Gordon, J.C.B. 114, 118, 121, 123·
Gouldner, A. 164
grammar 119
grammatical choice 119
Gramsci, A. 134
Grannis, J.C. 125
ground rules 15, 61, 98, 102; *see
also* recognition rules
guilds 218

habitus 3
Halliday, M.A.K. 97
Halsey, A.H. 166
Hartnett, A. 166
Hasan, R. 5, 10, 98
Henderson, D. 105
Hewitt, R. 215
hide and seek text 56–7, 58–9
hierarchical rules 52, 65–6, 67,
89; control 82–6
Holland, J. 6, 90, 98, 101, 112;
adolescent conceptions 4, 164;
ideology, field location and class
140; oppositional elaborated
codes 111; pedagogic
recontextualizing fields 202;
social basis of classification 18,
103

idées pédagogiques, les 166
ideology 13–14; agents of
symbolic control 140; social
class and 140; of tense 68–9
individualism 153, 157
instruction, theories of 72–3, 189,
212–14
instructional context 97
instructional discourse 108, 183–4,
188, 210–12
instrumental activities 210–11
insulation 28, 126–7; social
division of labour 23–6, 27–8,
99
integrated pedagogic practices
91–2
interactional principle 34–5
international field 216

invisible pedagogies 71, 90–1, 124;
charismatic education 217;
social class assumptions 80–6;
specialized practices 91–2
'IQ' 94–5
Islam 149–50, 151

Jackson, L.A. 121
Jenkins, C. 6, 89, 91; New
Education Fellowship 85, 124,
164
Jessop, B. 145
Johnson, R. 166
Judaism 148–9, 151

Kallos, D. 124
Karabel, J. 166
King, R. 90, 124, 125
knowledge: autonomous visible
pedagogies 63, 86–7;
organization of 150–1, 156,
160–3; orientation of 148–50,
155–6, 157; pedagogic device
181–3

labour, division of *see* division of
labour
Labov, W. 114–18
Landsheere, G. de 215
Leon 116–18
Lévi-Strauss, C. 89–90
lexical pedagogic practice 79,
80
local pedagogic discourse (LPD)
194
local pedagogic practices 217
location of codes 19–20, 62,
109–10, 111–12; communicative
context 34–5; modalities 44,
45–6
locational principle 34–5
London, University of 152, 164
Lundgren, U. 178, 215

manual practices 147–8, 153, 157,
201; transmission 218
Manpower Services Commission
204

market-based ideology 154, 155, 157
market-oriented visible pedagogies
63, 86–8, 91
Marx, K. 123, 133–4
material base 19, 103
meanings 95–6, 98, 181–2, 214;
relevant 14, 15, 102, 106; *see
also* orientations to meanings
mechanical solidarity 211–12
medieval universities 148–51, 161,
182, 218
message 23, 32; of pedagogy 190;
social relations, practice and
33–9
Mitterand, F. 204
modalities: codes 4–5, 41–6, 62,
101, 108–9, 214–15; culture
and gender 48–9; pedagogic
practice 67–70
Moore, R. 101, 109, 111, 165
Morrison, K.F. 149
mother–child control 57, 59

Namie, Y. 164
narrative 56, 78, 105
neo-medievalism 157, 160
New Education Fellowship 85, 124
normalization 138, 159, 163–4

official pedagogic discourse (OPD)
193–4, 195–6, 202, 203, 216
official recontextualizing field
(ORF) 192, 196, 200, 202,
208–9
opposition: pedagogic device
206–8; pedagogic practice
63–4, 86–8; symbolic control/
production 85–6, 140
organic solidarity 211–12
organization of knowledge 150–1,
156; teacher training 160–3
orientation of knowledge 148–50,
155–6, 157
orientations to meanings 15–17,
21, 30–1, 40; code formula 43,
108, 214; elaborated and
restricted codes 18–20
over-determining 8–9

pacing rules 52–3, 66, 89; visible pedagogies 74, 76–9
Paris, University of 150–1
Parsons, T. 210–11
Passeron, J.C. 167, 171, 174–5, 176, 215
pedagogemes 194
pedagogic device 180–90, 209–10, 217; realization 195–205; symbolic control 205–9
pedagogic discourse, definition of 183–4
pedagogic practice: as cultural relay 64, 65–7; evaluation rules 185–6; generating modalities 67–70; *see also* invisible pedagogies; visible pedagogies
pedagogic recontextualizing fields (PRF) 192, 200, 216; relative autonomy 198, 202, 209
pedagogic text 194
Pedro, E.R. 98, 107, 126; instructional and regulative discourse 7, 211
peer group 179
performance: theories of instruction 189, 207–9, 212–13; visible pedagogies 70, 71
performance rules 15, 61, 98, 102; *see also* realization rules
personal families 96–7, 121
physical resources 62, 194, 203, 206
physics 184–5
Piaget, J. 89–90, 202, 212, 213
Pickvance, R.E. 105
Plowden Report 67
pointillism 9
police 138–9, 164
positional families 96–7, 121
positioning 13, 175–6
Poulantzas, N. 134
power: control and 46–7, 73; elaborated and restricted codes 99–100, 101, 106–7, 108, 118; implicit hierarchies 67; pedagogic device 205–6; social division of labour 24–5,

99–101; syntax of generation of meaning 29–30
practices 22, 23
pre-capitalism 147–52, 160
primary context 59–60, 191, 193
prison service 138–9, 164
private sector 137
privileged meanings 15–16, 102
privileging meanings 15–16, 102
privileging text 172–8; relation to 175–6, 178; relations within 176–8
production: agents of 135–6; codes of: classification and framing of 49–52; location and distribution 111; dominant principles 40–1; education and 146, 160; classificatory relation 43–4, 195, 200–1, 204–5, 215; competitive capitalism 152; formation of consciousness 141–5; pre-capitalism 147–8, 152; reorganized capitalism 157, 159; transitional capitalism 153–4; field of 135; code modalities 45–6; social basis 21–2, 27, 170; symbolic control 135–40, 198
'progressive' pedagogic practice 72
public examinations 216
public expenditure 86, 92, 112, 140, 154
public language use 95–6; *see also* elaborated codes

Quadrivium 150–1, 155–6, 212

radical pedagogic practice 72–3
reading, theory of 69
reading, visible pedagogies and 75
realization 14, 31–2, 214; conditions 21, 40
realization rules 15, 35, 129, 189; framing 38–9, 55–9, 102, 103–7
recognition rules 29, 129; classification 35, 55–9, 102, 103–7
recontextualization 215

recontextualizers 8
recontextualizing of codes 122–30
recontextualizing context 60–1,
192–3
recontextualizing fields 60, 61,
196–200, 201–2, 208
recontextualizing grammar 188–9
recontextualizing rules 89, 180,
183–4, 193, 206; charismatic
education 217–18; official
pedagogic discourse 201, 203
regionalization of knowledge 156
regulative contexts 97
regulative discourse 108, 183–4,
188, 210–12; dominance 184–5
regulative rules 66, 70, 71; *see
also* hierarchical rules
regulators 138–9
reification of concepts 127–8
relative autonomy 174–5, 202,
209
relay: code as 182, 215; education
as 63, 64, 65–7, 168–9
religion 148–50, 151, 201;
education's link with 62, 111,
148, 152
religious cosmologies 62, 111,
181–2
religious field 188
relocation of discourse 60–1,
184, 192–3
reorganized capitalism 145, 157–9,
160
reorganizing (transitional)
capitalism 145, 153–7, 160
repair systems 74
repairers 139
reproducers 139
resistance 39, 129–30; theories of
168, 171, 178, 179
restricted codes 17–32; criticism
of theory 113–30; development
of theory 94–113
restricted orientations 62
Robins, C. 116, 117
Robinson, W.P. 97
roles 121, 128–9
ruling class 141–2

Said, E.W. 150
schizzing 8
school-based professional training
161, 163
Schools Council 163
secondary context 60, 191–2
secondary servicing 8
selective referencing 8
sequencing rules 52–3, 66, 67–9,
89; visible pedagogies 53, 74–6
service, agents of symbolic control
and 137
shapers 139
shared competences 71, 189,
207–8, 212–14
Silverman, D. 62
simple societies 62, 111, 181–2
Smith, A. 210
Smith, D.J. 123
social class *see* class
social division of labour *see*
division of labour
social messages 80–1
social relations 95, 99–100;
practice, message and 32, 33–9
Sociological Research Unit (SRU)
18–19, 119
space: invisible pedagogies 80–1;
privileging text 175
specialized interactional practices
15–17
specialized invisible-pedagogic
practices 91–2
specific codes 15–17; modalities
40–6, 214–15
specific instructional discourse
(SID) 194, 216–17
specific meaning potential 98
specific regulative discourse (SRD)
194, 216–17
speech, description of 5, 95–6
State: education and 152, 157,
160, 163, 202; pedagogic
recontextualizing field 208–9; as
field 45–6; role: production/
symbolic control opposition 140;
visible and invisible pedagogies
85–6; shift to symbolic control

88, 92–3, 139, 154–5, 209; *see also* public expenditure
stratification 70–1, 74, 77
structuralism 125–30
Stubbs, M. 119, 121–1, 125, 167
sub-voices 26
symbolic assumptions of invisible pedagogies 80–1, 81–2
symbolic control 45–6, 134–45; agents of 135–40; education and 146, 160; competitive capitalism 152–3; pre-capitalism 148–50; reorganized capitalism 158–9; transitional capitalism 154–5; invisible pedagogies 74, 85–6; public expenditure 85–6, 112; recontextualizing fields 198, 208–9; social division of labour 6, 133, 138–40, 143–5, 159–60; State's shift towards 88, 92–3, 139, 154–5, 209
symbolism pedagogic practice 79, 90
syntax of generation of meaning 29
systemic relation 194–5, 195, 204–5

tacit practice 30, 39
tautology 127–8
teachers 123, 139; training of 160–3
text, agents of symbolic control and 137–8
textual productions 15–17
theories 46
time, invisible pedagogies and 81–2
Tomlinson, S. 123
Torode, B. 62

Torstendal, R. 145
transition, rituals of 207
transitional capitalism 145, 153–7, 160
transmission: acquisition and 3, 6–7, 64–5, 65–6; pedagogic practice 186–7, 214; visible pedagogies 71
Trivium 149, 150–1, 155–6, 211–12
Trotin picture card 56, 58, 104–5
Trudghill, P. 120
Turner, G.J. 97, 98, 105
Tyler, W. 101, 124–5, 165, 167

universities, medieval 148–51, 161, 182, 218

visible pedagogies 53, 70–1, 84–5; autonomous and market-oriented 63, 86–8, 91; class assumptions 53–4, 74–9; control 82–3; space 80; time 81, 82
vocationalism 87–8, 92, 153–4, 204
voice 24, 62; classification and 25, 26, 28–32; message and 23, 33, 35; of pedagogy 190

Waller, W. 167
Weber, M. 188, 217
Wells, G. 97, 120
Whitty, G. 90
Willis, P.E. 166, 171
work, education and 204–5
working class 141, 142–3

Young, M.F.D. 166